GANDHINAGAR

Building National Identity
in Postcolonial India

GANDHINAGAR

Ravi Kalia

UNIVERSITY OF SOUTH CAROLINA PRESS

Published in Columbia, South Carolina, by the
University of South Carolina Press

Manufactured in the United States of America

08 07 06 05 04   5 4 3 2 1

Library of Congress Cataloging-in-Publication Data

Kalia, Ravi.
   Gandhinagar : building national identity in postcolonial India / Ravi Kalia.
   p. cm.
   Includes bibliographical references and index.
   ISBN 1-57003-544-X (cloth : alk. paper)
   1. City planning—India—Gāndhīnagar. 2. Urban policy—India. 3. Gāndhīnagar
(India)—Social conditions. I. Title.
   HT169.I52G265 2004
   307.1'216'095475—dc22

2004003488

To the unknown artisans and craftsmen of India
who continue to innovate and enrich the landscape

CONTENTS

List of Illustrations   ix

Acknowledgments   xi

Introduction   1

1   The Making of the Gujarat State   7

2   The Politics of Site   30

3   The Kahn Seminar in Ahmedabad   60

4   The Plan and Architecture   96

5   Conclusions   119

Notes   133

Selected Bibliography   143

Index   151

ILLUSTRATIONS

FOLLOWING PAGE 40

Location of Gujarat in India, identifying Gandhinagar

The Gandhinagar plan by H. K. Mewada

The planner H. K. Mewada

Le Corbusier with Prime Minister Nehru in Chandigarh, Punjab

Louis Kahn with Gautam Sarabhai at the Indian Institute of Management, Ahmedabad

The Millowners Association Building built by Le Corbusier

Classrooms at the Indian Institute of Management, Ahmedabad

The Capitol Complex, Gandhinagar

The assembly building, placed on a raised plinth by Mewada

The interior structure of the assembly, inspired by the lotus flower

Assembly chambers, inspired by the inner sanctums of the scores of Indian temples

Mahatma Gandhi's statue, in the foreground of the assembly

The assembly building at night

The secretariat block

The overhanging bridge that links the secretariat with the assembly

Intersection of the two grid axes

The auditorium in sector 17

A temple in sector 22

Layout of sector 21

ACKNOWLEDGMENTS

MY DEBT TO OLD and new colleagues and friends continues to grow in my exploration of urban and architectural developments in India. These friends and colleagues have answered my questions, suggested new angles of looking at issues, recommended ways out of deadlocks and bureaucratic obstacles, and demonstrated generous hospitality, all of which makes it very difficult to find suitable words to thank them. But thank them I must, howsoever inadequately, in bringing out yet another volume on an Indian city, this one on Gandhinagar, the capital of Gujarat State.

To Governor Naresh Chandra, who launched my research in Ahmedabad and Gandhinagar by introducing me to the Gujarat administration, I owe special gratitude—gratitude that multiplied as I continued to seek his wisdom later, in Washington, D.C., where he served as India's ambassador to the United States. I thank B. A. Patel, joint secretary to the governor, for many a courtesy. My special thanks are also due to Babubhai Jasubhai Patel, the former chief minister, for sharing his personal papers and for sitting through long interviews, explaining the textured complexities of Gujarat politics and the making of the new capital. I am equally indebted to Shrenik K. Lalbhai, the late Kasturbhai Lalbhai's son, for sharing the family papers, for providing insights about his father, and for his warm hospitality in Ahmedabad; and to Abhilasha Kasturbhai in Bombay (Mumbai) for her help.

I found a warm friend and a willing collaborator in Deepak Mewada, the chief architect and town planner for the Roads and Buildings Department, Gujarat, and the late H. K. Mewada's son, who worked tirelessly with me over several years, digging up family papers, introducing me to members of the family, and guiding me through the labyrinth bureaucracy to bring to light the story of Gandhinagar and his father's role in it. His affable wife, Bharati, introduced me to delightful Gujarati cuisine and to rich Gujarati culture. My heartfelt thanks to both of them for their support and friendship.

Principal Secretary H. B. Jamdar, of the Roads and Buildings Department, Gujarat, and Chief Town Planner J. H. Tamakuwala and his fine staff at the Town Planning and Valuation Department, Gujarat, were most helpful in letting me consult materials on Gandhinagar. Chief Architect S. A. Verma and his helpful staff facilitated my understanding of the architecture of Gandhinagar and supplied drawings. I also received assistance from the office of the superintending engineer of the Capital Project. In Ahmedabad, too, many individuals helped. They included Congressman Prabodh Rawal, J. K. Mewada, Virendra T. Purohit, the retired chief town planner and architectural adviser, Gujarat, and father-and-son architects Hansmukh and Bimal Patel; also Surit Sarabhai, L. R. Dalal, I. K. Modi, K. M. Shah, D. A. Kadia, R. K. Pathak (Ahmedabad Urban Development Authority), D. G. Pandaya, S. P. Bhatia, M. D. Gajjar, Joti Gajjar, and Professor Ramlal Parikh, vice-chancellor, Gujarat Vidyapith; and at the School of Planning, Centre for Environmental Planning and Technology (CEPT), I was indebted to Professors Miki and Madhavi Desai, Barjor E. Mehta, Anjana Vyas, and H. M. Shivanand Swamy. My many thanks to all.

Architects Anant Raje and Balkrishna Doshi, both of whom worked with the American architect Louis Kahn in Ahmedabad, were most illuminating on Kahn's work at the Indian Institute of Management, Ahmedabad. I thank both of them for liberally giving their valuable time. My heartfelt thanks are also extended to Chief Town Planner D. S. Meshram, of the Town and Country Planning Office, Government of India, New Delhi, and his successor K. T. Gurmukhi, Senior Town Planner P. M. Apte (Gandhinagar), and to architects Rahul Mehrotra, Hafeez Contractor, Raj Rewal, the late Achyut Kanvinde, Gautam Bhatia, Satish Gujral, and the late Joseph Allen Stein. I can never thank enough my good colleague and friend Edgar F. N. Riberio and his gracious wife, Flavia, for their support and warm hospitality since I first started investigating Indian urbanism and architecture more than two decades ago. I continue to benefit from illuminating discussions on Indian urbanism with Edgar, who even in his retirement remains actively involved in planning and scholarship. Thanks also to my good friend, the consummate administrator Jagdish Sagar, who served as chief administrator of Chandigarh and who was responsible for assembling distinguished architects and planners from around the world in Chandigarh on that city's fiftieth anniversary in 1999, and his accomplished Gujarati administrator-wife, Gita, for opening their house for lively discussions and Gujarati gourmet meals.

Other colleagues who have greatly helped me stay the course include Professors Judith Stein, Walter Struve and his wife, Cynthia, Joel Wiener and his wife, Susan, Irwin Yellowitz and his wife, Barbara, Thomas Lee and his wife, Nancy Lee, Philip Leonhard and his wife, Francee, and Jung Jing. My colleague and attorney friend at the Professional Staff Congress, Nicholas (Nick) Russo, also helped me to stay the course. Professor Robert Twombly and his gracious wife, Professor Jeanne Chase, supported me in many ways at a time when completion of this volume appeared doubtful. I incurred an additional debt to Robert for his reading of the manuscript and his valuable comments. Collectively, these individuals made me realize that it is possible to fight "city hall" and that individuals do make a difference when they choose to act out of conscience against evil.

I thank my distinguished colleague and friend Stanley Wolpert and his gracious wife, Dorothy, and Professors D. R. SarDesai, Eric Monkkonen, Melton and Sandra McLaurin, John Richards, Thomas and Barbara Metcalf, Giles Tillotson, Asish Nandi, Asish Bose, Ravi Sundram, Anthony King, Nihal Perera, Ainslie Embree, and Dwijender Tripathi for their support. My research would have been rendered dull and vapid without wonderful friends—Narain Sadhwani (Sadi), Deepak Raja, Jim and Eileen Ray, Ambassador T. C. A. Rangachari and his wife, Kokila, Ashok and Rita Beckaya, Sanju and Sweetie Beckaya, Professor R. P. and Shusheela Kaushik, Navin and Rekha Anand, Ajit and Rita Chadha, Dennis and Raj Wesley, Shammi Manik, Amar Gulati, Dr. Rajan Prasad, Neal Brickman, Bill House, Ethen Lenoard, Martha Maclennan: they all helped in providing distractions when I most needed them.

I also incurred debt to several institutions in the course of my research. I benefited in my research travel from the generous support of the Research Foundation, Professional Staff Congress—City University of New York, and from the Freeman Foundation grant to the Asian Studies Program at the City College of New York. I thank the staff of Perkins Library, Duke University, for once again giving me extended borrowing privileges, with special thanks to Rebecca Gomez for approving my countless requests. I thank Mounir Khalil, Herman Cline, and Evelyn Bodden and the interlibrary loan staff of Cohen Library at the City College of New York; and the Architectural Archives at the University of Pennsylvania, Philadelphia, with special thanks to William Whitaker, collections manager for the Louis Kahn Collection; the Nehru Memorial and Museum Library, New Delhi, with special thanks to the late Professor Ravinder Kumar; the Calico Museum, Ahmedabad; the General Administration Department, Gandhinagar; the Chief Architect's Office, Gandhinagar; the Chief Town Planner's Office, Gandhinagar; the Gujarat Vidyapith Archives, Ahmedabad; the Parliament Library, New Delhi; the Town and Country Planning Office Library, New Delhi; the Maharastra State Archives, Elphinstone College, Bombay; and the India Office Library and Records, London.

I also thank Curtis Clark, director of the University of South Carolina Press, Columbia, and his fine editorial and production departments, and Oxford University Press, New Delhi, for unfailing support in the publication and distribution of my scholarship, including this volume. I truly treasure the relationship with both presses, even as many old friends have moved on and new ones have come in.

I owe a special debt of gratitude to my wise and dear friend the Honorable Inder K. Gujaral, former prime minister of India, who has continued to encourage me in my scholarship and has steered me through the complexities of the Indian bureaucratic system for more than two decades, and his dear wife, Sheila, for her warm hospitality and affection in New Delhi.

Finally, I must thank Shantha, who embodies infinite patience and unselfish love, for forgiving me for spousal neglect in the preparation of this volume and, along with T. S. (Boogie), humoring me when I most needed it.

GANDHINAGAR

Introduction

MY EXPLORATION OF India's postcolonial capitals started with Chandigarh, Punjab; it extended to Bhubaneswar, Orissa; and it concludes with Gandhinagar, Gujarat. Over the course of this exploration, stretching some twenty years, besides excavating buried government files, blueprints, and drawings in the general administration departments of the respective state governments and sifting through the personal papers of many departed practitioners in libraries and their family homes, I interviewed surviving architects, planners, politicians, and their relatives in India, Europe, and America. Even as I researched and wrote the accounts of the three capital cities, I sought out construction workers in the three capitals. In Chandigarh, I shared meals with Punjabi carpenters, Rajasthani masons, and Bihari laborers, and I sensed fear among the Biharis who wore the famous five symbols of the Sikhs in an effort to blend in with the dominant population, even while chewing *pan*, the betel nut that betrayed their transplanted origin; and in Bhubaneswar and Gandhinagar I drank countless cups of tea with the Oriyas, the Biharis, and the Bengalis. To better understand the culture of the building industry, I worked with bricklayers, carpenters, and concrete workers when remodeling the family home in Delhi; and in California and New York when remodeling my houses there, I worked with workers from literally around the world, including Bangladeshi bricklayers—about whom architect Louis Kahn once remarked that they certainly know how to make arches out of bricks. Through these artisans, I discovered a common thread that ties together the global construction industry; and these faceless workers introduced me to their humanity and to the pride of their craft.

The larger meaning of India's experiments in urban planning—and the consequent development of Chandigarh, Bhubaneswar, and Gandhinagar—must be based on knowledge of a people and place emerging from a time of unremitting hardship, of values in transition, of broken families and shattered households wrought by the

1

partition, but most of all a time of reflection in which a people pause at a cross-roads to ponder the meaning of the past and the purpose of the future. Marveling at the miracle of modernism that the Frenchman Le Corbusier unleashed in Chandigarh and witnessing it faithfully followed in Bhubaneswar and Gandhinagar, as well as countless other cities, Indians might easily overlook that, in postcolonial India, Chandigarh is as much a city "unfettered by tradition"—a standard that Prime Minister Jawaharlal Nehru demanded—as it is a national political celebration for the New India. With political endorsement of Le Corbusier's ideas came a new appreciation for the aesthetic of the "international style" and the consequent visual variety in the Indian cityscape. But Chandigarh, and to a greater extent Bhubaneswar and Gandhinagar, also signaled a pervasive resistance to Western modernism and a frequent contentious confrontation with colonial legacies from New Delhi. Nehru himself called the national capital "un-Indian," and Chandigarh evidenced profound conflicts in values and a host of underlying political and social issues only marginally addressed, or not addressed at all, by architects and planners—a phenomenon emblematic of many developing countries. Even for middle-class Indians, modernism represented an unattainable ideal; it was neither an occasion to celebrate nor an opportunity for self-congratulation. The dichotomy of Chandigarh perpetuated itself in Bhubaneswar, Gandhinagar, and other Indian cities.

Still, because of the centralized control inherent in a new city's development, many national governments in the twentieth century have looked to planned cities as solutions for urban congestion, slowing rural depopulation, and restoring regional balance. The Indian government, recognizing the effectiveness of urban planning as a policy tool for modernization, economic growth, and social change, has erected not only three new capital cities—Bhubaneswar, Chandigarh, and Gandhinagar—but also other new towns, for refugees, lesser-administrative functions, and industry. In fact, the Indian government, in order to generate economic activity and provide balanced regional urbanization and settlement patterns for India, soon after independence in 1947 postulated building at least three hundred new cities, including several new state capitals, by the end of the century. It was hoped that these new cities would improve communication systems, raise economic standards, bring law and order to areas torn by communal passions, and provide social mobility to the economically depressed classes.

To Nehru and Le Corbusier, the machine age held the promise of liberating individuals and improving society, which was to be achieved by the simple but powerful dictum: modernize your house and your life will follow. For both men, India offered unimaginable freedoms played out in a vast and exotic landscape: skyscrapers and steel-chrome-aluminum factories announcing the aesthetic potential of new materials that were already transforming life outside the home. Modernism offered a shimmering vision of escape from everything conservative, traditional, and limited. But by the time that construction of Gandhinagar commenced in the mid-1960s, other realities appeared to mediate those earlier, more optimistic images: India's military debacle against China, uncontrollable famines, spiraling inflation, unrestrained population growth, unmanageable illiteracy, mindless communal violence, perpetual caste conflicts, the growing marginalization of women, the devalued Indian rupee, the battle to impose Hindi on a linguistically diverse national landscape, and so on. The India I inhabited in the late 1960s was less mythic than that of the earlier generation, more humbled by social and political realities, with India's history, or histories, increasingly obscured by waves of seekers more interested in the past than the future. Looking back over fifty-some years of independence, I find myself drawn back again to the unresolved, perhaps unresolvable, tensions between, on the one hand, mythologies of Westernization and the promise of industrialization and, on the other, the realities of the complex, multifaceted India that confronts us today.

India's experiments in urbanism and modernism accentuated the gap between what India professes and what India has achieved, beginning with the reminder that clean water, uninterrupted power, and basic housing remain unattainable for the bulk of the population, while the illiteracy rate stubbornly stays higher than 50 percent. Such defiant realities chastened and chastised the enthusiasm and sense of optimism that prevailed during the urban renaissance of the 1950s and the early 1960s, when an unrivaled number of cities, dams, institutions, and other public works were built, including Chandigarh and Bhubaneswar. The possibility that India's professed egalitarian sentiments and modernism's optimistic promises might turn out to be an illusion became evident during the construction of Gandhinagar. The conflicting visions—those of the cotton barons of Ahmedabad, who unsuccessfully tried to recruit Louis Kahn, an American, to build a new capital that, while respecting Indian tradition, would rival Le Corbusier's Chandigarh, and those of the political leaders of Gujarat, who felt duty-bound to build the capital as a monument to Gandhi's ideals—compress the entire significance of Gandhinagar into a dual between modernity and tradition.

Chandigarh, the archetype of a Garden City dressed in modernist architecture, becomes embattled in the old linguistic battles between Punjabi-speakers and Hindi-speakers, resulting in the bifurcation of the state—and the city—between the states of Punjab and Haryana. The outcome is urban sprawl engendered by both Punjab and Haryana. Bhubaneswar, the capital of Orissa in eastern India, represents the socioreligious conflict between a temple town (Old Bhubaneswar) and a secular city (New Bhubaneswar) and the counterforce of Oriya nationalism that ultimately shaped the outcome of the capital city. Bhubaneswar, because of its multiple relationships, provides a unique opportunity for an examination of rapid urbanization, showing how the resulting sociocultural changes have been adapted in a predominantly rural state (Orissa is 90 percent rural). The government hoped that Bhubaneswar, as a romantic city steeped in pious Hindu sentiment, would unify local sectarian sentiments, encourage economic growth, absorb excess population from the old town, and provide population stability in economically depressed Orissa.

Gandhinagar, the capital of Gujarat in western India, struggled to represent the influence of its native son Mohandas Karamchand Gandhi and his policy of *swadeshi* (Indian-made goods; literally, "of our own country") on the development of the city. Built nearly a generation after independence and Gandhi's death in 1948, Gandhinagar represents a purely indigenous effort in planning and development by Indians. Whereas in the cases of Bhubaneswar and Chandigarh, Indians were forced to acquire technical help from the West, in the case of Gandhinagar they were themselves prepared to undertake the planning.

Gandhinagar was built to serve as the capital of the new state of Gujarat after the bifurcation of bilingual Bombay in 1960. Gandhinagar's story focuses on the historical process through which independent India attempted transformation to modernization and self-sufficiency. Gandhinagar further explores the earlier debate that was central to the building of Bhubaneswar and Chandigarh—the traditionalists harking back to the historicism of the nineteenth century and the reformists calling for the brave new architecture of the modern international style for India's future. Before independence, to many British administrators the question of style was the question of how much "Indianization" to allow without appearing to make political concession to the subject people; but after independence, the question changed to how much "indigenization" could a newly independent nation afford without appearing backward and weak both in its own eyes and in the image it presented to the rest of the world. Where the architecture of Gandhinagar fits into this debate is the central question explored in this book. The other issues explored in Gandhinagar are the urban political tradition and popular participation in the planning process. Through fieldwork and government records, this book documents the aspirations of the people of the new state and the extent of their fulfillment.

Gujarat broadly covers the region of Kutch (bordering Pakistan), Saurastra (the maritime part), and the territories between the rivers Banas and Damanganga. Gujarat derives its name from the Prakrit (vernacular language) Gujjaratta—that is, the Gurjara Rastra, or "land of the Gurjaras." The Gurjaras are believed to have been an immigrant tribe that entered India along with Huns who settled in western Rajasthan. The areas in western India where, in time, Gurjaras came to settle came to be called Gujarat, a name that became popular around the tenth century. Under British rule, Gujarat was placed under the Bombay Presidency, and it was not until 1960 that the state was created in response to nationalist linguistic demands.

There were several sites proposed for the capital of the new state. Ultimately, the debate came to center on Gandhinagar, which was open agricultural fields, and Ahmedabad, an old commercial and educational center of the region. Owners of cotton mills in Ahmedabad, after trying very hard to pull the capital to their city, ultimately agreed to Gandhinagar because of its close proximity. They were equally keen that the new capital must rival Chandigarh, and for this reason they tried to recruit Kahn's services with the help of architect Balkrishna Doshi, albeit unsuccessfully. Doshi, who had studied with both Le Corbusier and Kahn, played a major role in the early discussion on Gandhinagar, arguing for Kahn's selection. Kahn had been active in India, had built the capital of East Pakistan (now Bangladesh), and his work could be seen in Ahmedabad, where he was building the Indian Institute of Management in redbrick. Ultimately, the Indian H. K. Mewada, who had the support of local politicians, was selected to build the city. Mewada had apprenticed with Le Corbusier in Chandigarh as a draftsman, was fiercely Gandhian, and attempted to recapture in the capitol complex the Gujarati past and the Mahatma's ideals.

The three capital cities—Bhubaneswar, Chandigarh, and Gandhinagar—in aggregate show that new designs and planning do not by themselves make the dream of building a modern urban environment come true. Collectively, the three capitals provide a needed antidote to the more familiar oratorical zeal that characterized modernism. Indian architects such as Charles Correa, Achyut Kanvinde, Balkrishna Doshi, and others who came under the spell of modernism later became critical of its utopian promises. The surge of enthusiasm for modernism in the 1950s and 1960s may make the measured reflections on its promises by the major practitioners like Doshi more pertinent now than ever before. Doshi, who in the mid-1960s fought so hard to recruit Louis Kahn to build Gandhinagar, has now come to question his Western-inspired building designs. "I have gradually discovered that the buildings that I have designed seem somewhat foreign and out of milieu; they do not appear to have their roots in the [Indian] soil. With the experience of my work over the years and my own observation, I am trying to understand a little about my people, their traditions, and social customs, and their philosophy of life."

In retrospect, planner H. K. Mewada's conceiving of the Gandhinagar plan in the image of Gandhi stands vindicated. Because Gandhi's own ashram was located downstream on the Sabarmati banks, Mewada placed the Gandhi monument (yet to be constructed) on the banks of the river overlooking the capitol complex along the main axis. "The monument would overlook the great expanse of the lake and the parks and [the] recreational areas along the Sabarmati . . . and would be seen from almost anywhere in the town." But Mewada, himself trained in the United States, was willing to borrow Western ideas wherever he felt they could be used appropriately.

Grumblings about modernism notwithstanding, Le Corbusier provided the designs for postcolonial India: since independence, the clean lines of modern architecture have been making their way fitfully into Indian buildings. They gained acceptance because of their parsimonious expression of design and the unadorned spaces that the modernists love never represented much of a threat to religiously pluralistic India, anxious to create a secular identity. One of the aims of both modernist Nehru and traditionalist Gandhi, after all, was to purify India, to clear out the bric-a-brac of communalism. For that same reason, Hindu nationalists have been more resistant, searching for traditional Hindu symbols. Mewada preferred the simplified forms of modernism, but he also recognized that cities are places of memory. Not just personal memory but of the collective past. At Gandhinagar he tried to express that feeling in traditional iconography, just as before him Julius Vaz had tried to do in Bhubaneswar. Mewada knew that his assignment in Gandhinagar was to provide a space not just for celebrating Gandhi's ideals but also for achieving communal peace, a place where people from different faiths—Hindus and Muslims—could coexist in harmony. That aim has been betrayed by the ca. 2002 religious violence in Gandhinagar—and by the state of Gujarat, which continues to witness the outbreak of tensions between the two communities. But as the city streets become crowded with Hondas, Toyotas, Fords, and other makes of autos and the city fathers pursue the economic promise of information technology as a rival to high-tech Bangalore in the south, it says something about the partial triumph of modernism.

What should an Indian city look like in the twenty-first century? Le Corbusier concluded in Chandigarh that "India had, and always has, a peasant culture that exists since a thousand years! India possessed Hindu temples . . . and Muslim [mosques] . . . the architectural beauty of which is very geometrical. But India hasn't yet created an architecture for modern civilization (offices, factories, buildings)." The past fifty-some years can be distilled into achieving what he spelled out at Chandigarh and for which he provided "some basic principles concerning habitation, which will be as clear as the basic principles of . . . the plan of Chandigarh." While Corbusian forms have been repeated ad infinitum, his message has become lost in modern India.

Meanwhile, Nehru probed the meaning of Indian independence. The socialist sensibility with which Nehru has come to be identified provides the backdrop of his remarks on Indian urbanism. "However well we may deal with the towns," he noted perceptively at the beginning of the experiment in modernism, "the problem of the villages of India will remain for a long time and any social standards that we seek to introduce will be judged ultimately not by what happens in Delhi but in the villages of India." It is as if Nehru's thrill of independence quickly faded. Instead of glory and liberty, he saw illiteracy and poverty and great draping clouds of despair that hung down like gray rags. Moved to exhort his countrymen to expand their lives to encompass new ideas to escape poverty, he blamed tradition for shackling India. The ensuing experiments in modernism took Nehru and the nation to a new world of ideas, and beyond the ugly thoughts that colonial India stirs.

1

The Making of the Gujarat State

GUJARAT, CALLED THE melting pot of India and treasure trove of architectural styles, derives its name from Gujjara-ratta, the form the name takes in Prakrit, the old Indic dialect: the Sanskrit term is Gurjjara-rastra—literally, the "country of the Gurjjaras." The Gurjjaras were a Central Asian tribe believed to have entered India along with the Huns in the mid–fifth century, when the imperial control of the Guptas was on the decline. The Gurjjaras passed through Punjab and settled in parts of Mount Arbuda in the Aravalli mountains, founding a new kingdom at Jodhpur in Rajasthan. The areas where the Gurjjaras had settled came to be called Gujarat by the tenth century, when Mularaja Solanki, the founder of the Hindu Chalukyan dynasty, established his capital at Anhilwada Patan. Anhilwada in time came to be replaced by Ahmedabad, which was picked by Muzaffar Khan as his sultanate's capital in 1412. In time, the city came to rival Manchester in textiles. Bombay became the capital of the region when the British placed Gujarat under the Bombay Presidency, and it was not until 1965, after the unilingual state of Gujarat had been created from the bilingual Bombay in 1960, that Gandhinagar, about 112 kilometers to the north of Ahmedabad, was selected as the site for the new state's capital.

Lying between 20°1' to 24°7' north latitude and 68°4' to 74°4' east longitude, and nestled between the hills of Maharastra and Rajasthan to the north and east, the Pakistan border to the west, and the Arabian Sea to the south, Gujarat includes two parts: Mainland Gujarat, or Gurjjara-rastra, and Peninsular Gujarat, the Sanskrit Saurastra, the Kathiawar of modern history. The total area is about 72,000 square miles, to which Mainland Gujarat contributes 45,000 square miles and Peninsular Gujarat 27,000 square miles. Characterized by a long coastline (it extends from north to south 155 miles, and from east to west 200 miles) and blessed by the Sabarmati, Mahi, Narbada, and Tapti that irrigate Mainland, Gujarat from the earliest times has been called the "granary of India," and this has drawn strangers, both as conquerors and as refugees.

Arriving by sea were probably some of the half-mythic Yadavas (1500–500 B.C.E.); contingents of Yavanas (300 B.C.E.–100 C.E.), including Greeks, Bactrians, Parthians, and Scythians; the pursued Parsis and the pursuing Arabs (600–800 C.E.); hordes of Sanganian pirates (900–1200 C.E.); Parsi and Navayat Muslim refugees from Hulagu Khan's sacking of Persia (1250–1300 C.E.); Portuguese and rival Turks (1500–1600 C.E.); Arab and Persian Gulf pirates (1600–1700 C.E.); African Arab Persians and Makran soldiers of fortune (1500–1800 C.E.); Armenian, Dutch, and French traders (1600–1750 C.E.), and the British (1750–1812 C.E.).[1]

By land from the north came the Scythians and Huns (200 B.C.E.–500 C.E.), the Gurjjaras (400–600 C.E.), the Jadejas and Kathis (750–1500 C.E.), hordes of Afghans, Turks, Mughals, and other northern Muslims (1000–1500 C.E.). Also from the north, the nomadic Aryans, whose early settlements date as far back as 1600 B.C.E., continued to send waves of settlers of Brahmans through modern times (100–1200 C.E.). From the east came the Mauryans (300 B.C.E.), the Guptas (380 C.E.), and other groups. And from the south came the Satakarnis (100 C.E.), the Chalukyans, and Rashtrakutas (650–950 C.E.), occasional Muslim raiders (1000–1600 C.E.), the Portuguese (1500 C.E.), the Marathas (1660–1760 C.E.), and the British (1780–1820 C.E.).[2]

Proximity to the sea and exposure to many cultures experienced through endless invasions has instilled in Gujaratis an enterprise, practicality, catholicity of taste, and social wisdom that has made them one of the more prosperous ethnic groups not only in India but also in other parts of the world, including the United States, where as new immigrants they have quickly assimilated and climbed up the economic ladder. Although not stout in physique, Gujaratis are strong-willed. The volatile history of Gujarat was also to instill in native son Mohandas Karamchand Gandhi the longing for *ahimsa* (nonviolence), which he would successfully translate into a spiritual war of *satyagraha* (his method of nonviolent noncooperation) on the British Raj, earning him the honorific title of Mahatma, the "Great-Souled One." Called a "naked fakir" by Sir Winston Churchill, the wartime prime minister, and "a coolie" by Edwin Samuel Montague, the English secretary of state for India who referred to himself as "an Oriental" because of his Jewish birth, Gandhi was to strip Great Britain of India, its proudest possession. He was to achieve this by finding the right mix between religion and politics that would galvanize his countrymen into a series of protest movements against the British, which may be one of the reasons why there is no consensus on whether he was a religious man or a politician. But in his youth, he spent endless hours looking out to sea, dreaming from the shores of the coastal town of Porbandar. Another Gujarati native son,

Vallabhbhai Patel, who as India's first home minister was instrumental in persuading even the most reluctant princely states to integrate with independent India, came to be known as "the Iron Man."

Based on archaeological finds at Lothal, near Dhandhuka, in Ahmedabad District, and at Rozdi, in Saurastra, the Gujarat region has intimate ties to the Indus Valley, which flourished between 2500 and 1600 B.C.E. The Epic Mahabharatha and Puranas (ancient tales of Hindu gods) tell the story of Lord Krishna and his brother Balrama evacuating Mathura in response to Jarasandha's invasions and of how they established themselves at Dwarka.[3] The Asoka edict engraved on the rock at Junagadh testifies to the influence of imperial Mauryas, while the recovery of old coins establishes the presence of Hellenistic influence in the region. The Rudradaman (150 C.E.) rock inscription in Junagadh suggests the influence of Satraps, who were overthrown by the conquering Guptas in the early fifth century. Chandragupta II (Vikramaditya) issued new silver coins after conquering Gujarat; and Sakandagupta left behind an inscription on the famous Junagadh rock.

By the middle of the fifth century B.C.E., the nomadic Central Asian Hsiung-nu began their first approach at the Khyber Pass, the historic entry point for peoples invading India. The ensuing protracted struggle against the Huns ultimately drained the royal treasury, prompting feudatories to declare independence from the imperial Guptas. By the end of the century, Guptan control was crumbling and much of North India reverted to political fragmentation. In Saurastra (peninsular Gujarat) the kingdom of Valabhi emerged independent of Magadha, with its capital at Valabhipura, a choice possibly influenced by its having a harbor on the Bhavnagar creek. Hiuen Tsang and I-tsing, the Chinese travelers who visited Gujarat in the seventh century, compared the university at Valabhipura with Nalanda in Bihar and with the best centers of learning in China; in time, Valabhi control would extend beyond Gujarat to Malwa. This claim is disputed by the *Gazetteer of the Bombay Presidency* (1896), which suggests that for want of sweet water, Valabhipura would have been rendered unfit to serve as the capital of so large a kingdom as Valabhi.[4] The Valabhi rulers nonetheless are remembered in Gujarati history as enlightened; and although Shaivites themselves, they also patronized Buddhism and Jainism.

The Cavadas (800–942 C.E.), or Capa of Bhinnmal, who were "supposed to have sprung from the bow of Shiva" and who were vassals of the Valabhis controlling parts of north Gujarat, taking advantage of the political instability in the region established the kingdom of Anhilwada (810 C.E.), thus overthrowing their overlords. The new dynasty produced eight rulers: Vanaraja, the founder, taking the credit for founding the capital of Gujarat at Anhilwada Patan on the sacred Sarasvati in northern Gujarat, which was destined to play a great role in the history of Gujarat as the seat of Hinduism. Legend has it that Vanaraja's father was a small chieftain of Capas, at Pancasar, who had been assassinated, and his wife gave birth to Vanaraja (Lord of the Forest) while wondering in the forest. Vanaraja avenged his father's death by establishing his kingdom at Anhilwada. Historical tradition suggests that Pancasar was destroyed by the Arabs in about 810.[5]

The Solankis, or Chalukyans, came to the throne of Gujarat as a result of the adoption of Mularaja by the last Cavada ruler, Samantasimha; Mularaja grew up to become a great patron of the Shaivism branch of Hinduism, and the Solanki kings, like their contemporary Kesari kings in Orissa,[6] attracted learned Brahmans with land grants from the north to Gujarat, just as the linguistic passions for a regional identity in Orissa in the nineteenth century were to have an echo in Gujarat. Gujarati Brahmans such as the Audicyas and Gaudas trace their origins to the time of the Solankis.

It was during Mularaja's reign that Anhilwada became the great seat of Hindu political power and that Lord Somnath (Shiva) became the chief god of the Solankis. The Solanki interlude, lasting nearly five hundred years, witnessed a great effort in public works, the Solanki kings building temples in praise of Hindu gods (mostly to commemorate Shiva and Durga), the finest example of which is the Temple of Somnath at Prabhasa Patan. The Solanki kings built other works of public utility: reservoirs, roads, and guest houses; and it was Bhima (Mularaja's grandson) who also founded the new city of Karnavati, dedicating it to the Hindu goddess Kali and designating it as his second capital. Karnavati is the old site of modern Ahmedabad,[7] which was destined to become a symbol of Hindu/Muslim amity and the best synthesis of the two religions represented in the local architecture.

The birth of Islam in the sands of Saudi Arabia in the year 622 was destined to change fundamentally the course of Indian history, and Gujarat, being a western province, was one of the first to face the fury of the new religion. For the first two decades of Islam's existence, the Muslim religious warriors remained apprehensive about raiding India, and Indian rulers remained blissfully indifferent to its existence. However, Arab merchants, who had been trading with South Asia for several centuries, continued to bring enough wealth to whet the appetites of cash-strapped Muslim rulers, who were finally provoked into action by attacks on Muslim shipping by Sindi—the people of Sind, or Kutch, neighboring Gujarat. The Arab commander of the first Islamic force to reach India reported from Sind to his caliph (the "deputy" of God) in 644 that "water is scarce, the fruits are poor, and the robbers are bold; if a few troops are sent they will be slain, if many, they will starve."

This pessimistic picture of South Asia notwithstanding, the Ummayad governor of Iraq in 711 responded to Sindi attacks on Muslim commercial vessels by conquering Brahmanabad and imposing Islamic rule on the local population. Significantly, Sind would not become the staging ground for Islam's expansion across India; the Arab indifference to maritime activities ruled out any invasions from the Arabian sea backwater. Rather, Islam would march into the Indian subcontinent from the Afghan high board of the Khyber Pass, the ancient gateway to India from the times of the Aryans, and then not before the tenth century.

By the tenth century, the Islamic world was no longer what it had been under the Abbasid caliphate in the mid-eighth century, when it was ruled from Baghdad rather than Damascus or Medina; it had turned into "an empire embellished by Persian civilization, protected by Turkish armed slaves, and enriched by commerce and industry." It had also become too large and unwieldy to control from a central point, and from its fringes, east and west, independent kingdoms emerged under regional rulers who, by the eleventh century, assumed the secular royal title of sultan. The Islamic world was also affected in the tenth century by China's expansion to the west, which drove into Afghanistan and Persia entire tribes of Turkish nomads who since the ninth century had filled the armies of Abbasid kings as slaves (*mamluks*). Out of this political turmoil emerged Alptigin, who founded the first independent Turkish Islamic kingdom at Ghazni in Afghanistan in 962, thereby establishing a dynasty that was to last nearly two hundred years. It was his grandson, Mahmud (971–1030), the "Sword of Islam," who led a series of bloody annual forays into India from his capital at Ghazni.[8]

Beginning in 997, Mahmud would leave frostbitten Ghazni each winter with mechanical regularity and descend into the plains of India, looting Indian cities of their wealth and women and plundering Hindu temples, which he viewed with Islamic iconoclastic fervor as an abomination to Allah. It was on one of these raids, in 1025, that Mahmud targeted the holy city of Somnath, in Peninsular Gujarat. He did so as much because he was lured to its temple treasures and maritime wealth generated from serving as a port of call for ships sailing between Africa and China as because of the promise of paradise for destroying Hindu idols.

Somnath (Prabhasa Patan) derives its name from Soma, the deified juice of the climbing plant *Ascepias acida,* a drink reverently mentioned in the Rig-Veda and popularized by the Brahmans, who thought of it as a panacea, an enlightener and enlivener. In Puranic tales later, Soma became identified with the Moon. Another local legend says that as the result of a quarrel, Soma's body was sliced in half by Shiva's trident, an episode presumably illustrating the victory at a certain point of Shiva's followers over the old shamans.[9] The Arab Ibni Asir (1121 C.E.), who provided a detailed account of the temple of Somnath and its ancient grandeur, speaks of "jewels of incalculable value" that were stored inside, and the temple was endowed with "more than 10,000 villages."[10]

Whatever its real ancestry, such wealth made Somnath ripe for sacking by Mahmud, who returned home to Ghazni with the famed silver gate of the temple, setting in motion a series of Muslim raids that would engulf the city and its rich temples. In 1297, the city was captured by Ala ud-Din Muhammad, the cruel shah of the Khilji dynasty. For nearly a century (1297 to 1392 C.E.), the sultans of Delhi sent governors to administer Gujarat, and they paid tribute to Delhi by plundering Hindu temples, building mosques in all the principal cities. In 1706, Somnath was again sacked, this time by the forces of the zealot Alamgir I (Aurangjeb). Alamgir, who self-righteously inflicted suffering on non-Muslim subjects in peacetime as well as in war, was reviled by Hindus even more than the Ghaznavids and Ghurs had been. Then in 1770 the city was annexed by Amarji, the diwan (minister) to the nawab of Junagadh. The modern temple of Somnath was built at the old site between the years 1950 and 1962, after India's independence—a reconstruction of the Solanki-period temple. This was achieved through the unfailing efforts of Sardar Patel, the native son of Gujarat mentioned above—albeit not without controversy. Prime Minister Nehru declined to inaugurate the temple on the grounds that that would violate India's commitment to secularism, and Nehru also (albeit unsuccessfully) encouraged Dr. Rajendra Prasad, the president of India, to follow his example. A travel guide describes the new temple: "The massive mandapa and the main shrine smaller in area but taller in gentle pyramidal stages loom in a vast courtyard which has the effect of minimizing by optical illusion the number and importance of visitors."[11]

One historian has argued that Islam succeeded in Gujarat because "Jainism, with its insistence on non-violence [ahimsa], and Buddhism, with its [emphasis] on renunciation, combined to create an atmosphere in which patriotism and the martial virtues withered and dropped—naturally."[12] In Gujarat, Buddhism had been introduced by the Mauryan rulers in the third century B.C.E.; Jainism gained currency under the Chalukya period in the second millennium. The Arab merchant Sulaiman in the ninth century confirms Buddhism's existence there: "The chief religion in Gujarat was Buddhism."[13] The Arabs did not fail to note that both Hindu kings and peoples showed toleration to Islam. "This was specially marked in the Rashtrakuta towns where[,] besides free use of mosques and Jama mosques, Musalman magistrates or kazis were appointed to settle disputes among Musalmans according to their own laws." Toleration by Hindu kings of Islam is also mentioned by Al Biruni, who notes that in "the ninth century (581 C.E.) when the Hindus recovered [Sind] . . . they spared the assembly mosque where long after the Faithful congregated on Fridays praying for their Khalifah without hindrance."[14] Moreover, the Arabs did not view Indian rulers as warlike. Sulaiman notes that Indian rulers lacked the drive to conquer or "cause war"; rather, Hindus were devoted to religion and science.[15]

In contrast, monotheistic Islam, powered by the twin doctrine of martial fervor (jihad, holy war) and the ethic of social unity (umma, Islamic brotherhood) that replaced Arab intertribal feuds, made Muslim forces ready to conquer distant lands. The concept of the last judgment day, which was clearly articulated by the prophet Muhammad, buttressed Islam's appetite to expand by promising better prospect of achieving Allah's paradise to those valiant warriors who died in righteous battles.

Iconoclastic Islam in its very nature was opposed to idolatrous Hinduism. Al Idrisi, the Arab traveler who visited Gujarat at the end of the eleventh century, observed that the local inhabitants are "idolators,"[16] which provided the necessary justification either to conquer the rich province or to die in the battle and achieve Allah's paradise.

Islamic rule in Gujarat commenced from the conquest of the province at the close of the thirteenth century by Ala-ud Din Khilji (1296–1316 C.E.), who had usurped the throne of the Delhi sultanate by having his uncle, Jalal-ud Din, murdered in 1296. Originally, Turkish slaves, the Khiljis, had moved to Afghanistan and then settled in India after the Ghaznavid and Ghur invasions. Alu-ud Din's cruelty in the province had earned him the epithet *khooni* (murderer), a name that Gujarati peasants still know him by. Islamic rule in Gujarat ended with the final defeat of the Mughal viceroy Momin Khan by marauding Marathas in February 1758. In 1761, following the Maratha defeat at Panipat, Momin Khan tried to recover the province, but he was unsuccessful, and Muslim rule in Gujarat came to a close.

The term of Muslim ascendancy in Gujarat, stretching over a little more than four and a half centuries, can be divided into three periods. During the first period, from 1297 to 1403 C.E., Gujarat was under the Delhi sultanate, the Khiljis and the Tughlaqs bringing the province under a tighter control of Delhi. During the second period, from 1403 C.E. to 1573 C.E., the province came under the rule of Ahmedabad kings, who had set up an independent kingdom after Muslim governors broke away from the Delhi sultanate. Under the Ahmedabad kings, Gujarat was divided politically into two main parts: one, the crown domain, was administered directly by the central authority at Ahmedabad; the other was left under the control of feudal chiefs who paid tribute to Ahmedabad—a practice that the British were to borrow later in their administration of India. In the third period, 1573–1760 C.E., Gujarat was governed by the Mughals, with Mughal viceroys administering the province. Thereafter, Gujarat would pass over first to the Marathas and then to the British.

If Muslim rule was to polarize the Gujarati society into two opposing religious groups, the Maratha interregnum, which imposed the punitive *chauth* and *sardesh-mukhi* taxes, was to leave a lasting memory that would make integration of Gujarat under the Bombay Presidency by the British impossible. "From first to last the Maratha interests in Gujarat were, except at one or two special junctures, simply pecuniary ones," the *Gazetteer of the Bombay Presidency* concluded. It added: "In comparison with other countries within reach of Maratha arms, Gujarat has always had a very large proportion of inhabitants engaged in commerce and manufacturing industries . . . hence the commercial classes and manufacturers presented the most favourable opportunities for pillage, and the agriculturists were at first only mulcted in forage and provisions."[17]

The Marathas in western India rose as a fierce Hindu opposition to Mughal rule in the second half of the seventeenth century under the leadership of Shivaji Bhonsle (1627–80), who was hailed by his people as the founding father of the Maratha "nation" but reviled by the Mughals as a Deccan "mountain rat." Raised in Poona (modern Pune), the future capital of Maratha power, Shivaji grew to manhood angry with his father, Shahji, for abandoning his adoring mother, Jaji Bai, when she was pregnant with him. The Hindu upbringing provided by his mother made him disapprove not only of Mughal rule itself but also his father's opportunistic career with Muslim Bijapur; however, it was from his father that he learned guerrilla warfare tactics. The diminutive Shivaji yearned to free Maharastra (Great Country) from all foreign rule and to return to it *svaraj* (self-rule) and *svadharma* (native religion)—ideas that later were to influence Gandhi in his political struggle against the British. To pay salaries to his guerrilla fighters, Shivaji devised two types of taxes: one was called *sardeshmukhi* and was only 10 percent of the tax assessment; the other was called *chauth* and made up an additional 25 percent for "Maratha protection."[18] It was the application of these taxes to Gujarat and their abuse amounting to extortion that was to build a lingering resentment among the Gujarati peasants—a resentment that would serve to separate the two peoples.

The connection of the Marathas with Gujarat commenced in 1664 with Shivaji's raids on Surat, then the richest town of western India. It was Shivaji's strategy to plunder and make a quick getaway. This period of Maratha predatory inroads lasted until 1743. In the second phase of their interaction with Gujarat, the British Bombay *Gazetteer* notes, the Marathas acted as mercenaries, when, partly by independent action "but far more by a course of judicious interference in the [local] quarrels of the Mohammedan officials and by loan of troops, [they] acquired considerable territorial advantages. Then came the time of domination, from 1760 to 1801, during which period the Gaekwad influence was occasionally greater than that of the Peshwa." After 1802, the internal power struggle between Poona, which was in control of the peshwa, and Baroda, which was in control of Gaekwad, so weakened the hold of the Marathas on Gujarat that the paramount power passed over to the British long before the downfall of Balajirao Peshwa and the final annexation of his territories in 1819.[19]

The British first came in contact with Gujarat on August 24, 1608, when three English ships led by the flagship *Hector* under Captain William Hawkins of the East India Company dropped anchor off Surat at the mouth of the Tapti River. Surat was a bustling city and principal port of the Mughal Empire. The western gateway to India, which had been sacked in turns by the Portuguese, the Muslims, and the Marathas, was about to undergo yet another transformation, as it did recently in the 1990s after the scare of the bubonic plague. Hawkins found the port city crowded with Muslim pilgrims waiting for a passage to Mecca. Its streets were filled with Indians, Arabs, Jews, Armenians, Portuguese, Dutch, and many other merchants, engaged in a trade of goods encompassing luxuries as well as necessities. Its warehouses bulged with indigo, cotton, carpets, kinkabs, and satin, ready for export; and its playhouses offered every amusement and creature comfort in return for specie.

In the midst of wealth and pleasure, Hawkins found himself an unwelcome guest: "First ignored, next humiliated, then robbed by Mughal officials (his ship and most of his crew were captured by Portuguese pirates while he was ashore at Surat)." He was discouraged to learn that British products were not desired in India, just as, in 1793, King George III's ambassador to China was to be disappointed by the Chinese; and he became fearful of Portuguese Jesuits at Agra and Delhi (the twin capitals of the Mughals), whom he believed "had helped convert Indian apathy and neutrality toward Englishmen into positive aversion." But in late November 1612, the British victory at sea over the Portuguese "shifted the balance of Anglo-Portuguese power in the Indian Ocean and effectively neutralized the influence of Portuguese Jesuits at [the Mughal Court]."[20]

By the time Sir Thomas Roe, King James's ambassador, visited Mughal Emperor Jhangir in 1616 to present his credentials, "there was a new mood . . . awaiting him [at the Mughal court]." Although the Mughals found Portuguese proselytizing practices annoying, in the absence of their own naval fleet they had depended on Portuguese protection for the safe passage of their annual pilgrim ship to Mecca. They "now looked instead toward the more seaworthy, less bigoted British for this religiously vital service," which ultimately allowed Roe "to win permission in 1619 for the English East India Company to build a factory at Surat." Roe, like the Arab commander who cautioned his caliph from Sind in 644 C.E., warned against any precipitous penetration of India, urging "rest content with profits derived from 'quiet trade.'"[21]

Quiet trade was quickly disturbed for the British by their defeat at the hands of the mercantilist Dutch in the Indies in the winter of 1623. The British defeat changed the course of Indian history by forcing the East India company "to abandon Southeast Asia and fall back on India as a second-best base of operation." Surat became the company's principal port, and from it British influence would extend to the Arabian Sea and the Persian Gulf, dismantling "Portuguese power in the latter in 1622 by seizing Ormuz. Thereafter, Persian silk competed with Gujarati calico as England's favorite textiles from the East . . . [and] English annual imports of Indian calico 'pieces' . . . jumped from fourteen thousand in 1619 to over two hundred thousand in 1625." However, the growing demand for indigo and saltpeter, which were produced in the eastern Gangetic plain, combined with the famine of 1630 in Surat, convinced the British to diversify their base operation in India. "Surat remained the company's west coast headquarters, but Bombay, which had been given to Charles II as part of Catherine of Braganza's dowry in 1661 and turned over to John Company [the East India Company] in 1668 for £10 annual rent, would soon displace it."[22]

In early 1759, two company clerks were murdered and the factory at Surat was plundered, setting the stage for a power struggle among rival Muslim factions for the control of the government. In retaliation, in March the company captured the city. From that year until 1800, the British were complete masters of Surat and its territories, sharing land revenue and sea customs with the nawab of Surat and the Marathas.[23] The British, true to their national character, had transformed themselves from merchants into rulers.[24]

In the logic of its new role, the British East India Company, in complete disregard of Roe's warning, was now lured into an imperial expansion, which came to be exemplified in Richard Colley Wellesley's (1761–1842) subsidiary alliance system. The subsidiary alliance system, as perfected and implemented in India, was intended to secure more real estate directly under British India. The logic of the system was that by persuading princely India to enter into a subsidiary alliance in return for "protection," the British would be killing two birds with one stone: restoring political peace to turbulent India and eliminating any European threat to their paramountcy, particularly from the French. So, in 1800, when the nawab of Surat died without an heir, the British annexed the port state. The Bombay Presidency proclamation of May 6, 1800, declared:

> This is therefore to give notice to all the inhabitants of the town of Surat and the dependencies that the Hon'ble Company's exclusive Government commences from this day being Thursday, the 15th May 1800 . . . all persons now in civil offices are to continue to act under the administration of the Hon'ble Company until further orders and their future permanency will of course in a great measure depend upon the good pleasure of Government, upon their diligence in their several duties and their fidelity to the English Sircar [government].[25]

Self-righteously, the proclamation concluded that Surat was being acquired to procure a just, wise, and efficient administration for the lives, properties, and promotion of happiness of all its inhabitants. The British insisted, incredibly, that "Oriental races are so accustomed to violent measures that they seldom appreciate moderation or forbearance"; on the other hand, "the national character for even-handed justice had made the English name respected throughout India and far across the steppes of Central Asia."[26]

Surat was now placed under the administration of the Bombay Presidency for the sake of administrative convenience, always of paramount concern to the British, in complete disregard of ethnic or linguistic considerations; it would remain with Bombay along with other territories of Gujarat as they came to be acquired gradually until May 1, 1960, when the new state was created. At the beginning of the nineteenth century, what stood between the British and the rest of the Gujarat territories was the divided Maratha Pentarchy. The same year that Surat was acquired by the British, Nana Phadnis (1742–1800), the wise adviser to the young and inexperienced peshwa, Baji Rao II (1775–1851), died. After the nana's death, the old rivalry between Daulat Rao Sindhia and Yeshwant Rao Holkar again erupted violently, forcing the puppet peshwa, who had nominally ruled Poona since his accession in 1796, to seek refuge aboard a British warship, which took him to Bassein, north of Bombay. By the Treaty of Bassein, signed on December 31, 1802, Baji Rao II became Wellesley's subsidiary ally, ceding the Maratha domain he had abandoned to the British. "This de jure surrender of Maratha power would be sealed in blood some sixteen years later. The Treaty of Bassein may, however, be said to herald a century of almost unchallenged rule over India's subcontinent by Britain's New Mughals."[27]

Capitalizing on their sudden good fortune, in August 1803 the British wrested the wealthy Broach state from Sindhia.[28] Sixteen years later, a Scot, Mountstuart Elphinstone (1779–1859), Lord Wellesley's trusted protégé and a political appointee of the Francophobic Henry Dundas, defeated Baji Rao II before he could translate his pretensions of reviving the Maratha authority into reality. By the treaty of Poona (1818), the British domination was conclusively established over India, and British rule was underwritten by the company's army, and consequently the open warfare of the eighteenth century was finally suppressed.

Elphinstone administered the newly conquered Gujarat territories, soon to be integrated into the presidency of Bombay, over which he presided, with impartiality and efficiency, as governor from 1819 to 1827. "Dependent on Indian clerks and subordinate officials, and beholden to Indian landholders or peasant leaders, the conquerors were strictly limited in what they could achieve, for to a great extent the British empire in India remained an empire run and garrisoned by Indians."[29] The British claim to fair and just administration in India rested not on the reduced land revenue that was collected but on "the methodical, evenhanded way in which newly conquered territories were 'settled.'"[30] After paying the company's share of the crop, *ryots* (peasants) could live out the rest of the year without fear of any further extortion. In contrast, the Marathas had been mainly interested in squeezing out as much revenue as possible from the cultivators through a class of middlemen called *manooteedars*, who were no better than *shaukars* (usurers), charging the ryots as much as 25 percent in interest.

British Gujarat occupied a small area in the sprawling Bombay Presidency, comprising about 10,082 square miles (roughly 8.10 percent of the whole). Its population density, however, was twice that of Bombay Deccan, and, as reported in 1872 in the first census of British India, it exceeded in population any other division of the presidency. Then there was Gujarat, made up of feudatory states subordinate to the British. Gujarat districts were redrawn based on the earlier experience of the British in Bengal; and in 1827 Elphinstone enacted a civil and criminal code that became the substantive law of the land. The *Gazetteer* reported: "[The code] was simple and admirably suited to the people, but justice was administered according to the spirit rather than the letter of the law. A district officer would have incurred severe censure if his decisions were found to be inequitable, however they might have been supported by the letter of the law."[31]

Still, the tranquil Gujarat erupted in violence in response to the outbreak of the mutiny in the north in 1857. The *Gazetteer of the Bombay Presidency* assessed the situation in Gujarat as follows:

Very soon after the outbreak of the mutinies in the North-west of India in May 1857, an uneasy feeling began to prevail in the Bombay Presidency, especially in Gujarat. The story of the greased cartridges had been industriously reported and found credulous listeners in every village. A similar incident occurred in Gujarat. A consignment of salt from the Ran of Kachh [Kutch] having been carried in bags which had previously held red ochre (*sindur*) had become discoloured. . . . [A] report was at once spread that the salt had been defiled with cow's blood. It was believed in Ahmedábád and throughout Gujarat that this was a device of the British Government to destroy the caste of the people as preliminary to their forcible conversion to Christianity. . . .

The native press, which had been merely disloyal, now assumed an attitude of decided hostility. . . . [A]bsurd rumours were circulated of the approach of a combined Russian and Persian army, which, it was said, had reached Attok and would shortly invade Hindustan. . . .

The native press was not the only source of sedition. The fall of the British Government was openly predicted in every masjid. . . .

. . . both Muslims and Hindus looked forward to a period of anarchy during which they might indulge that appetite for plunder which had been restrained for so many years. . . .

The operations of the Inám Commission and the Survey Department were also a fruitful cause of alarm and discontent. . . . When the Survey Department revealed the fact that nearly a fourth part of the fertile province of Gujarat was [illegally] [rent-free] . . . a due regard for the public interests demanded that there should be an investigation into the title on which the lands were held rent-free. . . . The Bráhmans and the priesthood of every sect [who held these lands] deeply resented the scrutiny of the Inám Commission . . . [and viewed] the inquiry as a sacrilegious attack on their religious endowments and a departure from the principle of neutrality and toleration which had been the policy of Government from a very early period.[32]

The *Gazetteer* provides a tacit admission of the failure of company rule, revealing the Gujarati people's growing discontentment with both administrative and land-revenue practices. The British bureaucracy in India also came under attack from the conservative lobby in Britain, particularly from legal minds, now that travel to India was easier because of the improved land route. The British administrator was viewed as inept in law and morally bankrupt because of the widespread practice of concubinage among British expatriates, which was viewed in Victorian Britain as "vulgar" and "immoral." The British press, too, was quick to raise an outcry against the Indian government.

But as everywhere else in agricultural British India, the fundamental source of discontent was land revenue. The British were not prepared to surrender this vital source of income, and the peasant had to borrow at such an exorbitant rate to fulfill his tax obligation that ultimately he became bankrupt. For the first sixteen years of their rule, ending in 1816, the British had made no ryotwari (peasant) settlement. The British continued with the old system in which they contracted with the desais (the middlemen), who collected the revenue in return for a percentage for their service. Under the Marathas, the desais had squeezed the ryots into poverty and had become petty rajas (rulers).

Also, all over Gujarat there were large tracts of lands called "alienated," the holders of which either paid no assessment at all or only a quit rent. These alienations, which originated as private landed property with the Mughal and Maratha conquests, meant a substantial loss to British India's treasury. The British divided all alienated lands into two categories: (1) lands privately held in return for service to the government or as religious endowments; and (2) lands occupied through extortion. Always looking to the standardization of practices, the British applied to these lands a "summary settlement." All those willing to pay quit rents varying in amount determined by the occupancy of tenure were confirmed in their titles under new deeds issued by the British government. In 1810, the Court of Directors suggested that holders of alienated lands be offered annuities equivalent to the income they derived from their estates, secured by the government and payable from the public treasury—thereby legalizing the ownership. Later, the British changed their position, declaring that no lands could be alienated.[33] Thus, the British had created a situation for political agitation.

Although by September 1857 the British had regained firm control of Delhi, the war lingered on over northern and central India until late in 1858, when peace was finally restored. The 1857 war proved to be a terminal point for three principal players of the preceding century: the Mughals, the peshwa, and the Honorable Company. The fiction of the Mughal government was finally ended. The peshwa renounced whatever pretensions he had of reviving his power at Poona. The character of British India was fundamentally altered when, by the Government of India Act of 1858, all rights of the company in India were transferred directly to the Crown.

No sooner had the British contained the Mutiny of 1857 than western India felt the seismic impact of the American Civil War, starting in 1861. Gujarat, as a principal cotton grower, experienced sudden prosperity, resulting from rising prices for cotton. There was fear that the spread of cotton cultivation would replace food cultivation, but this was ill-founded. As the prices of cotton started to fall after 1865, the economic boom in Gujarat vanished. After the opening of the Suez Canal in 1869, Indian cotton exports improved, but not enough to dislodge the hold of American cotton on Liverpool. Having tasted prosperity, the Gujaratis started to develop disaffection, which would find expression in regional and national political movements.

A lasting impact of British rule had been the introduction of English education and language, which in itself was not without controversy. Some Orientalist scholars in the tradition of Sir William Jones (1746–94), who founded the Asiatic Society of Bengal in Calcutta in 1784, argued that Indians would profit more from learning about Indian civilization through the study of Sanskrit, Persian, and indigenous languages. Utilitarians, driven by mercantile considerations and English pride, reasoned that the British were obliged to teach the English language to at least enough natives to facilitate the effective administration of a growing British India.[34] In the end, the implementation of English education resulted in accelerating "demands for the demise of British rule by arming India's elite with the words in which to call for it."[35] It was from the ranks of this elite class that Gujarat would provide a Gandhi (Mohandas Karamchand Gandhi) to spearhead India's struggle for independence; and a Patel (Vallabhbhai Patel) to persuade recalcitrant rulers of independent states to join the Indian Union. This elite also included a poet, Kavi Narmad, who articulated regional sentiment in the poem "Jai Jai Garvi Gujarat," which was to become the national anthem of Gujarat; and the leader Indulal Yagnik, who headed the Maha Gujarat Andolan (movement) for the creation of the new state.

Governor Elphinstone first introduced English-language education in Bombay and himself became president of the Bombay Education Society. In 1820, he formed a committee of the society, called the Native School and Schoolbook Committee. Two years later, this committee was transformed into an independent entity called the Native Schoolbook and School Society, the purpose of which was to produce books in native languages, to improve schools and create new ones, to prepare a cadre of qualified teachers, and to promote the study of English and Western sciences. In 1827, the society changed its name to the Bombay Native Education Society. In 1825–26, the society supplied the first batch of trained teachers to take up positions in schools in the Bombay Presidency. One of its first graduates was Runchhodlal Girdharadas (1803–73), of Broach, who joined the faculty of the society. It was his responsibility to recruit potential Gujarati teachers and to assist in the preparation of textbooks for schools. Ten Gujarati teachers completed their training in 1826, going on to occupy positions at new schools opened by the Bombay Presidency at Surat, Ahmedabad, Dholka, Broach, Kaira, and Nadiad. For this contribution, Girdharadas earned himself the lasting epithet "Father of Education in Gujarat."[36]

Bombay became a training school in English education and social reform for Indians long before it was to become the cotton capital of India, and the new ideas radiating from it spread slowly to western India, including Gujarat. The establishment of Bombay University in 1857 provided a new impetus to English-language education: Indians proving eager to learn the new language through their proficiency in English held out the promise of economic success and social mobility. By the end of the nineteenth century, there were 2 colleges, 4 high schools, 52 middle schools, and 1,339 primary schools in British Gujarat; and Gujarat states quickly duplicated these new temples of learning to create new opportunities for their citizens. With the spread of English-language education came printing presses, newspapers, periodicals, libraries, and cultural and political associations that would initiate reform movements in Gujarat.

The first Gujarati newspaper was the *Bombay Samachar* (Bombay news). Started in the summer of 1822, it was to be followed, in Ahmedabad in the summer of 1849, by the weekly *Vartaman*. By 1854, the *Samachar* had been taken over by the Gujarat Vernacular Society. The society had been founded in Ahmedabad in December 1848 by the Englishman Alexander Kinloch Forbes (1821–65). Influenced by the English educational system, the new urban Gujarati associations and societies differed from traditional ones in that they ignored caste considerations and propagated progressive reforms for lifting women and lower-caste groups up out of their social shackles. In time, these associations became training schools for political activism, and from among their ranks came the leaders to articulate regional sentiment as well as nationalistic aspirations. The evolution of regional sentiment in Gujarat was the result of its being placed in a presidency that comprised in the main two distinct linguistic groups, which created the need to maintain, even sharpen, the differences between them as a safeguard against one another. British administrative divisions had been created on the basis of efficiency rather than historical and ethnic sensitivity, and for Gujarat that meant living with the bitter memory of Maratha misrule, notwithstanding the efforts of the nationalists to reconstruct a past in which Shivaji was the national hero.

Arguably, the credit for first articulating the idea of Gujarati identity (*asmita*) is assigned to Narmadshankar Lalshankar Dave (1833–86), popularly known in Gujarat as Kavi (Poet) Narmad. A Brahman by birth, hailing from Surat, where he completed his primary education, Narmad intermittently attended the venerable Elphinstone College in Bombay, where he was exposed to progressive ideas such as remarriage for widows, female education, the liberalization of caste practices, and the readmission of Hindus who had converted to Christianity or Islam back to Hinduism. It was at Elphinstone that Narmad first formulated the dream of becoming a social reformer, and he subsequently started his Marathi weekly, the

Bombay Darpan (Bombay mirror), which was one of the earliest publications in western India to advocate social reform. He taught and wrote essays and poems to galvanize his people into action and founded the Budhivardhak Sabha (Intellectual society) for the propagation of his ideas.

But by the mid-1860s, Narmad had become disenchanted with the West-inspired reform movement and, as a result of his contact, albeit brief, with the Hindu revivalist Swami Dayanand Saraswati, began to reexamine his Hindu roots and Aryan origins. Reinventing himself, Narmad now became a crusader for the revivalist movement started by Mansukram Suryaram Tripathi (1840–1907). Returning to Bombay from Surat in 1875, the year that Swami Dayanand had founded Arya Samaj, a society promoting Hindu revivalism, in that city, he turned his home into a forum for Gujarati renaissance. Thinkers such as Manchharam Ghelabhai, Kikabhai Parbhudas, Ichharam Suryaram Desai, Ranchhodbhai Udayram, Nagindas, Ulsidas, Ganesh Shridhar Khapardo, Manilal Nabhubhai Dwivedi, and Mansukhram Suryaram Tripathi met in his home to debate Gujarati issues.[37] Tripathi was the first to search for cultural identity and exhort Gujaratis to take pride in their cultural tradition; Desai (1853–1912) provided the call for cultural identity by starting *Swatantra*, a monthly journal that was critical of British rule, and he narrowly escaped being convicted of treason; Narmad himself composed "Jai Jai Garvi Gujarat," which as Gujarat's first national anthem galvanized the people. The essence of these nationalist ideas was clearly not lost on Mohandas Karamchand Gandhi,[38] who employed both the vocabulary as well as the imagery used by these early Gujarati nationalists in his struggle against the raj. The same vocabulary and imagery would later help shape the movement for a separate state of Gujarat.

Cultural nationalism in Gujarat also received a fillip from the regional movements in Assam and Orissa. Annexation of Assam and Orissa by the British in the nineteenth century had resulted in those two provinces being placed under the Bengal government, with disastrous consequences. Bengali *bhadralok* ("gentle people"; intellectuals) had succeeded in persuading the British government that neither Assamese nor Oriya was an independent language and that both regions owed their development in religion, culture, language, and social practices to Bengal. Pressure from Bengalis had resulted in the introduction of Bengali in schools and law courts, marginalizing both Assamese and Oriya in their respective regions. The British physical and political dismemberment of Assam and Orissa and their deliberate neglect of the Assamese and Oriya languages resulted in producing separatist movements in the two provinces in the nineteenth century, which ultimately culminated in the formulation of separate states. Taking their cue from Assam and Orissa, the Gujaratis, too, concluded that there would really be no good done to Gujarat if Marathi were made compulsory for all and Gujarati were abolished.[39] Even Mahatma Gandhi, whose mother tongue was Gujarati, supported the demands from many regions for linguistic states, although he enthusiastically chose Hindi as the national language because it was spoken by a plurality of India's population and was closely related to all other modern Indo-Aryan languages of northern India. Whatever doubts Gujarat might have had on the demand for a separate state withered in the winter of 1952, when Potti Sitaramulu, the revered father of the Andhara movement, fasted to death, leading to the creation of Andhra the following year.

To be sure, in Gujarat, as in other regions, there was tension between, on the one hand, the regional instinct, embellished by linguistic passions and economic self-interest, and, on the other, a new nation-state, suspicious of divisive demands. Prime Minister Nehru was less supportive of the movement for linguistic provinces than Gandhi had been; and Morarjibhai Desai, the Gujarati chief minister of Bombay distinguished by his steel-rimmed glasses, came to personify the steel-trap mind untethered by insight. Counternational currents came to disdain "regionalism" as a mask for cultural chauvinism. Declaring that a separate state of Gujarat would be created only "over my dead body," Morarjibhai proceeded to mobilize resentment against "nattering nabobs of negativism," to use a phrase that U.S. Vice President Spiro T. Agnew uttered in another context. Morarjibhai did not suffer politically from his evident contempt for Gujarati regionalists, his ignorance of history, his reliance on crackpot ideas, and not even from his questionable Ayurvedic (Indian medicine) practices. That he was opposed by his own Gujarati people only inflated his aura, catapulting him to the prime ministership of India in the late 1970s.

In postindependence India, nationalist arrogance came in direct conflict with cultural chauvinism. Here lay a supremely Indian paradox: the same Indians who castigated the British for insensitivity to Indian culture were suspicious of regionalists and tricksters. Surely the English infusion into Indian politics—the premium on popular protest, the blending of economic self-interest with political participation—contributed to regional political awareness. A central force boosting regional politics since Charles Wood's "Education Dispatch" of July 1854 (which led to the birth of India's three presidency universities in 1857, as well as to many missionary-run vernacular schools funded by government grants-in-aid) had been the bulking up of popular politics and, in particular, the rise of a new middle class. It was this middle class that in the late nineteenth century came to see its self-interest in regional terms, rather than national ones. On the other hand, the Indian National Congress, in an effort to maintain its preeminent corporate position in national politics, frequently worked to depoliticize regional and local movements.[40]

But the more striking transformation in Indian politics since independence occurred within the fifty years from Pandit Nehru, a man of tremendous historical and philosophical sophistication, to Bal Thakare, an intelligent man who legitimizes Hindu revivalism and gives respect to regionalism, defending that choice on the ground that, after all, Indian civilization is Aryan in origin, and Shivaji, the Maratha hero, represents the Hindu ideals. Thus does regionalism make its peace with political populism.

With Nehru-Gandhi, *père et fille*, there is another turn in the history of the Indian aversion to regionalism: Congress's aristocratic disdain for practical intellectuals, the business types and regional leaders whose rising power displaces their own. At its Nagpur session of 1920, Congress had adopted Hindi as India's "national" language, sharing the platform with English and destined to be designated the "official language of the Union" by India's constitution. More significant, however, was the decision at Nagpur to substitute India's internal provincial boundaries drawn along regional linguistic lines for the more arbitrary administrative divisions created by the British. The decision was enthusiastically welcomed by several regional movements fighting for separate provinces. In Orissa, which at the time was under Bengal administration, the Utkal Union Conference passed the historic resolution accepting the Congress creed as one of its objectives.[41]

Congress's success with regional linguistic movements was due mainly to its finally having adopted the principle of linguistic nationalism for the formation of Indian provinces. Congress had then organized itself into twenty-one linguistic provincial committees, and after independence it was expected that the Congress government would take the necessary steps to implement such reorganization. The partition of India served to make the Congress leadership very suspicious of regional linguistic demands, however, and reorganization of provincial boundaries along linguistic lines came to be equated with balkanization of the new nation. But linguistic separatist demands continued to be made with evangelical zeal, and Prime Minister Nehru ultimately relented by conceding to the creation of Andhra in 1953. Conceding to the Telugu people, who had been bundled by the British under the Madras administration, set the precedent, and now Nehru was faced with a plethora of demands from many regions of India for linguistic states, including Gujarat.

Since 1908, Gujarati leaders like Ranjitram and K. M. Munshi, the nationally celebrated writer, spoke of Maha (Greater) Gujarat, and Gujarati cultural consciousness continued to deepen in the following decades with the introduction of responsible government by the British. At the close of British rule, Gujarat, a frontier state, was affected by the partition of India in 1947. Although it did not experience communal riots on the scale witnessed in Punjab and Calcutta, nearly two hundred thousand Gujaratis and more than one hundred thousand Hindu Sindis fled Pakistan to settle in Gujarat. Moving in the other direction, thousands of Muslims from Gujarat peacefully migrated to Pakistan. The credit for maintaining relative law and order in Gujarat goes to Sardar Patel, a criminal lawyer by training and a master of political maneuvering. Many members of the Congress Working Committee, which served as the executive committee of the Congress Party, considered the *sardar* (leader) to be a more worthy successor to Gandhi than Nehru, but in the end he accepted the position of deputy prime minister, a position especially created for him. He was obliged to remain in the shadow of the charismatic Nehru, just as Gujarat was to remain in the shadow of cosmopolitan Bombay. Peace notwithstanding, the road to separate statehood after independence proved tortuous for Gujarat.

Patel, as minister of states, assisted by his able secretary, V. P. Menon, persuaded all but one—Junagadh—of the independent states of Gujarat to accede to the new Indian dominion by August 15, 1947. (Hyderabad was the other state that refused to join the Indian dominion. The Hindu ruler of Kashmir vacillated until he came under direct attack from Pakistani troops. Because Gujarat borders Pakistan, the Indian government was extremely anxious about any Gujarati state raising the flag of independence.) Much smaller in size than most other states (roughly 3,200 square miles), situated on the coast of the Kathiawar peninsula some three hundred miles by sea from Karachi, the Junagadh population was nearly 80 percent Hindu, but had a Muslim ruler. The state had special significance for Hindus and Jains because of the location of the famous temple of Somnath and Jain temples on Mount Girnar. Diwan A. K. M. Hussain, who had shrewdly recommended to the nawab that the state accede to India, fell ill, to be succeeded by Sir Shah Nawaz Bhutto, the father of Berkeley-educated Zulfiqar Ali Bhutto, who later became Pakistan's prime minister and was subsequently executed. Shah Nawaz announced the accession of Junagadh to Pakistan on behalf of the nawab on August 15, 1947. The Indian government responded by imposing an economic blockade and subsequently armed a "liberation army" of Hindus émigrés to take control of the state. By the spring of 1948, Junagadh had been included into the Union of States of Saurastra, which had been newly created under the guidance of Sardar Patel and V. P. Menon to amalgamate Kathiawar's 222 states politically, after the example of the Eastern States of Orissa.[42]

On February 15, 1948, the United States of Kathiawar (Saurastra) was inaugurated by Sardar Patel. The unification had been agreed to by more than two hundred states, largely because the alternative would have been to be under the Bombay administration. This was the first political formulation of Gujarati-speaking states. It was also agreed that in the event of the formulation of a separate state of Gujarat on a linguistic basis, the Kathiawar union would automatically merge with it. As a temporary measure, the Kathiawar union accepted the jurisdiction of the Bombay High Court.

However, the future of Saurastra became uncertain when Baroda (modern Vadodara), the largest state in Gujarat (8,000 square miles), made a bid for the paramountcy of Gujarat. Maharaja Pratapsinghrao told the Indian government that, in return for assisting India against the secessionist Junagadh, he should be declared the paramount ruler of Saurastra and Gujarat. Sardar Patel refused to concede to

Pratapsinghrao, who was charged by the Indian government with misrule. After a series of political maneuverings, Pratapsinghrao agreed to join the Indian Union in January 1949. On March 29, 1949, the agreement was ratified, and on May 1 Baroda's administration was placed under the Bombay government.

Under the constitution of India (1950)—a document carefully crafted by Dr. B. R. Ambedkar, the distinguished leader of the Mahars of Maharastra, who had trained in law in London and completed his doctorate at Columbia University—Gujarat had been divided into three separate units, each with different administrative characteristics. Mainland Gujarat (North, Central, and South) was integrated with the A class state of Bombay. Saurastra was a B class state of the Indian federation, with its capital at Rajkot, while Kutch, being a border region with Pakistan, was placed under the administration of the Union government as a C class state without a local legislative assembly. The central government poured money into Kutch for both maintaining the army and for resettling Sindi refugees. The Kandala port came to replace the loss of Karachi, and the new town of Gandhidham was built next to it as the capital of the state to rehabilitate the government and the refugees. However, the Indian government refused to offer resettlement grants to the Gujarati migrants returning from Sind on the grounds that they were not "truly" refugees since they were "returning home." This was in contrast to the treatment afforded the Punjabis and the Bengalis, and the bitterness of this political inequity was to linger in the Gujarati memory, which would have its revenge ten years later in the local elections of 1957.

Patel handpicked his most trusted men to administer Saurastra, which had practically no administrative infrastructure or financial resources. Shri Uchhrang-rai Dheber was selected to head the state government, and he confessed that "when we assembled at our new Capital of Rajkot, we had neither a chair to sit upon nor an office to stand in."[43] Money had to be borrowed from a local *shaukar* (businessman) to pay salaries, and a hospital building had to be requisitioned and hastily converted into a secretariat. The administrative hierarchy was a patchwork of administrators borrowed from a number of states. The matters were made worse by the princes, who, angry about the loss of their estates, retaliated by sponsoring gangsters to disrupt law and order.

Bombay continued to exert its political influence on Saurastra. In the first general elections of 1951, Saurastra had six seats in the Lok Sabha (the house of the people, or lower house). Congress, which swept the polls, secured five seats, of which two members (Chimanlal Chakubhai and Narendra Nathwani) were from Bombay and had absolutely no roots in Saurastra. By the late 1950s, Congress began to lose its appeal, even though it held on to its provincial majority in the 1957 general elections in Gujarat. However, Saurastra remained relatively quiet until linguistic passions broke out in Bombay, where two new political parties suddenly rose to prominence—the Samyukta Maharastra Samiti (United Maharastra party) and the Maha Gujarat Janata Parishad (Greater Gujarat people party)—gaining widespread appeal and displacing Congress on linguistic loyalties.

Congress's codification of Indian nationalism and Nehru's long ascendancy had not changed the fundamentals of pluralistic India. Nehru was not especially serious about the linguistic demands, even though he was elegant, witty, and, by all accounts, sensitive to regional differences. In its report, the Dhar Commission, which had been appointed by the Nehru government, completely rejected the very idea of linguistic units, handing New Delhi its worst public relations disaster. Widespread political protests broke out throughout the country, ushering in a riotous decade. Moved by growing political unrest, the prime minister appointed another committee to study the linguistic demand. The new committee consisted of Nehru himself, Patel, and Congress historian Pattabhi Sitarammaiya. The JVP Committee, as it came to be called, accepted the principle of linguistic units, but recommended that its implementation should be deferred to an unspecified later date, ostensibly in the national interest. However, the committee made an exception in the case of Andhra, which could be created as soon as the Telugus and the Tamils could reach an accord on the city of Madras. Even the Constituent Assembly had given its nod to the principle of linguistic units in article 3, which empowered the parliament to reorganize political boundaries as and when it became necessary and expedient. However, matters were to remain moribund until Potti Sitaramulu fasted to death.

By the mid-1950s, "linguistic nationalism" had become an all-purpose epithet, used by neoconservatives against the "new class" (the "new class" consisted of all political intellectuals except themselves), by hard-nosed provincial leaders against the central government, and by nationalists in general against regionalists in general. Populist resentment flourished even as (and perhaps, in part, because) populist egalitarianism of an economic stripe was dwindling. Provincial politics had introduced suspicion of centralized rationality—enhancing the reputation of "regional" politics and elevating the demand for the reorganization of states along linguistic lines. Nehru was finally forced to appoint a commission—the State Reorganization Commission (SRC)—which delivered its report in October 1955. Another year elapsed before the SRC recommendations were implemented, as a consequence of which India was reapportioned into fourteen states and six centrally administered union territories. Each of the Indian states was now supposed to represent a population speaking a common language.

The linguistic demand initially did not impassion the Gujaratis, however, who greatly profited from their association with Bombay. Bombay had been the educational and economic hub of the Gujaratis from the time of British rule. Wealthy Gujaratis, moreover, had set up cotton mills and businesses in Bombay. The Gujaratis from North Gujarat, Kutch, and Saurastra had closer ties to Bombay than to Mainland Gujarat. Morarji Desai, the leader of the Gujarat Congress

Party, was strongly opposed to a separate Gujarat on financial grounds. The Maha Gujarat Parishad did not yet have a widespread appeal among the Gujaratis, although the Samyukta Maharastra Samiti demanded the integration of all Marathi-speaking areas, with Bombay as the capital.

Again, there is continuity from the earlier nation under the British. The SRC recommended that the state of Bombay be made bilingual, despite the fact that the territory was, linguistically, divided geographically: the Deccan portion of its population overwhelmingly spoke Marathi, while the region north of the city of Bombay, including the Kathiawar peninsula (Saurastra), predominantly spoke Gujarati. The bilingual arrangement was to be achieved by excluding Kannada-speaking districts and by including Saurastra and Kutch. Viderbha, a Marathi-speaking region, was to be maintained as a separate unit. The SRC report outraged the Maharastrians, who were now a minority in their own state. The report had unwittingly made the same mistake the British had made in Bengal at the beginning of the twentieth century when they bifurcated the province. Bombay became a center of blind fury, and in 1956 anti-Gujarati riots broke out throughout the city, resulting in loss of life and property. The emotional divide between Gujarat and Maharastra was complete. Ashok Mehta, the astute Gujarati Congressman who was to play a prominent role on the national scene, endorsed the recommendation made by the Gujarat Pradesh Congress Committee (1955) that Maharastra, Gujarat, and the city of Bombay be turned into separate units. Morarji Desai fasted to register his opposition to the loss of Bombay to Gujarat. Y. B. Chavan, the shrewd Maharastrian chief minister of Bombay who was later to hold several cabinet positions in Congress governments, including the portfolio of defense minister, declared that there was no emotional integration of the Marathi- and the Gujarati-speaking areas.[44] The compromise that was finally worked out provided the inclusion of Viderbha and Marathawada within the state of Bombay, which thus turned Gujaratis into a minority. By transferring the Abu and Sirohi districts of Gujarat to Rajasthan, the Gujaratis were made more vulnerable in the state of Bombay.

For a short time the artless compromise worked. The acceptance of the compromise by the Gujarat Pradesh Congress in 1956 however provoked widespread riots throughout Gujarat, and Gujaratis came to view Congress's decision as a great act of betrayal. Matters were made worse when police, attempting to control violence, shot four dead and wounded several hundred, inciting further violence. Indulal Yagnik, a young and relatively unknown politician, suddenly emerged as the firebrand leader of the youth; he would be elected four times to the Lok Sabha (1957–77). In the fall of 1956, the left-wing-tinged Maha Gujarat Janata Parishad was founded to oppose Congress in the forthcoming elections. Capitalizing on populist resentment accumulated since independence, Maha Gujarat Janata Parishad emerged as the major opposition party in the Gujarat region in the elections of 1957. Central Gujarat, Kheda, Mehsana, and the city of Ahmedabad were lost to

Congress for a long time. Congress managed narrowly to win in Saurastra, Kutch, and South Gujarat, where the demand for a separate state and the severing of relations with Bombay found little support because of their economic dependence on that city. Congress also did poorly in the Gujarati region of the state of Bombay, where it lost 32 of 132 seats. Nehru, who visited Ahmedabad to win the youth over to Congress with his charisma and charm, was scoffed at.

It has been suggested that Morarji Desai was opposed to the creation of a separate Gujarat because of his personal ambition to become the prime minister by counterbalancing the larger United Provinces (UP) with the smaller Bombay state. The other, more favorable, argument offered is that he wanted to protect the rupees 9 crore (10 million equals 1 crore) that Bombay spent on Gujarat out of its total revenue of rupees 24 crore.[45] Regardless, Morarjibhai's political stock remained depressed, and he would have to wait another two decades to become prime minister, and then it would be only briefly. In his long life—he died at age ninety-nine—it would remain Morarjibhai's abiding disappointment.

Meanwhile, at the beginning of 1959, political agitation had broken out again, leading to the passage of the Bombay Reorganization Act by the state legislature in March 1960. The credit for the legislation has been assigned to Indira Gandhi, who twenty four years later would be assassinated by a minority Sikh bodyguard in retaliation for her manipulating minority Punjab politics. The Bombay Reorganization Act became effective on May 1, 1960, and Jivraj Mehta took office as the first chief minister. For the time being, the new state government made its home in Ahmedabad, but the desire to replace the splendor of Bombay with a new Gujarat capital would continue to incubate until the construction of Gandhinagar.

2

The Politics of Site

EVEN BEFORE THE new state was officially inaugurated on May 1, 1960, Dr. Jivraj Narayan Mehta, the chief minister-designate, had announced nearly two months earlier, on March 19, 1960,[1] that the capital of Gujarat would be at Gandhinagar. The capital was named after the late Mahatma Gandhi, the native son of the new state and father of the young nation. As yet no more than a cluster of some dozen dusty villages inhabited by ryots living in predominantly tumbledown shacks, fifteen miles north of Ahmedabad on the right bank of the Sabarmati, Gandhinagar was to be the third state capital of independent India, albeit not without political struggle between princely Baroda (modern Vadodara) and industrial Ahmedabad, which wanted to win that proud status. The city was also to be another experiment in urbanization, initiated by Le Corbusier in Chandigarh and reinforced by Otto Koenigsberger in Bhubaneswar; and the new capital would renew the search for architectural style over which Indians have debated ad infinitum. Nevertheless, the development of Gandhinagar, like its older cousins Chandigarh (originally the capital of Punjab, but now the joint capital of Punjab and Haryana, and itself administered as a Union Territory) and Bhubaneswar (Orissa), was equal parts educational experiment, social welfare project, and prod to the profession of planning and architecture.

Before arriving at the decision to place the capital at Gandhinagar, the 1961 preliminary report on Gandhinagar noted, "various alternative sites near about Baroda and Ahmedabad were considered, a rapid reconnaissance was carried out and the advantages and disadvantages of these sites were carefully examined."[2] Insofar as alternative sites were considered, the process parallels the experiences of Chandigarh and Bhubaneswar. But unlike Chandigarh and Bhubaneswar, the official literature does not provide the detailed discussion on the alternative sites that ought to have taken place in the Capital Project Circle, the apex body created to implement the development of the capital. This scantiness of documentation might, in part, reflect the change that occurred in the quality of administrators almost a generation after Chandigarh and Bhubaneswar were built—a period during which the British-invented Indian Civil Service (ICS) had transformed into the Indian Administrative Service (IAS): there was no Fletcher or Trevidi or Thapar scrupulously to maintain records of all discussions; on the other hand, the decision to place the capital at Gandhinagar was not as protracted as had been the case for Chandigarh and Bhubaneswar.[3] And the old Gujarati practice of doing business by way of word, to which so many studies have pointed, must have weighed in as well. The process of site selection was not any the less contentious, however.

Baroda (modern Vadodara)—which derives its name from the older Vatapadraka; literally, "a dwelling by the banyans"[4] and is situated at the division of the Bombay-Delhi and Bombay-Ahmedabad railway lines (392 kilometers north of Bombay and 100 kilometers southeast of Ahmedabad)—first gained its prominence in the region in the eighteenth century. It was not until the reign of its fourteenth ruler, Sayajirao Gaekwad III (1881–1939), however, that the city witnessed a large-scale building effort, growing to its full urban character in the late nineteenth and early twentieth centuries.[5] It was during those six decades that several large-scale building complexes were erected in Baroda: palaces, including the sprawling Laxmi Villas Palace, Baroda College and Kalabhavan (art school), the Nyaya and other temples, the Mandavi tower, parks, and gates, and bridges across the Vishwamitri River.

The Gaekwads trace their origins to Poona (modern Pune) to a Maratha *kshatriya* clan by the name of Matre, which was corrupted to Mantri, meaning minister. Legend has it that in the seventeenth century a prosperous farmer, Nadaji, became a militant protector of cows, gaining the nickname *gae-kaiwari* ("one who protects cows"). The label stuck to the family and simplified into Gaekwad.[6] It was Pilaji Gaekwad who "rescued" Baroda from the clutches of an oppressive Mughal governor in 1725 and restored order. Pilaji is believed to have lost his life fighting both the Mughals and the peshwa (the Maratha prime minister, who had his power base in Poona) to defend Gujarat against exploitation by these outsiders.

It was not uncommon for Indian rulers and princes to undertake public works projects, and even to develop an abiding interest in city beautification, at least in their capital. The Mughal passion for parks, gardens, and lakes had survived into the British period, and it received a fresh impetus from Ebenezer Howard's Garden City movement, which in late-nineteenth-century England aimed at intermarrying town and country. The publication of Howard's *To-Morrow: A Peaceful Path to Real Reform* (London, 1898) influenced Britain and British India alike, which is reflected in the British efforts in New Delhi a dozen years later. Such urban schemes and new architectural designs were not lost on the Anglophile Indian rulers, and they did not hesitate to duplicate them in their own territories.

Sayajirao Gaekwad (also spelled Gaikwad or Gaekwar) was born into a modest peasant branch of the Gaekwad family in Kavlana village some three hundred miles from Baroda in 1853. On May 27, 1875, at the age of thirteen, Sayajirao was adopted by Matushri Jamnabai Saheb, the widow of the late Khanderao Gaekwad, an adoption that was approved by the British. Sayajirao's adoption turned his fate from that of a farmhand into that of a crown prince. It also secured Jamnabai's political future in Baroda against the cunning and maneuvering of her brother-in-law Malharrao. Grandson biographer Fatesinghrao P. Gaekwad has compared Sayajirao to Joseph Conrad (Theodor Josef Konrad Nalecz, 1857–1924), the novelist and writer of short stories, a naturalized British citizen who was the son of the Polish aristocrat and militant nationalist Count Apollo Korzeniowski. Conrad, adopted and raised by his uncle Tadeusz Bobrowski, taught himself English by reading the London *Times* and Shakespeare.[7]

One of the duties of the British resident in an Indian princely state was to protect British interests; and what better way to ensure that than to provide English education to the local ruler? Thus, under both his mother and the British resident, commenced the English education of the unlettered and rustic Sayajirao. English biographer Stanley Rice mentions Sayajirao's insatiable desire to learn through self-study and his passion for books.[8] The Reverend Edward St. Clair Weeden, Sayajirao's English friend and biographer, who spent a year with the maharaja in 1913, confirmed that he and Sayajirao would read books to each other every morning. Weeden said he was "half afraid" to recommend a book to Sayajirao because it "might not appeal to the Oriental imagination, but the Gaekwar's alert mind revels in grasping new ideas and penetrating subtleties of thought and expression."[9]

The precocious prince's education was entrusted to Diwan Sir T. Madhav Rao, who had replaced the Parsi Dadabhai Naoroji (1825–1917). Naoroji had been hired by the incompetent Malharrao Gaekwad to correct the failing affairs of the Baroda state; but Naoroji later resigned under British pressure and moved to London to practice law, where, in 1892, he became the first Indian to be elected to Parliament in Britain. Later, Naoroji was chosen three times to serve as president of the Indian National Congress and earned the sobriquet Grand Old Man of Indian nationalism. The new diwan, Rao, was quick to win the confidence of the British resident, having already acquired substantial administrative experience and familiarity with the British system as diwan of Travancore and Indore. The other influence on Sayajirao's education was that of F. A. H. Elliot, a British civil servant who had also served as the director of education in the state of Berar. The two teachers instilled a love for books and appreciation for the arts in the young Sayajirao, although it remained his lifelong regret that he could not attend Oxford University. As a young ruler, Sayajirao could not have escaped the influence of Naoroji, the former diwan, when, in 1906 Naoroji assumed the Congress presidency for the first time, thus averting a rift between the moderates and extremists (Congress had been founded in 1885, just four years after Sayajirao's accession).

Another influence on Sayajirao was Maharaja Chamarajendra Wodeyar (1863–94), of Mysore. The two were the same age. Chamarajendra, who had been adopted by Maharaja Krishnaraja Wodeyar, was invested as head of the Mysore state upon turning eighteen, in 1881, the same year that Sayajirao was invested in Baroda. In early 1876, the two princes befriended each other in Bombay on the occasion of the visit of Edward, the Prince of Wales, Queen Victoria's eldest son, who would succeed her as Edward VII, emperor of India.[10] The princes' friendship lasted a lifetime. The Wodeyars, with the assistance of able diwans who recruited European architects and planners, contributed richly to the architecture and urbanization of Mysore.[11]

Sayajirao's travels to Europe and the United States in 1906 and 1910 deepened his interest in education and architecture, and thereafter he became a regular traveler to Europe. On his first visit to the United States in 1906 he noted that "the problems in my country are many and grave. . . . I have learned already a great deal during my stay here that I think will be of profit to me in the government of my people, and I hope to learn a great deal more."[12] On the same visit, in New York, he met with Booker T. Washington, the black American social reformer who had risen from slavery to complete his education at the Hampton Institute, Virginia, and founded the Tuskegee Institute in the old cotton belt region of Alabama. The Tuskegee Institute, which relied heavily on North American philanthropists, provided agricultural and industrial training to blacks to help them improve their socioeconomic lot by developing trade and agricultural skills. Unlike W. E. B. Du Bois, who asked for full citizenship rights for blacks, Washington accepted the separation between blacks and whites, but campaigned for programs that offered socioeconomic mobility to blacks, ideas that were to leave a lasting imprint on the Indian prince. On both his visits to the United States, Sayajirao traveled extensively throughout the country, visiting Washington, D.C., Philadelphia, Chicago, Denver, and San Francisco. He made a special point of visiting the museums of natural history in New York, at Harvard University, and at the University of Chicago. "All aspects of life in the United States interested him keenly, and he was constantly on the look-out for ideas which might be adapted to . . . Baroda. In particular, he studied the system of education, and secured the services of . . . [the] educationalist Dr. Cuthbert Hall to come to India to inspect the schools of Baroda and to suggest improvements."[13] On a later visit to Europe, in 1923, the British ambassador in Rome arranged meetings between Sayajirao and King Victor Emmanuel and Benito Mussolini. Sayajirao was impressed by Italy's rapid recovery after World War I, and he congratulated Mussolini, the Fascist dictator, who after making a devil's pact with the monarchy and the church had triumphantly marched into Rome in 1922. Sayajirao was especially fascinated by the postwar buildings, stadiums, parks, and wide roads—emblems of a robust, urban civilization.

These exposures to America and Europe left him with the conviction that education was the basis for all reforms—that it was the only way to improve the condition of his people and territories. His belief prompted him to introduce in Baroda free and compulsory primary education, and a state-supported, free public library system. He even committed state support for the promotion of indigenous industries, albeit with limited success.[14] The July 23, 1910, issue of the *Outlook* (New York) noted:

> The Maharaja [of Baroda] is one of the three most influential native rulers
> of India, the other [sic] being the Nizam of Hyderabad and the Maharaja of
> Mysore. . . . But politically, educationally, and industrially [Baroda] is the most
> advanced of any of the Indian native states and its ruler is more alive to cosmo-
> politan influences than is the Nizam of Hyderabad or the Maharaja of Mysore.
> . . . Since the present Maharaja took the reigns of government in 1881, he has
> abolished some two hundred unnecessarily burdensome taxes, lessened others,
> established an income tax, revised the revenue system, provided for a scientific
> land survey, started the first cotton mills, built hospitals, and improved the
> military service.[15]

The *Outlook* also reported the efforts of the maharani (the queen) to make education accessible to women, and pointedly noted that the princess's impending education at the University of Bombay would make her the first Indian princess ever
to attend public lectures. That Sayajirao was educating his sons at Harvard and
Oxford was viewed favorably by the U.S. press, as were the maharani's efforts to
raise the minimum age of marriage for girls to fourteen—a minimum that she promised ultimately to raise to eighteen.

Sayajirao recruited British engineers R. F. Chisolm and Major R. N. Mant as
state architects to implement his architectural vision, and even appointed a cus-
todian for the upkeep of public buildings. Drawing on Saracenic sources (domes,
chhatris, or umbrellas, towers, and courtyards) and on classical schemes, they produced unusually diverse architectural forms, spaces, scale, and imagery. Their work
included the Laxmi Villas Palace, Kamati (Committee) Bagh, and the Residency
(home of the British resident). Chisolm and Mant might have influenced the Indo-
Saracenic vernacular that Edward Lutyens later employed in New Delhi. In the
belief that India could not make progress without industrial development, Sayajirao approved the use, wherever possible, of new industrial materials such as steel
and glass in place of the old brick and mortar.

The modernization of Baroda was put on firmer ground with the founding of
Baroda College and Kalabhavan (art school), which heavily emphasized engineer-
ing and architecture while teaching art, and that represented a synthesis of ideas
borrowed from America's Tuskegee Institute and Europe's Staatliches Bauhaus.
Education in Baroda got a new lift with the establishment of a public library by the
American William Alanson Borden in 1910. (Western ideas continued to influence
Baroda even after Sayajirao. In 1941, Herman Goetz, a German émigré, took over

the directorship of the Baroda Museum. Goetz supported contemporary Indian art, and used the museum to promote visual education for the people of Baroda. The Maharaja Fatesinghrao Museum was founded in 1961, the year that the Gujarat state was created, in the Laxmi Villas Palace complex.)

Sadly for Sayajirao, his sons did not do so well in Western education. His Oxford-educated youngest son, Shivajirao, remained a dilettante even after completing college and never took life seriously; Shivajirao died of pneumonia in 1919. Sayajirao's Harvard-educated eldest son, Jaisinghrao, who turned out to be an alcoholic, died in August 1923 while under treatment for the disease in Germany, at a time when Jaisinghrao's wife, Padmavati, was fighting a losing battle with cancer. Jaisinghrao was cremated at the Paris Cimiterie, his ashes being taken home for immersion in the sacred rivers of India in accordance with the Hindu tradition.

Although the death of his sons shook Sayajirao's faith in a Western lifestyle, he never forsook the West. However, now responsible for raising and educating his grandson Pratapsinghrao, the crown prince, Sayajirao was wary of sending his grandson to the West, where he might go astray: Pratapsinghrao was educated at home, in the manner that Sayajirao had been educated in his youth. Prince Pratapsinghrao's education was entrusted to the great Maratha historian G. S. Sardesai, a member of the distinguished Maratha Chitpavan Brahman community that would provide leadership to India's National Congress, and to Major Webber, a retired British army officer known only by his last name, who also became the young prince's guardian. Like so many Western-educated, affluent Indians, Sayajirao, looked to the West for inspiration and economic development. And yet the same Western education would breed disaffection with British rule and stoke the fires of nationalism. One fed on the other; it was a symbiotic relationship.

After World War I, Sayajirao was spending more time in Europe, in his French and English houses, than in his Baroda palace, partly to avoid growing political tensions with the British resident, which seemed to multiply with every satyagraha campaign that English-educated Gujarati Mohandas Karamchand Gandhi launched. Caught in the new nationalist mood and drawn to the ideas of the Enlightenment as well to American progressivism, Sayajirao could not condemn the British treatment of Indians without condemning the Indian treatment of the untouchables: "In our country, large communities of human beings are regarded as untouchables. Our progress is no progress at all if we refuse to extend the feelings of equality and brotherhood to the antyajas (untouchables) [sic] and other backward communities. Men like Mr. Gandhi and his followers have done much and said much in this connection. If people have failed to follow Gandhi's wise counsels in this direction, they have themselves to blame."[16]

Sayajirao believed, like Booker T. Washington, that it is "no use blaming the people for their ignorance if they [have] no opportunity of learning."[17] Opportunity for learning he was always willing to provide, as he demonstrated by helping an untouchable boy belonging to the Mahars of Maharastra. Dr. Bhimrao Ramji Ambedkar (1891–1956) was able to complete his high school on a scholarship of rupees 50 a month from Sayajirao, who later also funded Ambedkar's education in Britain and America. After successfully completing his education, Ambedkar returned to India and joined the Baroda Assembly (Ambedkar could be nominated by Sayajirao to the assembly only after the passing of a law requiring candidates to be willing to sit in the assembly next to untouchable members). He later played a prominent role in the drafting of India's constitution and served as law minister in independent India's first cabinet.[18] Long before Gandhi was to espouse the cause of the Harijans (the Children of God, Gandhi's name for untouchables), Sayajirao built schools for untouchables, and temples in Baroda were thrown open to them. Sayajirao must have come to compare the Harijans with American blacks.

By any measure, Baroda's credentials for becoming the capital of Gujarat were impressive, given the museums, parks, playgrounds, colleges, temples, hospitals, industry (albeit nascent), progressive policies, and the cosmopolitan population of the city. An Englishman who spent a year as guest of Maharaja Sayajirao described the city and lamented the growing American influence in the Baroda court:

> Baroda is a fortified city which reminds me in many ways of Chester; it is built in the form of a cross, with lofty gateways at the end of the four principal streets and a fine pavilion of Mohammedan architecture in the centre, over which the blood-red flag of the State floats.
>
> The streets are broad and picturesque with quaint shops and houses, many of which are adorned with specimens of fine old wood-carvings. The shops are for the most part open to the street up a few steps, and each street has its own special commodity; on one side is a row of shops filled with nothing but shoes, on the other the workers in brass and copper drown the clamour of voices with hammering.
>
> . . . The bazaar swarms with quaint specimens of humanity in every kind of dress and undress, flowing up and down like a many-coloured tide. The air is laden with strange spicy scents and is filled with incessant din of many voices bargaining for the goods spread out in profusion on the ground—fruit, vegetables, grain, brass, silver, clothes, and every other commodity that forms a necessity or a luxury in native life.
>
> Near to the central pavilion are the long rambling galleries of the Old Palace, with its steep, narrow staircases of painted wood. On the other side of the road is a similar building, which now contains the fine library. . . . Round the corner, in its green and spacious gardens is the Nazarbagh Palace, a graceful pile of white marble in which the priceless jewels are guarded, and which is used to lodge native Princes when they visit the Gaekwar; beyond this are the white wards of the Marchioness of Dufferin's Hospital, a modern building [named after

the paternalistic viceroy Lord Dufferin, who condemned Congress as a "microscopic minority"] looking contemptuously down on the ancient mud walls of the Guard House, in which gold and silver guns are kept. . . .

It is the Maharaja's desire that Baroda should be laid out spaciously, and ever since his accession he has been striving to prevent the great curse of overcrowding, which is one of the principal causes of the rapid spread of plague and other diseases. The work must necessarily be slow owing to the density of the population and the stubborn tenacity with which they cling to old ideas and associations. . . .

The Gaekwar has lately taken a fancy to having a good many Americans in his service. . . . [There is] an American [who] is continually devising new schemes for bringing Baroda up to date.[19]

Winning capital city status for Baroda would inevitably infuse much-needed new capital into the city and provide the opportunity to upgrade it. But Maharaja Pratapsinghrao might have committed a strategic mistake in 1949 when the process of forming an Indian nation started. For precisely the reason that Baroda was progressive and the largest among Gujarat's princely states, with the city its urban jewel, Pratapsinghrao had asked the newly formed Indian government to declare him the paramount ruler of Saurastra and Gujarat, thus raising questions about his political motives. After all, he was of Maratha origins, and the Gujarati home minister, Sardar Patel, refused the maharaja. Although the maharaja joined the Indian Union in 1949, the incident would not be forgotten when search for a new capital site started in early 1960.

In 1949, after independence, Baroda had been placed under the Bombay government. Following the reorganization of states in 1956, Bombay became the capital of the bilingual state of Bombay. Under this arrangement, the city of Baroda continued to be administered as a borough municipality of Bombay. The city was upgraded to the status of municipal corporation on April 1, 1966, six years after Gujarat State was created, and has since been administered in accordance with the provisions of the Bombay Provincial Municipal Corporation Act of 1949. As early as 1892, Sayajirao, inspired by Viceroy Ripon's measures for local self-government a decade earlier, had introduced the electoral principle for the formation of state praja mandals (People's councils, or forums), and the panchayats (a council of five in a Hindu village) in 1901. In 1908, a legislative council called the Dhara Sabha, composed of both nominated and elected members, had been instituted. These reforms by Sayajirao were intended to train the people in the art of self-government.[20] After independence, in 1948 Baroda's first (and only) popular ministry was formed by Dr. Jivraj Mehta, who would later also form the first popular ministry of the new Gujarat in 1960. Still, in the first general elections of 1952, the best Baroda could do was to elect to the Lok Sabha only the independent Indubhai Amin, a *patidar* (a Hindu caste of Kanbi agriculturalists) industrialist. It was not until the second general elections, in 1957, that Maharaja Fatesinghrao P. Gaekwad, who had joined the Congress Party the previous year, won the Baroda Lok Sabha seat.[21] Jivraj Mehta, who had formed Baroda's only popular ministry, had transferred to Bombay in 1957, becoming minister of public works in Morarji Desai's government. During the crucial years for Gujarat politics between 1955 and 1960, Baroda had no political voice in national affairs or in Bombay.

Nationally and in Gujarat, little note was taken of Baroda and its promise in national affairs, notwithstanding the contributions of Sayajirao, including "a very generous policy towards industrialists."[22] Sayajirao had been aided in his economic efforts by R. C. Dutt, a strong critic of British laissez-faire who, after taking over as the revenue minister of Baroda in 1904, had tried to transform Baroda into a model princely state that exemplified economic development. All hopes for economic development had rested on Ahmedabad, however—the "Manchester of India." Evidence suggests that Sayajirao in particular and his successors, while being ardent supporters of Gandhi's swadeshi movement, in general were strongly attracted to Western education and technology, and they considered it crucial for "India to develop technologically advanced industries." In fact, Sayajirao felt that "an economy based on local handicraft industry was doomed to failure"—a position closer to Nehru's than to Gandhi's.[23] But in Gandhi's Gujarat this was not a politically popular viewpoint, and it worked against Baroda to claim the capital status. There were other reasons on which Baroda was disqualified: its high density (a population of more than 400,000), its inadequate electrical power (which was blamed on the pro-Maharastra policy of Bombay State, and that had caused industrialists and businessmen in both Baroda and Ahmedabad to support the demand for a separate state), and its princely status, which could not be considered consistent with democratic ideas. It is quite another thing that the Ahmedabad industrial elite itself lived a princely lifestyle, one of them (Surottam Hutheesingh) even requesting that the cocky, colorful, Swiss-born French architect Le Corbusier build him a wealthy bachelor house suitable for entertaining on a grand scale, possibly because Le Corbusier himself was famous for his dalliances.

Ahmedabad on the banks of the Sabarmati was founded by Ahmed Shah, the second ruler of the Ahmedabad sultanate, in 1411 as his capital, but in the nineteenth and twentieth centuries the city came under the control of Jain and Vaishnava Bania merchants. The present city is believed to be on the site of much older Hindu trading center of Asaval (Karnavati), replacing the historic capital of Hindu Gujarat at Anhilwada Patan, seventy miles to the northeast. G. W. Forrest, the director of records to the government of India, in his *Cities of India* (1903), described Ahmedabad as "a citadel of much strength and beauty . . . and laid out . . . in broad, fair streets. Bringing marble and other rich building materials from a long distance [the sultan] raised magnificent mosques, palaces and tombs, and by encouraging merchants, weavers and skilled craftsmen he made Ahmedabad a centre of trade and manufacture."[24] And Ahmedabad stayed the center of trade and manufacture, its transplanted skilled workers in time raising the city to rival Manchester in textiles. Trading and manufacturing activities created a hereditary bourgeois elite early in the history of Ahmedabad, the city developing a corporate culture and a class of indigenous bankers and financiers who helped it survive England's laissez-faire practices. Nevertheless, "Ahmedabad's social and political response to the West was delayed and not at first remarkable," one study on the city has concluded. "Ahmedabad had one of the earliest municipal organizations in India, but this [development] does not tell a story which would differ significantly from that of other second-rank cities in nineteenth century India, except possibly in the civic-mindedness displayed by the old leading families (if not by the voters and elected commissioners, who opposed improvements and brought about the suppression of Municipality for incompetence). . . . Until the First World War, Ahmedabad's economic progress was achieved within a society which remained socially conservative and politically backward."[25] Essentially, the merchant community of Ahmedabad remained fiscally too conservative to embrace industry because it considered industry riskier than the trading and banking to which it was long accustomed. It can be added that Ahmedabad remained architecturally stagnant as well, its many old Hindu and Muslim monuments notwithstanding.

Ahmedabad fell on hard times for the 150 years preceding the city's annexation by the British after they finally crushed the Maratha power in 1818. In the intervening years, the city's fate had alternated between benign neglect at the hands of the Mughals and economic exploitation at the hands of the Marathas. Surat and Cambay emerged as rivals to Ahmedabad in trade in Gujarat, and in time the city's textile exports were challenged by Sind, Punjab, and other Indian states. The Peshwa of Poona and the Gaekwad of Baroda had been sharing revenue from Ahmedabad between 1800 and 1814. Thereafter, the "Peshwa had leased his part of the revenue to the Gaekwads for an annual payment of Rupees 500,000," thus placing the entire city under the Gaekwad administration. Because Baroda "was allied to the East India Company, which influenced much of the government of the Baroda State, and under this fairly competent administration, [Ahmedabad] recovered some of its prosperity."[26] In 1814, the peshwa refused to renew the lease, turning Ahmedabad into a bone of contention between himself and the Gaekwad; the issue was resolved finally when the British took over the city in 1818 under the Treaty of Poona, and the peshwa surrendered the revenue of Ahmedabad in perpetuity to Baroda; and later the Gaekwad family surrendered the city to John Company in return for territories near Baroda.

John Andrew Dunlop, the first British collector of Ahmedabad, found the city in a shambles and its economy in ruins. Nevertheless, Ahmedabad's mercantilist spirit experienced renaissance under British rule as a result of a series of measurers introduced by John Company: reduced tariff and taxes, infusion of capital in handloom and handicraft industry, introduction of the railway (1864), the establishment of Western institutions and better law and order—arguably making Gujaratis more conscious of Indian culture in this transformation to Westernization. There were only a small number of English in the city at any given time, which also limited full British impact, however. Ahmedabad also generated income through the opium trade (which picked up after 1819 with increasing British exports of the commodity to China), gambling, and speculation. By the end of the nineteenth century, the city's population had rebounded to nearly 150,000 from a paltry 80,000 in 1818. With the improved business climate, the city also acquired a more cosmopolitan character, seeing an influx of Parsis, Jews, and Christians, although correspondingly the size of the Muslim population declined.[27]

The combination of improved business climate and Gujarati entrepreneurship resulted in the transformation of the merchant capital into the industrial capital, which made its debut with the establishing of the Ahmedabad Spinning and Weaving Mill in 1858 by, ironically, Runchhodlal Chotala,[28] a Nagar brahman administrator who had been shabbily treated by the British, and his three partners. Up to this point, the merchant class of traders and bankers, composed of Jains and Vaishnava Banias, had shunned industry. The timing proved fortuitous because the American Civil War broke out in 1861, increasing demand for Indian cotton. Even though demand for Indian cotton declined after that war, the textile industry was well-established in Ahmedabad by the end of the nineteenth century. And the new seths (financiers, merchants, and mill owners) invested their wealth in English-style bungalows with wide glass windows, and even adopted Western dress[29]—the visible, even if superficial, emblems of modernization that follows economic success. But the acceptance of Western higher education was slow in Ahmedabad, slower than in Bombay, which explains the different paths of development taken by the two cities and why Bombay became, and remained, the beacon of higher education for the middle-class Gujaratis well after independence.

English influence and proliferation of textile mills notwithstanding, when Gandhi elected to settle in Ahmedabad upon his return from South Africa and established the Satyagraha Ashram (later renamed the Sabarmati Ashram) there in 1915, the place looked and felt very much like a medieval Indian city—predominantly bucolic in appearance, rather than urban and industrial in shape, despite mill chimneys belching smoke into the sky. One important factor that alone made the difference between Ahmedabad and Baroda was that the whole city of Baroda belonged to the English-groomed Gaekwad; "He not only rules it, but it is his own private property."[30] On the other hand, the Ahmedabad Municipality, which had been created in 1884, was a languid body, its monumental failure exemplified in its inability to deal with the plague of 1917–18, which was caused by poor sanitation and the absence of chlorinated drinking water.[31]

Location of Gujarat in India, identifying Gandhinagar

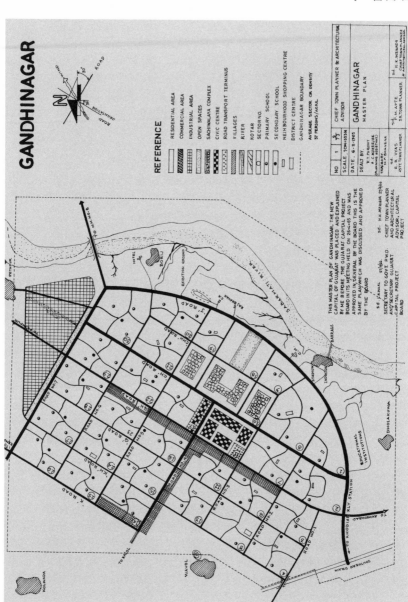

The Gandhinagar plan by H. K. Mewada. Courtesy Deepak Mewada.

LEFT: The planner H. K. Mewada. Courtesy Deepak Mewada.

Le Corbusier with Prime Minister Nehru in Chandigarh, Punjab. Courtesy Government Museum and Art Gallery, Chandigarh, and the Chandigarh Administration Chief Architect.

Louis Kahn with Gautam Sarabhai at the Indian Institute of Management, Ahmedabad. Courtesy Louis I. Kahn Collection, University of Pennsylvania and the Pennsylvania Historical and Museum Commission, Philadelphia.

The Millowners Association Building built by the modernist architect Le Corbusier —one of his first buildings in Ahmedabad and in India. Note the use of reinforced concrete as the building material. This is a significant building in Ahmedabad and stands as a counterpoint to Kahn's work. Photograph by the author.

Classrooms at the Indian Institute of Management, Ahmedabad, built by Louis Kahn, who tried to adapt his transcendental modernist architecture to local tradition by using the vernacular brick. Note the use of arches, cylinders, squares, and straight lines. Photograph by the author.

The Capital Complex, Gandhinagar. H. K. Mewada placed the assembly building between secretariat blocks, linking the two secretariat blocks to the assembly by overhanging bridges. The bridges have never been used by either the elected officials or the administrators for fear of terrorism. By placing the assembly between the two secretariat blocks, Mewada was departing from the capitol complexes in Chandigarh and Bhubaneswar. Photograph by the author.

Mewada placed the assembly building on a raised plinth to give it prominence, a traditional technique frequently used in building temples. Photograph by the author.

The interior structure of the assembly is inspired by the lotus flower, which in Hindu mythology is associated with Lord Vishnu. Note the central column holds the weight of the entire building. Photograph by the author.

Assembly chambers are inspired by the inner sanctums of the scores of Indian temples. Courtesy Deepak Mewada.

Mahatma Gandhi's statue is in the foreground of the assembly. Photograph by the author.

The assembly building at night. Photograph by the author.

The secretariat block. Photograph by the author.

The overhanging bridge that links the secretariat with the assembly. Photograph by the author.

Intersection of the two grid axes. Note the use of roundabouts, a lingering British influence common at intersections in India. Photograph by the author.

The auditorium in sector 17. Photograph by the author.

A temple in sector 22. Many unauthorized temples have cropped
in the capital, but authorities are afraid to demolish them for fear of
political backlash. Photograph by the author.

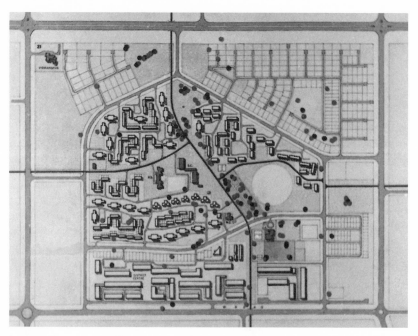

Layout of sector 21. All sectors are self-contained, having schools, libraries,
shopping, and a dispensary. Courtesy Deepak Mewada.

Still, Gandhi had elected to live in Ahmedabad precisely because it was representative of India and her culture: it had *Indianness,* a word that shaped the debate over architectural style and other cultural issues in postcolonial India. True, after Ahmedabad was connected to the railway in 1864, the city became more integrated with the market economy of the country, and therefore the world, but the Ahmedabad sarafs (bankers) who had built the city stayed tied to the hearth, retaining their "Indianness." Ahmedabad's economic success has been attributed to its stable population and labor, even during hard times,[32] and to its diverse population: a small Hindu "aristocracy" of warpers; the handloom Muslim weavers; a mass of landless laborers from the hinterland, who, being mostly untouchables, were confined to spinning. And then there was the indigenous elite of sarafs. It is equally possible that Gandhi found such a social mix well suited for launching his social reform and political campaign.

Even though Ahmedabad is not quite the Emerald City, and certainly not what millennial utopians had in mind, it provides closer to an equitable distribution of rank than other Indian cities do. Always the pragmatist, Gandhi was drawn to Ahmedabad's utilitarian and materialistic qualities; its multireligious population, particularly the presence of a large Muslim population;[33] its large working class and legions of peasants in surrounding villages, from which he could recruit his satyagrahi soldiers; its wealthy Jain and Bania business communities, which would bankroll his satyagraha in return for the profits promised by his doctrine of swadeshi; and its coarse homespun cloth that was popular with residents and that Gandhi would use to emphasize national pride. In his autobiography, Gandhi himself quite forthrightly explained his reasons for settling in Ahmedabad: "I had a predilection for Ahmedabad. Being a Gujarati I thought I should be able to render the greatest service to the country through the Gujarati language. And . . . as Ahmedabad was an ancient centre of handloom weaving, it was likely to be the most favourable field for the revival of the cottage industry of hand-spinning. There was also the hope that, the city being the capital of Gujarat, monetary help from its wealthy citizens would be more available here than elsewhere."[34]

The Gujarati writer Yashodhar Mehta has noted about his own community that "wherever there is money or even possibility of money, there always is a Gujarati."[35] But Gandhi's was a social decision, not a moral one, and only incidentally an economic one. Even though he came from a merchant family, Gandhi had decided to define himself in terms of the peasantry, which made up more than 80 percent of India's population. He wanted what his peasant community wanted. Moreover, Ahmedabad did not have any special religious significance, as Bhubaneswar did, for either the Hindu or the Muslim community; and it had been an administrative capital for much of its history. The Mahatma had another tie with Ahmedabad: a year before sailing for England in the fall of 1888, he had traveled to the city for the first time to take his matriculation examination. By the time he returned to India in 1915, both his brothers were dead and his hometown princely Rajkot must have appeared nothing more than a reminder of faded memories and courtly intrigues. The suggestion by one American writer that Gandhi rejected the backwaters of Kathiawar in favor of the urban dynamism of Ahmedabad belies the city's true character, for Ahmedabad was not quite the City on the Hill.[36] Another study more accurately assesses the urban scene in Ahmedabad: among the Jain mill owners and other businessmen Gandhi met a largely literate, but by no means Anglicized group, "while among the workers he would address a largely illiterate and almost solidly Gujarati-speaking population."[37]

Milltown Ahmedabad was a contrary urban oasis in the farmlands of Gujarat, Gandhi's Sabarmati Ashram being the campus where pacifism was revered: it is an ideology at the heart of the Jain community and in the hearts of many industrialists and mill workers there. Violence, to such believers, is both against God's will and a futile way to resolve conflict, which is not to suggest that either Ahmedabad or Gujarat has not seen violence. To the contrary. But Gandhi's message to the peasants and workers was "to curb anger, never to do violence and even to suffer violence done to us"[38]—a message that appealed to the city's industrial elite. Cocooned on a campus on the banks of the Sabarmati on the outskirts of Ahmedabad, the ashram became a research center for Gandhi to perfect pacifism as a political instrument to effect social change without violence. It is therefore not surprising that the city's capitalist class saw no contradiction in bankrolling the Mahatma in his social program of uplifting the Harijans; of finding a solution to the ever-elusive Hindu-Muslim communal conflict, which threatened and continues to threaten the economy of the city; of opposing European planters in Champaran, near India's border with Nepal, who imposed illegal levies on tenant farmers and forced them to practice the *tinkathia* system, under which the farmers were required to plant one-seventh of their holdings with indigo in return for a lump sum of money fixed by the planters;[39] and of seeking, albeit as a necessary evil, the Mahatma's intervention whenever the mill workers struck. The industrialists in Ahmedabad were practical enough to recognize conflict with the working class as inevitable: they saw in Gandhi the man who could contain labor unrest; and they saw advantages for the Indian textile industry in Gandhi's doctrine of swadeshi—a doctrine that came to permeate every aspect of the economy in post-colonial India and for which India has been criticized, ironically by another Gujarati in recent years, the Bombay-born, Cambridge-Oxford-MIT-educated and Columbia University–based Jagdish Bhagvati, youngest son of a distinguished legal family from Bombay.

A politician as shrewd as Gandhi could not have disregarded the possibility in 1915 through 1918 of inducting both peasants and industrial workers in the nationalist movement. Subalternist scholarship has documented that the nineteenth and early twentieth centuries witnessed an epidemic of peasant revolts, and extremists in Congress were already working to fuse peasant grievances with Indian nationalism. Ahmedabad, without urban pretensions, offered Gandhi a perfect place to craft a persona for himself that would make him appealing to the working class as well as to the countless peasants; while that pluralistic city served as a laboratory for him to experiment with finding a lasting Hindu-Muslim accord. He never did find a permanent solution to the communal conflict, a militant Hindu assassinating him in 1948 and the scourge of communal violence stubbornly refusing to disappear from India. But also in Ahmedabad he found his humanitarian friend and ashram benefactor Anasuyanbehn Sarabhai, the unhappily married sister of Ahmedabad millionaire mill owner Ambalal Sarabhai. Ambalal's eldest daughter, Mirdula, affectionately called "the Boss" within the family and described as the "Joan of Arc of Gujarat" by Sarojini Naidu, India's "poetess-*stayagrahi*" (freedom-fighter), would also follow in Gandhi's footsteps.

In Ahmedabad, Gandhi's impress of satyagraha first fell on the local mill owners in 1918, when he and Anasuyanbehn persuaded Ambalal Sarabhai and other industrialists to raise workers' wages by 35 percent; later, Gandhi redirected his satyagraha at the British in Kheda district (near Ahmedabad, to the southeast) for excessive land revenue; and later still, at the viceroy, to persuade him to release two militant Muslim brothers, Shaukat and Muhammad Ali, imprisoned for "seditious" writings, whom he would accept as his brothers. Such iconoclastic experiments would only portray Gandhi differently to different audiences: as the Mahatma to his peasant supporters and as a traitor to the Hindu hotheads.

In the industrial restructuring of Ahmedabad, two families had emerged in the twentieth century that would play a prominent role in the city's history and also in the capital city project. (Two other families—those of Surottam Hutheesingh and Chinubhai Chimanbhai—also were prominent and involved in the city's affairs, but all were interrelated by ties of birth and marriage.) Ambalal Sarabhai (1890–1967), who dominated the city when Gandhi arrived in Ahmedabad, had been only five years old when both his parents died, and he was adopted by his uncle Chimanlal Nagindas, a Dasa Shrimali Jain of the old financier family of Karamchand Premchand, a pioneer in the machine production of cloth in India. Noted in Ahmedabad for their wealth and philanthropy, the Sarabhais had been a source for social change as well. The self-willed Ambalal had received his schooling privately at home, after which he enrolled in Gujarat College, but had to drop out to take over the family business when his uncle died in 1908.

Ambalal would not only emerge as one of the leading progressive industrialists in the city but he also became very close to Gandhi—a man more than twice his age—and was always ready to match wits with the Mahatma. One day, still in his twenties, he turned up at Gandhi's ashram with a fistful of rupees to support the Mahatma's fledgling ashram and his controversial campaign for the upliftment of Harijans, which, for a young man of means, in itself was socially alien. Equally iconoclastic was Ambalal's decision to marry Sarladevi, a girl outside his own caste, and to treat her as his social equal. Ambalal was among the first Indians to take his wife with him to public events in Ahmedabad: at that time, Indian women rarely, if ever, accompanied their husbands at social occasions. Ambalal displayed the same liberal qualities with his children, encouraging them to participate in the family's social schedule, always prodding them to intermingle with intellectuals of all hues—Motilal Nehru, Rabindranath Tagore, C. F. Andrews, M. K. Gandhi, and the many other visitors who frequented Ambalal's residences,[40] Malden House in the prestigious enclave of Marine Lines, in Bombay, and the Retreat, the ancestral home in Ahmedabad, on nineteen sprawling acres of farmland in the picturesque Shahibagh, the great Mughal gardens that had been laid out by Shah Jhan when he was governor of Gujarat in the seventeenth century and who would later build the Taj Mahal as a memorial to his lovely wife, Mumtaj.

Perhaps because he himself was not able to complete his education, Sarabhai encouraged intellectual discussions in the family and provided individualistic upbringing for his children. The family dinner table was a locus of discussion for the expression of ideas, if not necessarily for their free exchange. Because grown-ups expected the Sarabhai children to be able to converse, or at least to listen, they were comfortable conversing with grown-ups. By listening, they achieved a level of passive knowledge about subjects and ideas beyond the ken of what was expected of their peers, especially by their teachers. Precociousness was an obvious byproduct. There were also values issues. The family was exposed to endless conversations about swadeshi, but never questioned the benefits of English education. There was rarely any talk about money, except that it was there to pay for the best of everything. The family business was viewed as a means to an end, not an end in itself. Playing sports was not applauded; practicing the sitar or the violin was. Of course, there was a concomitant—if abstract—respect for the laboring classes. Many of the Sarabhais espoused the cause of workers, wore *khadi* (homespun cloth), marched lockstep with Gandhi in his satyagraha campaigns, and studied in English schools and British universities. It was difficult for them to experience Britannia without a sense of irony. But for their part, the offspring of Ambalal never doubted that their lives would follow the comfortable path already trodden by their parents. They were led to believe that being smart was enough—and was certainly superior to being rich. They held to the quaint notion of meritocracy that permeated the zeitgeist of the children of privileged Indians. This was accepted without irony.

As a young, impressionistic man, in 1912 and again in 1920, Ambalal traveled with his family to London, where he explored the city's educational, economic, and cultural opportunities. On these extended visits to London, he enrolled his children in private schools, where they experienced color prejudice, which must have been a disconcerting experience for a wealthy Indian family. The London stay also exposed the Sarabhais to the popular Montessori school system, which he liked so much that he imported it to Ahmedabad. Later still, Ambalal would dispatch his children and family members to Britain for higher education, his youngest son, Vikram, graduating from Cambridge, and his sister, Anasuya, imbibing Fabian and suffragette ideas in London. Ambalal indulged his sister, even embraced her socialistic and nationalistic ideas, to which she committed her life following a marriage gone sour. Ambalal, as a shrewd and progressive businessman, saw in Anasuya's campaign to improve the lot of workers, educating their children and women, an opportunity to establish a better relationship between workers and mill owners; and in Gandhi he saw the man who could control labor unrest and thus safeguard the owners' economic interests.[41]

As a progressive business leader, Ambalal was also interested in social issues and in shaping Ahmedabad in the context of Gujarat's and India's future. In pursuit of this goal, raising the city's primacy was important, and it was possible if Ahmedabad could be turned into a modern educational and cultural center. All his life, "[Ambalal] Sarabhai had been arguing for an alternative politics for the city [of Ahmedabad], a politics which did not locate itself in caste, community and class matters but [one that] tried to realize, instead, the potentialities of each and every individual in the city."[42] The Sarabhai children grew up ingesting the work world of their parents, whether it was talking about Gandhi as if he were a member of the family or discussing the future of India: what was clear was that the Sarabhais would play an important role in local and national affairs. So when Gujarat was formed in the summer of 1960, the Sarabhais saw the "potential" for Ahmedabad to be the leader, not only in Gujarat but the nation. Ahmedabad would house the new Gujarat government, albeit temporarily.

The other prominent industrialist to play an important role in Ahmedabad was Kasturbhai Lalbhai (ca. 1894–1980), the son of Sardar Seth Lalbhai Dalpatbhai, an Oswal Jain from Ahmedabad, claiming his family links to the notable Ahmedabad merchant Shantidas Zaveri (Jawahari).[43] In the seventh or eighth century, the Oswals—who are considered to be one of the "richest" merchant tribes of India (they are believed to have been originally Kshatriyas, possibly descendants of one of the Rajput clans from Central Asia, and according to tradition take their name from Osian, a small railway town in Rajasthan, about forty-five kilometers northwest of Jodhpur) converted to Jainism, the puritanical sect founded in the sixth century B.C.E. by the Kshatriya Prince Vardhamana Mahavira (ca. 540–468 B.C.E.) Initially, Mahavira's teaching was confined to the Gangetic valley, but because of its emphasis on balanced life and its atheistic nature, the existence of God being irrelevant to its doctrine, it soon spread to western India (where to this day it has the largest following), parts of northern India, and to the south, in the Karnataka region. Because of Jainism's obsession with ahimsa, a teaching that made it a sin to crush even an insect while walking, its appeal was largely confined to the trading community (since agriculture involved killing insects and pests). Trade and commerce thus became possible occupations for Jains, and the encouragement of frugality in Jainism coincided with a similar sentiment in commercial activity. The Jains specialized in the trading of manufactured goods and acting as middlemen, confining themselves to financial transactions. Thus Jains came to be associated with the spread of urban culture, settling on the west coast of India because of the opportunities there for maritime commerce. Because Indian caste hierarchy prevented converts to Hinduism having upward mobility, many tribal transplants to India from Central Asia eventually embraced either Jainism or Buddhism, the latter being the other heterodox religion that challenged hierarchical Brahmanical orthodoxy in the sixth century. Ambedkar, the Indian legal brain from a lower caste from Maharastra, himself had converted with fifty thousand untouchables to Buddhism in a mass ceremony in 1954 to protest against the hierarchical Hinduism.

Whatever their origin, Kasturbhai Lalbhai's ancestors had moved to Ahmedabad because of the city's abundant economic opportunities, and the family prospered through money lending and trading. The family fortune soared during the American Civil War as the price of Indian cotton skyrocketed, even though Lalbhai Dalpatbhai, Kasturbhai's grandfather, had not yet entered the cotton industry. Instead, Dalpatbhai prudently established a *pedhi* (banking) firm, remaining in the relatively safe banking business rather than jumping into the vagaries of industrial production. The new wealth also opened many doors to higher social and political places for Dalpatbhai, and he began to expand his influence by financially supporting social reforms and education in the city. Through his participation in the Gujarat Vernacular Society (founded in 1848 by progressive Englishmen and Indians), Dalpatbhai was exposed to Western ideas, and he passed them on to his three sons—Lalbhai, Manibhai, and Jagabhai. The education of the eldest, Lalbhai, was interrupted because of his father's death in 1885.

By the time Seth Lalbhai had taken charge of the family business in 1886, Ahmedabad had turned into a textile mill city, had been connected by the railway to other Indian cities (1864), and the broadly based Indian National Congress, which would soon become the organizational vehicle for India's as yet nascent nationalist movement, had had its first annual meeting, at Bombay City on December 28, 1885. Seth Lalbhai took another twelve years to establish his first yarn manufacturing company, the Sarspur Manufacturing Company. That was in 1897. Raipur Mills, which was to become the foundation stone on which the Lalbhai industrial empire would be built, was established in 1905. Although the initial response of Ahmedabad mill owners to Congress and its programs was guarded, in the long run their behavior was guided by the industry's interests and pressures from the working class. It was not too long before they were to realize that *swadeshi* and *swaraj*, the two faces of the Indian nationalist coin that Gandhi minted upon his return from South Africa, not only promised home rule to India's teeming millions but also opened new economic opportunities for Indian business, and Seth Lalbhai and his brothers were quick to capitalize on the rising demand for homemade cloth from proud nationalist Indians. Following in the footsteps of his father and adhering to the dictates of his Jain faith, Seth Lalbhai contributed generously to social, educational, and religious causes in the city. But the family business in the end became a victim of the deadly virus of family disputes that has destroyed, and continues to destroy, so many Indian business houses. The business of Seth Lalbhai was divided between the brothers, an event that killed Seth Lalbhai: he literally died of a broken heart in June 1912. He was only forty-nine.

Kasturbhai Lalbhai, the second son of Seth Lalbhai, only seventeen years old at the time of his father's death, was forced to terminate his education at Gujarat College in Ahmedabad to take charge of Raipur Mills, the only surviving company in the family business. Kasturbhai had been raised with his six other siblings and two dozen other family members in a traditional Indian joint-family home: display of affection, even privately, was deemed immoral, and emphasis was on *dharma* (duty), which was considered a religious responsibility (not only required for the smooth functioning of hierarchical relationships of the joint family system but also necessary for ultimate personal *moksha* (salvation). From his father, he inherited the Puritan and Victorian values of diligence, discipline, and frugality; from his mother, Mohinibehn (who came from the industrialist-philanthropist Hutheesingh family), he inherited a talent for munificence. From his English-Sanskrit teacher, Keshav Harshad Dhruva, at Runchhodlal High School, he acquired a catholic taste that led him to read biographies of Abraham Lincoln, Swami Vivekananda, and other world leaders, and he became a crusader for education throughout his life.

Kasturbhai received his business training on the job. First, working with his older brother, Chimanbhai, he consolidated the affairs of Raipur Mills. Next, the two brothers expanded the company's operations by adding more spindles, even when domestic cotton faced stiff competition from Britain. The outbreak of World War I in 1914, however, created shortages of imported goods, which were filled by domestic production. Raipur Mills directly benefitted from this change, Kasturbhai Lalbhai utilizing the windfall profits to expand his business to related operations. In 1915, he married Shardabehn, a traditional girl to whom he had been betrothed when he was eight years old, and when she was two. He quickly hired a tutor to teach her English, which he considered a necessary skill for personal and public life in British India.

Kasturbhai's education continued through his business ventures. He successfully steered his business operations through the Great Depression, buying machinery from economically prostrated Britain at deeply discounted prices, taking full advantage of rising global demand for cotton during World War II and, with the help of the New York–based American Cyanamid, diversifying his business into the chemical dyestuffs industry; in fact, he persuaded the U.S. company to buy equity interest in his company by making direct investment. Thus was born, in 1947, Atul Products Ltd. He rewarded the American company by appointing Herbert Edward Lorenz to the board of directors of his new chemical company—a move he must have viewed as a good business strategy to please his American collaborator as well as to gain the benefit of his managerial skills. Kasturbhai placed Atul Products at Valsad, about three hundred kilometers south of Ahmedabad, because it was well connected to both Ahmedabad and Bombay, the two principal consumers of dyestuffs.

Kasturbhai's vision for Valsad was to transform this nondescript village on the western railway line into an industrial township like Jamshedpur, the steel company town in Bihar developed by the Parsi industrialist Sir Jamsetjee Jeejeebhoy Tata. Jamshedpur was originally, in 1911, planned by the American Axel S. Kennedy, and it had gone through two replanning efforts by British civil engineers before the Tatas recruited the German Otto Koenigsberger in 1943 to relieve congestion and improve traffic. Valsad was to be a city with housing for workers and managers, schools, shopping centers, religious, medical and recreational facilities, municipal and postal services—in sum, it was to be a modern urban infrastructure, built on nine hundred acres of essentially fallow land. The Valsad project exposed Kasturbhai to urban and architectural issues, preparing him for his role in the construction of Gujarat's new capital. His own abiding interest in horticulture led him to plant about one hundred thousand trees of two hundred different varieties in Valsad, a project that was expected to balance industry with nature, long before the United Nations–sponsored plant-a-tree campaign became a crusading cause of the Indian elite (it resulted in more than a million trees being planted in more than two thousand villages between 1996 and 2002).

On March 17, 1952, the Atul Products industrial complex was inaugurated by Prime Minister Nehru, who himself was intimately involved at the time with Le Corbusier in the construction of Chandigarh. Fabian socialist Nehru and the capitalist Kasturbhai had different visions for India: Kasturbhai, like several Indian industrialists, was privately critical of the Nehru government's economic policies, which Nehru himself supervised as the head of India's planning commission. But the two men also had family ties through the marriage of Nehru's sister, Krishna, to Gautam Hutheesingh, Kasturbhai's nephew. Downplaying the basic fact that every businessman invests in new ventures for profit, Nehru characteristically preached in his inaugural address: "I have come here to join your rejoicing because Sheth [Seth] Kasturbhai has set up a basic industrial unit which will go a long way towards our industrial progress. The dyestuffs and chemical industry has a special significance in our total economy. I view this project in a broader national perspective, the advantage it would bring to the nation, and not in terms of profits to an individual or a company set up by an individual."[44]

Postcolonial India was riddled with contradictions born of feudalism, colonialism, modern secular democracy, private enterprise, and socialistic ideas—

contradictions that are still being worked out. In the urban-architectural area, Le Corbusier had defined the problem as early as 1950 in Chandigarh: "India had, and always has, a peasant culture that exists since a thousand years! India possessed Hindu temples (generally in carved stones) and Muslim temples [sic] in red stone, the architectural beauty of which is very geometrical. But India hasn't yet created an architecture for modern civilization (offices, factories, [public] buildings)."[45] Even before Le Corbusier had articulated his thinking, political and business leaders were beginning to grapple with the problem of ushering India into modernity. Nehru himself noted in 1954 at the third meeting of the National Development Council of the Planning Commission that the major difficulty facing India is the lack of "trained personnel. . . . We want trained personnel in hundreds of thousands. . . . Apart from the apparatus of training, institutions, etc., that have to be built up, the training itself takes time."[46] Business leaders like Kasturbhai had come to the realization that the paternalistic, individualized, informal, Indian management system was too outdated to carry forward India (vis-à-vis their own business interests) into the free-market world: that it was in their own interest to build institutions to train Indians in the "hundreds of thousands" that Nehru was calling for. Kasturbhai himself had educated his two sons, Siddhartha and Shrenik at the Brooklyn Institute of Technology and at Harvard University (in chemical engineering and business administration, respectively). But the demand for professional engineers and managers was vast, and again the importance of modern education made itself apparent to Kasturbhai. To meet the challenge, he first became involved with building educational institutions in Ahmedabad and, later, in the building of the new capital. In both instances, his experience in planning the Atul industrial complex at Valsad served him well.

For the Indian industrialist, balancing personal gain with social good has proved, and continues to prove, difficult, even elusive. Like Renaissance patrons in Italy, industrialist-philanthropists in India have been far more interested in the next life than in this life: consequently, they have channeled charity to building temples, libraries, primary schools, and orphanages to memorialize the family name by naming them for the departed family members or donating money to these institutions, thereby earning good karma, a necessary ingredient for personal salvation. They have been far less imaginative in espousing bold and progressive projects for the greater good of the nation through well-trained future generations. Kasturbhai transcended this peculiarly Indian barrier in his public life, although he cannot be portrayed as the champion of the working poor, given his stubborn disagreement with Gandhi over the demand for a wage increase by mill workers in the 1918 strike in Ahmedabad (salaries and wages in the Lalbhai industries had been historically low). Nor can he be credited for transforming his essentially feudalistic business operations into a modern management system, notwithstanding his undertaking to educate his sons in the United States and his involvement with the development of the Indian Institutes of Management (IIM), modeled after the Harvard Business School. Ironically, young MBA graduates of IIM preferred to seek, and continue to seek, career opportunities in the financially rewarding and more glamorous multinationals or India's modern business houses, shunning the Kasturbhai Lalbhai group of companies, thus defeating Kasturbhai's hope of recruiting modern managers from IIM, the institution that he helped build.

It was the 1918 mill workers' strike that gained public attention for Kasturbhai, particularly among his peers, most of whom felt that Gandhi had no business meddling with the affairs of mill owners. Only a very small group, which Ambalal Sarabhai later joined, reluctantly, was astute enough to foresee how Gandhi could be helpful in disciplining the labor in Ahmedabad.[47] Gandhi was supporting the workers in their fight to maintain the wage increases they had won during the war but that the mill owners, led by Ambalal Sarabhai, wanted to roll back because of the slackening sales of cotton after the war. Also, Gandhi demanded the appointment of a neutral arbitrator whose decision should be binding on both parties, with future conflicts to be resolved through arbitration rather than by strikes or violence. It was Kasturbhai's position that the workers struck because of Gandhi, and that Gandhi was coercing the mill owners into submission by fasting—which he thought was unfair. (Gandhi effectively used the technique of fasting against the British or whenever there was an outbreak of communal violence.) In the end, Gandhi prevailed, not because mill owners relented but because they needed Gandhi as much as Gandhi needed them. Gandhi's message to the nation to fight the British through swadeshi, resonated with the Indian masses, and it clearly translated into greater profits for textile mill owners. For his part, Gandhi needed benefactors to bankroll his satyagraha movement, and what better cause could mill owners find to win them nationalist honors and also improve the sales of domestic cotton in an otherwise sluggish market.

Ambalal and Kasturbhai came from different backgrounds, but both worked in the same industry. The cosmopolitan Ambalal was impressed by the resolve displayed throughout the strike by the simple but sturdy Kasturbhai, who saw his own position as a matter of principle as well as one of economic interest. As president of the Ahmedabad Millowners Association (AMA), Ambalal appointed Kasturbhai to the managing committee of the association. Over the next four decades, until Gujarat State was created in May 1960, Kasturbhai's public portfolio diversified. He served on a number of committees, including the Famine Relief Committee (1918); he was vice president of the AMA (1923–28, 1930–34); president of the AMA (1935–39); secretary of the Gujarat Pradesh Congress Flood Relief Committee (1928); a member of the Federation of Indian Chambers of Commerce and Industry (1933); and, for the years 1923 to 1926, he was elected to the Central Legislative Committee on the ticket of the Swaraj Party, the party founded by Motilal Nehru and C. R. Das.

Kasturbhai's connection with the Swaraj Party is interesting. The Swarajists disapproved of Gandhi's constructive program of hand spinning and called instead for the paralyzing of the British India government from within by getting supporters elected to provincial legislative councils (this had become possible in the wake of the 1921 Government of India Act). The Swarajists also opposed the heavy tax burden—their key platform during the 1923–24 elections—winning a plurality in the Central Legislative Assembly and sufficient seats in Bengal and Bombay to prevent the government from establishing ministries in either of those key provinces. Das was elected mayor of Calcutta, and Jawaharlal Nehru mayor of Allahabad (the Swarajists, however, lost their steam after the death of Das in 1925). Kasturbhai, as a businessman, was naturally against the taxes, and the anti-tax attitude of Indian business carried over to postcolonial India.

All this public work not only put Kasturbhai in the national limelight but also sharpened his public-speaking skills. The prestigious national daily newspaper, the *Times of India,* came to label his speeches as "the most apposite."[48] What he had lost in formal education from having to drop out from Gujarat College in 1912, he more than made up through practical experience, willingness to learn from others, and international business travel. In his own mind, however, nothing could compensate for his lack of college education. At the time of India's independence in 1947, Kasturbhai was a wiser, middle-aged man, a nationally recognized figure, acutely aware of his Gujarati origins and educational limitations. Following World War II, the global textile industry had fallen on hard times, and matters for Indian textiles were further aggravated by wars with neighboring Pakistan and China. A further burden was placed on Indian textiles by rising inflation in the 1960s because of a series of crop failures. Industrialists were also burdened with a number of new welfare measures by the Congress government, adding to production costs. Devaluation of the Indian rupee stretched the industry to its limits as imported items became more expensive. Kasturbhai and other industrialists tried to take advantage of the government incentives offered for exports, but having a monopoly in the domestic market left them ill-prepared to compete internationally—a problem that neither the Indian government nor Indian industry was to address until the late 1980s. This was one reason why Kasturbhai, abandoning the old strategy of diversifying into related product lines, now explored (albeit unsuccessfully) the possibilities for expanding into nontextile goods, such as crockery, low-density polyethylene, and PVC. Clearly, the "*gaddi* [literally, "throne"] system" of management, as one biographer of Kasturbhai has called his personalized and informal management style, had become irrelevant (the system nevertheless still persists in Indian business houses, recent new economic liberalization measures notwithstanding). It was in such a state of flux that Ambalal Sarabhai's Cambridge-educated youngest son Vikram returned to India after finishing his doctorate in physics in 1947.

Precisely because Kasturbhai, despite his brief stint with the Swaraj Party, remained apolitical throughout his life, he enjoyed the authority to speak out on local and national issues. Before independence, he had been an ardent advocate for the protection of Indian textiles, opposing excise duties on Indian cotton by the British government; after independence, he became an indefatigable defender of Gujarati identity against Maratha Bombay. When the Bombay government that controlled Gujarat made Marathi the official language of the Dangs in 1949—tribals who lived in a region near Valsad (near Bombay), where Atul Products is located—Kasturbhai opposed the decision because Dangri is a dialect of Gujarati. The Dangs incident may be viewed as lighting the fire to the language controversy between Maharastra and Gujarat. In 1952, Kasturbhai once again clashed with the Bombay government, when it imposed a blanket sales tax, covering all sectors of the Gujarati economy; and the Ahmedabadi industrialists were quick to defend Gujarat against economic or cultural threats that would undermine the region's interests or identity, or both. Rich Gujaratis, who had long sent their bright young children to Bombay for higher education, now felt vulnerable in the absence of modern educational institutions of their own. Opposing the introduction of Marathi as the official language in Gujarat and wanting Western educational institutions of their own were seen as two separate things by the middle-class Gujaratis. They found no contradiction in the two positions. Gandhi's dream of *sarvodaya* (Gandhian socialism, which called for the "uplifting" of all) had faded, if not crumbled, by the late 1950s, to be replaced by what the Fabian Nehru called "socialization of the vacuum," which largely left private entrepreneurs alone in the country to thrive as a reward for their support for Congress. Gujarat Vidyapith, founded by Gandhi in 1920 for the teaching of vernacular studies and for recruiting satyagrahi soldiers and swadeshi supporters, was not seen by the Ahmedabad industrialists as meeting the needs of the new nation (nor is it seen to do so today, although deference to the late Mahatma is scrupulously maintained in every public pronouncement by politicians of all hues). Other colleges (Gujarat College, M. R. College, and R. C. Technical Institute, of which Gujarat College, founded in 1879, was the oldest) were woefully ill-equipped to serve as modern educational institutions. For most educated Indians, opposing British rule was one thing; it was quite another to discredit the benefits of Western education in nation building, which is how middle-class Indians view education today. In a perverse sense, Thomas Babington Macaulay's dream of creating a class of persons "who would be Indian in blood and colour, but English in taste, in opinions, in morals, and in intellect" survived into postcolonial India. Nirad C. Chaudhry, the unabashed critic of India and an implacable Anglophile, is often cited as the worst example of what Macaulay had in mind—but, in truth, all upper-class Indians from Rabindranath Tagore to Arundhati Roy benefitted from the Western educational system.

Education, not politics, was Kasturbhai's passion: because of his professional stature (he also had high physical stature—he was more than six feet tall, and lean), he was quite willing to use his political connections to achieve his goals. As a businessman, he understood the significance of the lack of modern educational institutions in Ahmedabad. As early as 1936, in order to overcome this drawback Kasturbhai and some other progressive Gujaratis had established the Ahmedabad Education Society, which has been responsible for the creation of Gujarat University, its other notable achievement being Lalbhai Dalpatbhai Arts College, established in 1937 and named after Kasturbhai's father. Under Kasturbhai's leadership, the society established educational institutions in a variety of disciplines: education, science, commerce, pharmacy, engineering, and the arts. Kasturbhai was instrumental in establishing the Lalbhai Dalpatbhai Institute of Indology, home to classic Jain literature, teaching, and philosophy. Restoration and maintenance of Jain temples also became a part of his efforts. In 1962, the society established the School of Architecture, which was later (1972) merged with the School of Urban Studies and Planning. Kasturbhai himself contributed liberally and exhorted other industrialists to contribute generously to education.

Ahmedabad owners of textile mills created a formidable financial war chest in the form of charitable trusts, which became a major source for funding educational and cultural initiatives in Gujarat, particularly in Ahmedabad. As early as 1922, Kasturbhai, who was driven as much by profit as by munificence, had successfully sought from the government of India under the Income Tax Law individual tax exemption for up to 50 percent of the amount donated to recognized charities. The Finance Act of 1948 also brought company donations under the exemption provision, providing additional inducement to the wealthy to contribute to charities; every millionaire wanted a charitable trust of his own, however, and invariably created it to memorialize a departed family member. In 1976, the various Kasturbhai Lalbhai family trusts alone stood at a staggering sum of rupees 230.5 lakh (1 lakh is equal to 100,000; hence, 230.5 x 100,000 rupees). Between 1948 and 1976, the Kasturbhai Lalbhai family and the Lalbhai industries together had contributed about rupees 478 lakh to various causes, mostly for education in Ahmedabad.[49] In concert with the Indian government, these charitable trusts were also responsible for the creation of the Ahmedabad Textile Industry Research Association (ATIRA), the Physical Research Laboratory (PRL), and IIM, the last having been founded in 1959.

Vikram Sarabhai (1919–71), one of the Kasturbhai clan, returned from England in 1947, just in time to join Kasturkaka, as he reverently addressed his uncle (*kaka* [Gujarati]: uncle) in a flurry of activities that followed independence. In Vikram, Kasturbhai saw the promising young man who could push forward his agenda for the modernization of education in Ahmedabad, just as he had earlier found the talented London School of Economics graduate B. K. Muzumdar to run Atul, the Indo-American venture. To the Sarabhais he owed an old debt incurred when Ambalal had ushered him (Kasturbhai) into public life. One remarkable feature of the Jain-Bania industrialists of Ahmedabad was that, operating as a hereditary plutocracy, most of them were related to each other by birth and marriage: consequently, cooperation rather than competition characterized their behavior in business, as well as in public dealings with each other. "Ever since childhood I have known Kasturkaka as one of my family members. . . . I am trying to imbibe his ideals in my life," Vikram Sarabhai noted in a speech on the occasion of the seventy-fifth birthday of Kasturbhai.[50]

Vikram received his early education in the Montessori system, which had been imported to Ahmedabad by his parents. On completing his secondary school examinations, Vikram attended Gujarat College, Ahmedabad, but later transferred to Saint John's College, Cambridge, and in 1940 he took his tripos in natural sciences. The outbreak of World War II took him back to India, where he took up research in physics at the Indian Institute of Science, Bangalore, working under the Noble Laureate Sir C. V. Raman. In Bangalore, he met and married Mrinalini Swaminathan, a classical Indian dancer, with whom he had a son, Kartikeya, and a daughter, Mallika. After the war, he returned to Cambridge, completing his doctoral dissertation in photo fission at the Cavendish Laboratory in 1947. Kasturbhai and Vikram Sarabhai collaborated in the founding of the PRL in Ahmedabad, which Vikram personally directed until his death in 1971. Together, they also founded ATIRA, of which Vikram was the first honorary director.

From 1950 to 1966, Vikram Sarabhai was instrumental in establishing a number of industries in Baroda, including Sarabhai Chemicals, Sarabhai Glass, Suhrid Geigy Ltd., Symbiotics Ltd., Sarabhai Merck Ltd., and the Sarabhai Engineering Group. In Bombay, he took over Swastik Oil Mills, introducing new techniques of oil extraction and the manufacture of synthetic detergents and cosmetics. In Calcutta, he assumed control of Standard Pharmaceuticals Ltd., where he introduced the large-scale manufacture of penicillin, besides increasing the range of pharmaceutical products. In 1960, in Baroda, he set up the Sarabhai Research Centre for the investigation of natural and synthetic medicines.

Vikram was particularly drawn to issues of management, a subject that also interested Kasturbhai; thus was born, in 1957, the Ahmedabad Management Association, and in 1960 the Operations Research Group, now located in Baroda. In 1959, it was the Kasturbhai-Sarabhai team that was responsible for persuading the Indian government to locate the Indian Institute of Management at Ahmedabad, rather than at Bombay, to train India's professional managers; IIM was inaugurated in 1962, and Sarabhai served as its honorary director until 1965.

In 1962, Vikram Sarabhai took over the chairmanship of the Indian National Committee for Space Research, and in 1966 he became chairman of the Atomic Energy Commission and secretary to the Department of Atomic Energy for the government of India, thus becoming the architect of India's nuclear program. By way of contrast, his oldest sister, Mirdula, like his aunt Anasuya, took the path of ahimsa, becoming Gandhi's dearest disciple. In later life, she was preoccupied with the Kashmir dispute between India and Pakistan, searching for a solution that would be acceptable to India, Pakistan, and the Kashmiris—both Hindus and Muslims—a dispute that has remained unresolved and taken countless lives.

Vikram saw tremendous potential in using science to help the process of development in India. Long before the advent of the internet and distance learning, he envisioned plans for introducing modern education to the remotest villages by using satellite television, later implemented as the Satellite Instructional Television Experiment. He established the Community Science Centre in Ahmedabad for the promotion of science among schoolchildren, as well as assuming responsibility for the creation of the Nehru Foundation for Development. Winner of several awards, including the Shanti Swaroop Bhatnagar Memorial Award for Physics, the Padma Bhushan, and the Padma Vibhushan (posthumously), he searched for ways to link atomic power with the industrial development of large, backward areas, such as his proposal concerning the development of agroindustrial complexes in the Gangetic plain and the arid area of Kutch. No less imaginative was his plan for the use of satellite communication to bring the benefits of television to the hundreds of villages in India on an economical basis.

Vikram Sarabhai was a Renaissance man. His interests transcended science to include music, photography, archaeology, and the performing arts. With his wife, Mrinalini, he started Darpana, an institute devoted to the performing arts, the propagation of Indian cultures, and the creation of a free environment where artists could fully express their talent. The institute is now managed by his daughter, Mallika. Among his other pursuits was the promotion of family planning and rural education. All these measures were light-years ahead of the traditional mentality of the textile mills with which he had grown up in Ahmedabad.

The Kasturbhai-Sarabhai team found a political ally in Dr. Jivraj Mehta (1886–1977), a doctor-turned-politician who would head Gujarat's first elected Congress government as chief minister. Soft-spoken, suave, sartorial Jivraj Mehta was born in Amreli, Saurastra. Son of wealthy Baroda Bania parents, Narayanbhai and Zamakbehn, Jivraj excelled in studies and dreamed of becoming a doctor. His parents financed his medical education in London, where he met Gandhi soon after the start of World War I in 1914. After Gandhi informed a gathering of Indians in London that "English students had volunteered to serve in the army, and Indians might do no less,"[51] Jivraj was among those who volunteered to help the British war effort. He trained under the distinguished Dr. James Cantlie, who established the Society of Tropical Medicine and Hygiene in London in 1907 and who also trained the Chinese nationalist Sun Yat-sen.

Upon his return to India, Jivraj married the beautiful daughter of the diwan of Baroda, Hansabhehn, who was much younger than him (she later became the first vice-chancellor of Maharaja Sayajirao University of Baroda, founded in 1949). Family connections helped Jivraj to secure the position of diwan (minister) of

Baroda. While serving as the diwan, he remained active in the nationalist movement and also continued with the medical profession. The British Indian Medical Service denied Indian doctors professional positions in medical colleges teaching Western medicine. With the help of the Bombay financier Seth Gordhandas Sunderdas and support from the Parsi lawyer Sir Pherozshah Mehta (1845–1915—popularly known in the city as the "Uncrowned King of Bombay"), the Bombay Municipality opened the two-tiered Seth Gordhandas Sunderdas Medical College and King Edward Memorial Hospital, named after the late King Edward VII, in the summer of 1925 (however, the institution celebrated its first Foundation Day the following year on January 22, and it has ritually done so ever since). Dr. Jivraj Mehta was appointed the first dean. The teaching-medical hospital was needed particularly for treating the mill workers of Bombay, who were the backbone of the city's economy. Common diseases that were treated included the bubonic plague, smallpox, malaria, cholera, dysentery, leprosy—all this at a time when antibiotics had yet to be invented.

Living up to the Hippocratic oath, the good doctor also started several medical camps, treating the poor and the famous alike, including the moderate modernist nationalist Gopal Krishna Gokhale (1866–1915) and the Mahatma himself, for appendicitis, in the Yeravda jail. In 1928, Jivraj furthered Gandhi's cause of swadeshi by inventing Babuline Gripe Water to replace the British Woodward Gripe Water, used by Indian mothers for treating colic babies. He gave production rights to the businessman-chemist Bhavanishankar Atmaram Oza, from his native Saurastra. Drawing on his experience in English hospitals, he also experimented with architectural design for the Seth G. S. Medical College and the K. E. M. Hospital by integrating the two functions—teaching and treatment (including the outpatient block)—in a single building, rather than segregating them as had been the practice in India. The two sections of the building were connected by covered concrete corridors so that patients, students, and staff, going back and forth, would be protected from rain and sun. The English architect W. A. Pite, who had earlier designed King's College Hospital in London, executed the design plan. Pite had built his reputation by designing a new village for boys—twenty-eight houses on thirty-nine acres of land at Woodford Bridge, intended to make boys into better citizens. In Bombay, Pite was assisted by the Bombay-based English architect George Wittet (1880–1926), who "achieved a thoroughgoing Anglo-Indian synthesis for the Prince of Wales Museum in 1905 and the Gateway of India some twenty-two years later."[52]

Jivraj acquired electoral experience when, on the strong suggestion of his friend and political mentor, Vallabhbhai Patel, he successfully contested a seat in the Baroda State Praja Mandal (lit., citizens' forum) and formed Baroda's first representative government in September 1948. Ruler Sayajirao III had introduced (albeit in a limited way) the Ripon-inspired electoral principal for municipalities as early as 1892, with a view to preparing people in self-government. On December 31, 1916, at a conference, the Baroda state panchayats passed a resolution that called for the establishment of the praja mandal, which was created shortly thereafter—and from time to time it "espoused such policies and programmes of the Indian National Congress as were applicable to the princely state."[53] After Baroda was merged with Bombay State on May 1, 1949, Morarji Desai appointed Jivraj to be minister for public works in the Bombay government, the much-maligned colonial department that transferred to postcolonial India with all its contradictions and corruption.

In the late 1950s, when talks started about creating the new state of Gujarat, Dr. Jivraj, because he was acceptable to all parties, appeared to be the best candidate to head the new government: he had served with the Gaekwads of Baroda, with the Ahmedabadi mill owners, the Bombay government, and Congress. Gentle, perhaps too gentle for the noise of Indian politics, but bright, personable, and loyal, Jivraj had acquired considerable experience in government, particularly in public works. As minister of public works in the Bombay government, he had overseen urban and architectural projects throughout the state, and he had kept a close watch on projects in Ahmedabad, which had turned into a center of international attention in architecture (along with Chandigarh) because of the work there by Le Corbusier and, later, the American Louis Kahn. He had worked closely with Kasturbhai on the development of the free-trade zone Kandala Port in the Gulf of Kutch after Karachi harbor was lost to Pakistan in partition. Kasturbhai had been appointed chairman of the West Coast Major Port Committee by Deputy Prime Minister Vallabhbhai Patel after Patel rejected several names submitted by Finance Minister John Matthai; and in turn Kasturbhai had rejected several suggested sites by interested parties, including Balwantrai Mehta's choice of his hometown of Bhavnagar (Mehta was to later succeed Jivraj as chief minister), and Jam Sahib's recommendation for Sika on the northern coast of his principality of Jamnagar.[54]

In the decades immediately following independence, India witnessed a flurry of building projects, including the state capital cities of Chandigarh[55] and Bhubaneswar,[56] refugee towns, industrial towns, hydroelectric projects, and much more. Ahmedabad itself was a center of building projects by European and Indian architects, including Le Corbusier's designs for the Millowners Association Building, the Ahmedabad Museum, and the Sarabhai and Shodhan houses (the Shodhan house plan was originally drawn for Surottam Hutheesingh, but later sold to mill owner Shyamubhai Shodhan)—all Ahmedabad patrons of Le Corbusier and close relatives of Kasturbhai, either by birth or marriage. In fact, Le Corbusier had been invited to Ahmedabad by Chinubhai Chimanbhai, a nephew of Kasturbhai and mayor of the city between 1950 and 1962, who commissioned the architect with two projects: the museum and his own residence.[57] During Mayor Chimanbhai's tenure, several major projects were implemented by various architects: libraries, playgrounds, a stadium, an auditorium, and the Gandhi Smarak Sanghralaya, by Charles Correa, who had set up his practice in Bombay in 1958 after finishing his master's degree in architecture at Massachusetts Institute of Technology in 1955. Like the neighboring Sabarmati Ashram (designed by Gandhi's nephew Maganlal Gandhi, who had also designed the Phoenix Ashram in Durban, South Africa, where Gandhi launched his public career), the Gandhi Samarak Sanghralaya symbolizes the asceticism, minimalism, and functionalism that characterized Mahatma's life. Also in 1958, Balkrishna Vithaldas Doshi, a graduate of the J. J. School of Art, Bombay, one of the oldest and premier institutions to offer a degree in architecture in India, established his own architectural firm, Vastu-Shilpa, in Ahmedabad, changing its name in 1962 to the Vastu-Shilpa Foundation for Environmental Design. Before relocating to Ahmedabad, Doshi had apprenticed with Le Corbusier in Paris, which later gave him the opportunity to serve as a site architect on his mentor's buildings in Ahmedabad. Doshi's fluency in Indian and European languages and his understanding of Indian culture allowed him to serve as interpreter between the maestro and his Indian clients. He was exactly the person the Ahmedabad mill owners needed to translate for them the new architectural language. In time, Doshi would play an important role in many a building project in the city, including the establishing of the Centre for Environmental Planning and Technology (CEPT) in Ahmedabad.

Gautam and Gira Sarabhai, the brother-and-sister team that had been designated to succeed the old patriarch Ambalal, launched Ahmedabad's renaissance in independent India by establishing the Calico Museum in 1949. Called the Wonder House, a name that evokes an image more from a Walt Disney extravaganza than from a house celebrating linen, its purpose was as much to preserve the textile family's history as to showcase the skills of master craftsmen—and, of course, selected family heirlooms. For a historical narrative of the cotton industry in India, the Sarabhais recruited the distinguished Indian art historian Ananda Coomaraswamy. A volume produced on the centenary of the Calico Mills in 1980 explains the museum's purpose: "Let our . . . young learn . . . in an age when we are being alienated by the machine civilization . . . [that only] those who can [appreciate] . . . nature . . . can be trusted to run the machines."[58] This is not how Le Corbusier would have interpreted the machine age: and, happily, the museum of textiles was placed not in one of Le Corbusier's buildings but in the Retreat, the ancestral home of the Sarabhais designed in 1936 by Surendranath Kar (1892–1970), the gifted painter-architect who had built Rabindranath Tagore's house and who drew his artistic inspiration from the poet laureate in much of his work.

Ahmedabad's renaissance was fueled by industrial capital, but the arrival of Le Corbusier and other messengers of the international modern movement held out the promise of transforming the decaying urban structure into a modern metropolis with broad boulevards, stylistically advanced buildings, well-planned residential sectors, institutes, theaters, and convention halls that would make Ahmedabad a sparkling capital and a desirable business destination. With Kasturbhai as the lord of the city, the fellowship of the Ahmedabadi industrialist, and the family network that extended throughout the city, the balance was tilted in favor of Ahmedabad to resume its old status as the capital city. "The civic leadership of the city," as one writer on Ahmedabad and its industrial elite has observed, "had been traditionally identified with the business leadership. . . . Kasturbhai had a secret desire not only to bring back to his family the business leadership of the city but also revive the social preeminence that his ancestors once enjoyed."[59] Expecting Ahmedabad to become the capital of Gujarat, several industrialists, including Kasturbhai, had acquired large tracts of land on the western side of the city, hoping to benefit from the rise in land values that would inevitably follow.

But even the deep pockets of the city's industrialists, their intricate family network, and their access to the famous architect-planners could not change the overcrowded character of Ahmedabad. The best alternative was Gandhinagar, fifteen miles north of the city. This was announced by chief minister designate Jivraj Mehta on March 19, 1960, two months before the new state was officially born. A biographer of Kasturbhai has pointed to the patriarch's compulsion to keep his factories and businesses within the city so as to allow him personally to supervise operations, the only exception being Atul Products, which was placed at Valsad because of its close proximity to Bombay.[60] It seems clear, given Kasturbhai's involvement with the capital project, that his desire for its placement in Ahmedabad—or near enough for close proximity to the political establishment—was inevitable. As a member of the Capital Project Committee, Kasturbhai could protect the economic interests of Ahmedabad and also influence the urban future of the new state. Jivraj, who had come to be viewed as a stooge of the city's industrial elite and who found himself in an adversarial position with Bombay's Morarji Desai, who had opposed the bifurcation of Bombay State, in the heat of internecine political warfare resigned from the chief ministership early in his second term. This loyal soldier of Congress was dispatched to London as India's high commissioner by his close friend Prime Minister Nehru—away from the din of Gujarat politics. He would later return to politics to represent his hometown constituency of Amreli in the Fifth Lok Sabha (the lower house of the Indian parliament). Meanwhile, Ahmedabad would serve as the temporary capital until Gandhinagar was ready to house the Gujarat government.

3

The Kahn Seminar in Ahmedabad

LE CORBUSIER'S VISIT to Ahmedabad in 1951 had introduced mill owners to modernism in architecture: the arrival in the city of the American architect Louis Kahn in 1962 started a seminar in modern architecture that would last the rest of the decade. Ahmedabad became not only the focal point of Kahn's creative expression but also served as the principal place from which he would direct his large-scale projects on the subcontinent, including the building of the Indian Institute of Management in Ahmedabad and, in Dhaka, the second capitol complex of Pakistan. As Gandhi had established his Sabarmati ashram in Ahmedabad, whence he launched the national campaign of satyagraha, Kahn would use the National Institute of Design (NID) to introduce Indians to his transcendental architecture. Kahn's subcontinental projects drew international attention to the old, rustic, mill town of Ahmedabad. It was there that the Gujarat government was temporarily located, and it was in the homes of Kasturbhai Lalbhai, the Sarabhais, and NID that the first negotiations started on recruiting Kahn for the planning and designing of Gandhinagar, the capital of Gujarat. But like Indian civilization itself, the search for the architect-planner of Gandhinagar was shrouded in mystery, enriched by myths, and burdened with paradoxes, eluding even the mystic Kahn himself. But Kahn's relationship with his patrons in Ahmedabad was not one of simplicity of purpose; rather, it was a relationship born of mutual dependencies, textured by competing interests, and energized by personal ambitions. Kahn's substantial subcontinental oeuvre would catapult him to the pantheon of twentieth-century architects, and the mill owners made their mark on the twentieth century riding the crest of modern architecture. Somewhere in between fell Gandhinagar, promising artistic immortality for Kahn and material gain for the mill owners, local architects, and contractors.

Gandhinagar is located fifteen miles (twenty-three kilometers) north of Ahmedabad on the right bank of the Sabarmati River in Kalol Taluka (the Kalol division) of the Mehsana District. The capital city covers an area of about twenty-five square miles, or nearly sixteen thousand square acres. *The Preliminary Report on Gandhinagar,* which was issued in 1961, defined the size and the character of the capital: "This area is considered sufficient for a garden city . . . of [150,000] souls."[1] The site was selected because it is level, but with a gentle slope, allowing for good drainage, running northeast to southwest. The ground is about seventy-five to eighty feet above average ground level at Ahmedabad. The soil is sandy loam, considered good for the foundations of buildings and road construction, as well as for horticultural projects (in neighboring Pethpur, mango groves abounded). But the chief criterion was, as is usual, the cost, which was "comparatively less" than any other site near Ahmedabad. Close proximity to the Sabarmati assured ample water supply. The site also had good transportation connection to National Highway 8 (which links Ahmedabad with Delhi), to the Ahmedabad-Kalol State Highway (which links the capital with Mount Abu in Rajasthan), and to an approach road linking Gandhinagar with Ahmedabad via the Sabarmati, Koba, and Dholakuwa; and to the meter-gauge railway line near Ahmedabad. A provision was made to place the airport near Ahmedabad Cantonment. Southwest breezes cooled the capital in the hot months.[2]

On June 16, 1960, the Gandhian governor of Gujarat, Shriman Narayan, issued ordinance no. 7, requisitioning the capital site for development; the ordinance's reach extended to a distance of five miles from the outer boundary of the capital on all sides in order to secure a green belt around the city along the lines of one in Chandigarh. On June 11, 1960, the Capital Project Circle was created by the Gujarat government. Consisting of the Office of the Superintendent Engineer, three divisional engineering offices, and nine subdivisional engineering offices, charged with the task of conducting land surveys, landscaping, gardening, planting of trees, supplying electricity and water, providing sewerage, building materials, and so on, the Capital Project Circle was the apex authority for the planning and designing of Gandhinagar. G. K. Patil was appointed the superintendent engineer on July 8, 1960. The speed with which government decisions were reached to set up an organizational structure suggests the influence of the experience gained from the planning of Chandigarh and Bhubaneswar. The Capital Project board included, among other members, the old patriarch of Ahmedabad Kasturbhai Lalbhai, who, along with architect Balkrishna Doshi would exercise his influence in the selection of a planner-architect.

Gandhinagar's year has three seasons: summer (February 15 to June 15), the rainy season (June 15 to October 15), and winter (October 15 to February 15). Although the meteorological department in Ahmedabad records wind velocity in

Gandhinagar at under ten miles an hour for most of the year, the city can occasionally experience gusty winds rising up to thirty-five miles an hour, and even cyclonical conditions of winds as high as sixty miles an hour. In the summer, the temperature can reach as high as 118 degrees Fahrenheit, falling to a minimum of 40 degrees in the winter, with the maximum temperature variation in a day being about 33 degrees. The average rainfall in the Gandhinagar region is between fourteen inches and fifty-seven inches, which explains the constant problem of water shortages in the city.

The preliminary report provided for three types of buildings in the capital: (1) the administrative buildings, which included the secretariat (the Sachivalya), the Legislative Assembly (the Vidhan Sabha), the Raj Bhavan (Governor's House), the High Court, with lawyers' chambers, the Government Guest House, the Central Office, and the District Office; (2) the civic buildings, which included the municipality library, theater, town hall, museum, educational institutions, medical offices and hospitals, police stations, guest houses, hotels, stadiums, and other recreational buildings; and (3) housing for public employees built by the government and assigned on the basis of pay scale and rank, challenging Gandhi's egalitarian philosophy of sarvodaya, while private housing was to be regulated by the Capital Project Circle. In the end, however, the plan succeeded in achieving a segregated settlement for government officials—exactly what the German planner Koenigsberger had opposed, unsuccessfully, in Bhubaneswar.[3]

In Bhubaneswar, Koenigsberger, even more than Le Corbusier and the American Albert Mayer in Chandigarh, had provided the clearest definition of a postcolonial, postwar capital city. "In 1946, the term 'administrative capital' means much more: It describes the lively nerve centre of provincial activities where workers and their representatives, manufacturers, businessmen, meet and collaborate in the development of all aspects of provincial life."[4] Koenigsberger strongly felt that it was important to mix members of different professions in a capital city, to avoid segregated settlements, like cantonments, and the civil lines that were built in India by the British to insulate a handful of Europeans from Indians.

Built almost a generation after Chandigarh and Bhubaneswar, Gandhinagar is essentially a carbon copy of the Garden City plan that was drawn for its older cousins. "Apart from meeting the needs of the Government, it was felt necessary to provide a suitable nucleus around which the business[,] educational and cultural interests of the New Capital could be rehabilitated," the preliminary report declared in 1960. "The basic concept underlying the plan is that each sector will be practically self-sufficient in its daily requirement[s] such as shopping centers, markets, schools, health and community centre and recreation grounds." Even before a planner or an architect had been selected, the planning details had been worked out, dividing the city into four functional areas in accordance with Corbusian pedagogy,[5] which calls for separation of functions between automobile traffic and the pedestrian and between work, business, residential, and recreational activities. There was some mixing of functions, however, to suit the Indian taste for living close to work:

Sector I—All important Government buildings with [a] residential area [for] the Ministers, Deputy Ministers and Class I and Class II Officers.

Sector II—Residential zones for Class III and Class IV servants and certain Public Buildings.

Sector III—Cottage Industries zone and Railway Station.

Sector IV—Business centers and residential accommodation for private sector.

The four sectors are bounded on all sides by main roads for fast moving vehicles which give the town the Ring and Grid pattern. No fast moving traffic will thus enter any of the residential sectors, the life within which will be safe, quiet and social and free from danger of accidents.

The town will be dominated by a group of buildings consisting [of] the High Court, the Assembly chamber, the Sachivalya [the secretariat] and [the] Raj Bhavan and a group of central offices, situated on the highest ground in the north of the town.

The Commercial hub of the town will be located in the centre of the town where the two principal traffic roads cross each other at the centre of which it is proposed to erect a magnificent statute of Mahatma Gandhi to increase the grandeur of the central area.

The area [for] Cottage industries [in] the Capital is located in the southwest corner [in the direction of Ahmedabad] and is separated entirely from the residential sector. Its physical situation permits the expansion of industries side by side with the expansion of the town. A Railway siding connecting this area to the main railway lines has also been provided to facilitate the incoming of raw materials and to take away the finished products. The industrial area is also connected by direct roads to the other regions without crossing other sectors of the city.

Adequate reservations have been made in all sectors, for parks and open spaces, health and community centres, swimming pools, playing grounds and other similar amenities.[6]

The road system was modeled after the "7 V Rule" introduced in Chandigarh by Le Corbusier, who aimed at curbing urban congestion by separating automobiles and pedestrians.[7] The city roads were classified into six categories: principal traffic roads, the fast-moving "ring" road, main city streets, compound (or sector) roads, and sidewalks (footpaths) running through parks and gardens. Guiding the development of Gandhinagar was not only the experience of Chandigarh and Bhubaneswar but also experience gained from several new, postcolonial townships in Gujarat itself. Soon after independence, the refugee town of Gandhidham, which also serves the nearby free port of Kandala, in the Gulf of Kutch, that replaced the loss of Karachi to Pakistan had been planned by Koenigsberger, who attempted to fuse the Garden City planning principles of Ebenezer Howard with those of the Congrès Internationaux d'Architecture Moderne (CIAM), inserting three basic ingredients—sun, space, and greenery—into modern urban life. Created in 1928, CIAM had been a major influence on the many housing programs in Germany before World War II to which Koenigsberger had been exposed growing up in Berlin—programs that he would utilize not only in Gandhidhar but in other towns and housing projects he helped build as director of housing for the government of India's Ministry of Health from 1948 to 1951. An admirer of Clarence Arthur Perry, who had helped popularize the "neighborhood unit" as a solution to the decaying state of Western cities and the growing menace of the automobile, Koenigsberger had effectively used neighborhood in his planning of Indian cities, including Bhubaneswar, but with a variation on how it had been used by both Mayer and Le Corbusier in Chandigarh. In his critique of the Chandigarh plan, he noted that "separation of function and improved design may not be enough" in economically depressed countries. "Residential neighbourhoods may have to be designed as walking units, not only because of the poverty of the inhabitants, who will include but few cars owners, but also because groups of 'walking neighbour-hoods' connected by efficient systems of public transport, may ultimately prove to be better and more humane solutions than towns for private motorcars." In fact, he saw a blessing in the economic backwardness of developing countries: it pre-vented the menace of the automobile. That simplistic argument certainly did not win any converts to the doctrine of asceticism, but in the second half of the twen-tieth century, several Indian cities were developed "by stringing rows of neigh-bourhoods together along one major line of public transport."[8] Among them were Valsad, in Gujarat, home to Kasturbhai's Atul Industries, near Bombay, where middle-class suburban comforts made it a visual oasis.

Meanwhile, in Ahmedabad, the founding of the Calico Museum in 1949 had ushered in a cultural renaissance as a result of the funding provided for building projects by the mill owners. The Kasturbhai Lalbhai and Sarabhai families were the undisputed leaders of Ahmedabad's urban minirevolution. Competing ideas in planning and architecture began pouring in from all corners of the world. The Cambridge-educated mathematician Gautam Sarabhai himself dabbled in engi-neering and architectural issues when, in the 1940s, he and his sister Gira Sara-bhai studied with the American Frank Lloyd Wright at Taliesin, his home in Spring Green, Wisconsin. Wright named his house Taliesin (Welsh for "shining brow," Welsh being his ethnic heritage) because he had built the house around the brow of the hill, rather than on its top, and that, like the brow, was to be emblematic of thinking—the thinking part of his practice. At Taliesin, Wright, always idiosyn-cratic and authoritarian, experimented in the self-sufficient utopian community that represented his educational ideal of developing "a well-correlated human being"—a kind of Renaissance man as opposed to a professional man—and the result was the Taliesin Fellowship.[9] This fellowship and Gandhi's Sabarmati Ashram in Ahmedabad had several similarities, especially the emphasis on self-reliance, communal living, and the union of physical and mental labor. Apprentices at Taliesin and residents at the Sabarmati Ashram (and Gandhi's other ashrams around the country) built their own quarters, worked, studied, farmed, cooked, and cleaned. Like Gandhi, Wright hated religious dogma, but unlike Gandhi, Wright, the son and grandson of Unitarian ministers, remained suspicious of organized religion and believed that all churches were "essentially undemocratic." Both men searched for a shared universal worship, which, however, eluded them both. Later, while designing the dome for the Calico Shop (1962) with Gira in Ahmedabad, Gautam Sarabhai is reported to have corresponded with another American visionary, the techno-architect Richard Buckminster Fuller,[10] who spent a lifetime inventing new structural systems and who had the grand vision of covering the whole of Manhattan with a glazed dome. The dome idea may have sown the seed in the minds of U.S. political leaders to build a nuclear shield over the country. Such a concept gained a certain attention and urgency, not only in the United States but also in many other countries, after the crashing of two airliners into the World Trade Center on September 11, 2001.

Ahmedabad's architecture would never have been able to develop in such an eclectic fashion without the peculiar political situation of the time. After independence, there was a growing demand from many regions, including Gujarat, for administrative autonomy. The influx of refugees and the increase in rural-urban migration spurred by industrialization contributed to demands for city expansion and low-cost housing. Gujarati capitalism, based on the boom in commercial businesses and industrial production, had taken off in World War I, and with it came industrial concentration, urbanization, the emergence of trade unions, and a general political awareness among the working classes. The newly wealthy feared losing their sudden cornucopia, while those less fortunate had less and less to lose. The danger of urban unrest created by a lack of low-cost housing and the absence of institutional infrastructure to train India's future managers demanded new policies to address a volatile situation. The Indian government arranged scholarship programs for several Indian students to study architecture and engineering courses in Western countries.

The Harvard-educated Achyut P. Kanvinde, one of the new crop of Western-educated Indians, returned home to design the Ahmedabad Textile Industries Research Association (ATIRA) in 1950, about ten years before MIT-educated Charles Correa designed Gandhi Samarak Sanghralaya, also in Ahmedabad. Kanvinde's ATIRA shows the clear influence of the Bauhaus school, which attempted to integrate craft and industry and to which he had been exposed at the Graduate

School of Design at Harvard University, where Walter Gropius, the founder of the Bauhaus in 1919, taught. Other influences on Kanvinde at Harvard were Joseph Hudnut and the Hungarian-born Marcel Breuer, who, along with Gropius, helped transform the curriculum from Beaux Arts classical precedent to the appreciation of modern aesthetics with its social and technical imperatives. Charles Correa, too, came under the spell of the modern movement at MIT, the first U.S. university to start a formal architectural program (in 1868), where he studied under William Wilson Wurster, who was born in Stockton, California, and who distinguished himself as a major designer of town and country dwellings in the roomy and comfortable West Coast aesthetic. Wurster's buildings were carefully integrated with the surrounding environment, a technique that Correa would use effectively in his many buildings, including the Gandhi Samarak Sanghralaya, where he successfully integrated the Corbusian-inspired open grid plan and pyramidal roofs with the surrounding environment. The other influence on Correa was the genial and popular Lawrence B. Anderson, under whose leadership changes were made in the curriculum of the architecture program at MIT. The School of Architecture and Planning also rethought its role as part of a technological institution, adding studies of illumination, solar heating, procurement specifications for mobile housing, the application of modern plastics in construction, and acoustics to its curriculum —all of which would show up in Correa's works.

Soon after arriving in India to finish building Chandigarh, which had been started by Mayer, Le Corbusier was invited to Ahmedabad by Mayor Chinubhai Chimanbhai, Kasturbhai Lalbhai's nephew. Le Corbusier arrived in March 1951, and he would remain involved with the city until his death in August 1965. He designed four buildings there in the 1950s. He was also to be the messenger of the modern movement to the cotton plutocrats of Ahmedabad. World War II had disrupted the modern movement in Europe, with two of its three leading advocates— Walter Gropius and Ludwig Mies van der Rohe—leaving for North America and Europe itself becoming disillusioned. Le Corbusier, with the conviction of the evangelist, championed the strong moral and social imperatives of the modern movement, extending to postcolonial India its promise of unlimited possibilities and a better life through good design and planning. Proclaiming himself "Spiritual Director" of the Chandigarh enterprise, he declared that his aim was to make that city a finishing school for Indians by providing "them an education of the university type."[11] However, what transferred to India was only an awareness of the modern movement's product, not the process.

One of the earliest converts to the modernist mainstream in India was Balkrishna Vithaldas Doshi, who would be instrumental in linking India to Western architectural thought in a matrix of mutual dependencies. Born in 1927, Doshi has led a peripatetic life—first as that most improbable of creatures in colonial India, a liberal arts and architectural student. He finished studies at Fergusson College,

Poona, the capital of the Peshwa, and at the J. J. School of Art, Bombay, the repository of British-inspired Gothic architecture, and became an itinerant apprentice, living in London, Paris, Philadelphia, and Chicago, eventually settling in Ahmedabad. His decision to set up offices in Ahmedabad in 1958 was clearly influenced by his mentor Le Corbusier. Doshi first met Le Corbusier in London. He persuaded the French master to let him apprentice with him in Paris from 1951 to 1954, and during those years he assisted Le Corbusier (whom he playfully called "Acrobat") with his designs for Chandigarh. Experience gained at 35, rue de Sèvres, Le Corbusier's Paris atelier, allowed Doshi to replace the French Jean-Louis Véret as the site architect for Le Corbusier's buildings in Ahmedabad. Doshi was able to ease his way into the textured Ahmedabad establishment and win the hearts of the city's cotton elite because of his Gujarati Bania origins—in much the same way that the Swiss-born Le Corbusier had eased his way into the insular Parisian society because of his Francophone background. In 1958, Doshi established Vastu-Shilpa, a semiautonomous, environmentally-conscious study cell named after the ancient Indian science of building, to provide emotional dimension to the fresh ways that architectural students map the world. In 1980, the Vastu-Shilpa Foundation was moved to Sangath ("moving together"), his office complex, twenty-five hundred meters square, in Ahmedabad, which he himself designed in the local low-rise vernacular. For this complex he used Kahn-inspired cylindrical structures, but in terra-cotta tiles sandwiched between thin ferro-cement shells covered with shards of white ceramics, which served as heat-reflecting, waterproof casing for the structure, which was set in Mughal-inspired, tiered gardens that merged with lily ponds and other bodies of water. In Ahmedabad, Doshi felt the urge to encourage local mill owners to live with a more encompassing sense of what constituted their world.

Among his contemporaries, Doshi is perhaps the only Indian architect to have either studied under or forged working relationships with four Western architects: the English Claude Batley, the French Le Corbusier, and the Americans Louis Kahn and Joseph Stein. He was thus the first Indian architect to integrate into a wider world. Doshi was exposed to Batley's ideas at the J. J. School of Art in Bombay, and they left a lasting impression on him. Batley was a product of the English arts and crafts movement, which believed that the traditional art of architecture had been "crippled" by the utilitarian brutality of industrialization. A leading influence on Batley had been the British architectural historian Howard Robertson, who in 1933 renovated a hotel in Knightsbridge, London, named the Berkeley, where Charles Dickens reportedly once spent a night; and who in 1949 was a member of the international team that designed the United Nations Building in New York (the team also included Le Corbusier, the American Wallace K. Harrison, and the Brazilian Oscar Niemeyer).

Batley had been a strong influence on young Indian architects and planners in the 1930s and 1940s, cautioning them against the modern movement and against "the hastily developed, inadequately tested but ready to hand ideas of the West."[12] Batley believed that Indians should search for solutions to their building needs in their own tradition, not in the international style. This message clearly influenced his student Julius Vaz in Bhubaneswar, the capital of Orissa; however, it would also make Indians recoil from "foreign" ideas associated with the unfathomable or the threateningly remote. Not surprisingly, Batley's message produced revivalism in postcolonial Indian architectural and urban thought as a parallel force to the international style. Doshi, the prodigal student who experimented with Le Corbusier and Louis Kahn, never lost the lesson learned from Batley, however, naming his study cell Vastu-Shilpa, after the ancient Sanskrit word for building. Late in his career, Doshi would reflect on the impact of his Western training, as Batley had instructed his students to do:

> From Le Corbusier I learnt to observe and react to climate, to tradition, to function, to structure, to economy, and to the landscape. I know how to build buildings and create spaces and forms. And from Kahn I understood the spirit of architecture. But in the last two decades, I have gradually discovered that the buildings that I have designed seem somewhat foreign and out of milieu; they do not appear to have their roots in the Indian soil. With the experience of my work over the years and my own observation, I am trying to understand a little about my people, their traditions, and social customs, and their philosophy of life.[13]

In Ahmedabad, Doshi's first independent assignment (1958) was to build the joint housing complex for ATIRA and the Physical Research Laboratories—an assignment arranged by the mill owner Kasturbhai, who became Doshi's benefactor. The same year, Doshi won a Graham Foundation Fellowship to the University of Chicago. It was during his stay in the United States, in 1958, that Doshi first met the rationalist mystic Louis Kahn, whom he would reverently call "the Yogi." The two men resonated with each other: Kahn the son of Russian Jewish immigrant parents trying to find his place in race-conscious, capitalist America, and Doshi, the son of Hindu parents, trying to define himself in caste-conscious, secular-socialist India. Kahn frequently spoke about seeking out "beginnings": it was through a sense of history that he "sought a 'timeless' architecture that tapped into primal dissatisfaction with abstract detachment." Called the "prototypical new modernist" by architectural historian James Steele, Kahn served as "the transitional figure between Modernism and Post-Modernism";[14] for Kahn, light was a sacred substance that sanctified life through spirituality.

Like many other Westerners in the 1960s, Kahn was drawn to India wanting to escape materialism and find spirituality in the East. The combination of the anti–Vietnam War movement and Civil Rights activism in the 1960s prompted many Americans to reject capitalist consumerism and search for spiritual solutions to myriad personal and societal problems. The belief systems of that decade challenged repressive hierarchical power structure, accepting a universal belief system that transcended the social, political, and moral norms of any established structure, whether it be a class, a church, or a government. The new creed, exemplified by hippies, prevented imposing one's beliefs on others; it sought, instead, to change the world through reason and by personal example. Kahn displayed many of these qualities in his personal behavior, searching for inner vision to provide answers to his personal and professional problems. When Doshi arranged for him to design the Indian Institute of Management in Ahmedabad, Kahn could not refuse the offer. According to Doshi:

> In 1962, the grand old man of Indian industry and a great patron of architecture, Kasturbhai Lalbhai, who had invited [Le] Corbusier to design the Museum [of Ahmedabad] and the Mill Owners' [Association] building at Ahmedabad, asked me to design the Indian Institute of Management. Its director, Dr. Vikram Sarabhai, a noted scientist and industrialist, wanted me to prepare the programme after studying the management school at Harvard. He also desired that like [Punjab had invited Le] Corbusier [to build Chandigarh], we should invite another comparable architect to help me on the design of the institute. Since the names suggested by them were not comparable to [Le] Corbusier, I persuaded them about Lou[is] [Kahn] and his great work, [which is] comparable to [Frank Lloyd] Wright about whom they had heard a great deal. They agreed. Having obtained the consent from the client, I sent a telegram to Lou and requested him to undertake this assignment with the assurance that I will act as his local associate if he so desired.[15]

Considering that Wright died in April 1959, it is not likely that Vikram Sarabhai would have suggested his name in 1962. Moreover, Vikram Sarabhai knew Wright well through his brother Gautam and sister Gira, who had studied at Taliesin in the 1940s. Furthermore, Wright had been asked by the Sarabhais to design the administrative offices of Calico Mills sometime in the 1950s (Wright declined).[16] It is possible that when the cotton plutocrats prevailed on Prime Minister Nehru to place IIM in Ahmedabad and not in Bombay in early 1959, however, Wright's name was again mentioned. But by then Wright was past ninety, and it is unlikely he would have been willing to decamp to Ahmedabad. A few of Wright's associates did come and build in India: Walter Burley Griffin, who had worked with Wright in Chicago, and Antonin Raymond, who had worked with him in Japan. Wright's ideas, which were freely circulating in Indian architectural circles, are best represented in the works of the American Joseph Stein. Wright's spiritual search did take him to India, not to build but to meet Swami Nitya Swaroopananda in Calcutta—a visit that was ostensibly facilitated by the Sarabhais. It was on that visit that he is reported to have referred to Le Corbusier, who was then building in Chandigarh, as "the other architect."

It appears that the industrial elite also had a Shanghai-born Chinese American, the MIT-Harvard-educated Ieoh Ming Pei (Ieoh Ming translates as "to inscribe brightly") in mind.[17] But Pei was a less serious contender for the assignment because of his tendency to use large, abstract forms and sharp, geometric designs, and his use of glass-clad structures must have appeared unintelligible to Ahmedabad's Bania-Jain cotton barons, who jealously guarded their privacy and who would have considered Pei's transparent structures anathema to their religion. It is also questionable how well-suited Pei's designs would have been in India's intense sunlight.

The loss of metropolitan Bombay as a consequence of the bifurcation of Bombay State when Gujarat was created in 1960 must have played on the collective imagination of the cotton barons of Ahmedabad, which must have persuaded them to patronize Western practitioners of modernism to build brave new buildings in their own city. Gautam, Gira, Vikram Sarabhai, and Kasturbhai formed a discussion group, which also included Doshi, Correa, Kanvinde, and Anant Raje (who would later become the curator of Kahn's work in Ahmedabad), and together they tried to hammer out an urban vision for the city, while finding ways of making architecture intelligible to the ruling elite. There was nothing unusual about these discussions: after all, the earlier ruling elite, both Hindu and Muslim, had erected several monuments in the city as enduring testimony to their names. It was not even unusual that the newly wealthy should be searching for the European modernist style in which to build monuments of their own. "Native rulers adopted western palace types in whole or in part, with state rooms incorporating antechambers, salons, banqueting halls and vast saloon-like *durbar* halls, designed to cater [to] Westernized manners and European guests. It was certainly not lost upon the 'Model Prince' that European building types could be interpreted in a wide diversity of western, eastern and hybrid styles and at their service the fecundity of the Anglo-Indian imagination was to know no bounds."[18] Invariably, the results were eclectic, ranging from Italianate classicism to neo–High Renaissance to neo-baroque; native merchants went beyond the bounds of their status in aping the European style by using high ceilings and wide verandas for their stately bungalows. Their taste, like their politics, was determined largely by considerations of legitimizing wealth and perpetuating the social conventions that affirmed their sense of superiority.

In independent, democratic India, however, modernism made more sense because of its social and moral imperatives, its international application, and its promise of material progress for the maximum number. Because of his associations with Le Corbusier and Louis Kahn and his Gujarati origins, Doshi emerged as the most influential in the discussion group and the best suited for interpreting Western ideas. In recommending Kahn to the new patrons of the modern movement, Doshi was exchanging one teacher for another. Moreover, Kahn's presence in

Ahmedabad would afford an opportunity for architecture students at the newly created National Institute of Design.[19] Of course, Kahn helped by agreeing to all the terms of the Indians, including making concessions in foreign-exchange payments, always, until more recently, an issue for India. So Kahn had already begun work at the IIM complex long before the construction work started at Gandhinagar in 1965, which would make him a potential choice for the planning and designing of Gandhinagar as well.

After Kahn's death in March 1974, Doshi was to forge yet another relationship with an American architect, Joseph Stein. This was to be a partnership, rather than a student-teacher, arrangement. Stein, a midwesterner, had studied at Cranbrook, which had been founded by the newspaper baron George Booth in Michigan in the late 1920s. Cranbrook encouraged personal growth, spiritual development, and a commitment to community service—values that remained with Stein throughout his life. He had also worked with famous architects like the Michigan-based Finnish American Eero Saarinen, noted for the TWA terminal building at Kennedy Airport, New York, and the Los Angeles–based Richard Neutra, noted for his modernist vocabulary. Stein settled in his own practice in San Francisco in 1938 and also became involved with Telesis (from the Greek, meaning progressive; intelligently planned), a progressive environmental movement in the San Francisco Bay Area. In 1952, on Neutra's suggestion, he took over the directorship of the newly formed architectural department at B. E. College, Calcutta, whence he moved to Delhi a few years later to work with Benjamin Polk, an American who had a large practice in India, and later set up his own practice to capitalize on the building boom that had followed independence. Noted for his designs of the India International Centre, New Delhi, Stein cleverly fused an environmentalist discourse (born out of the deforestation of India's Himalayan region) with a powerful vocabulary of ethnocentric regionalism. Together, the two languages gave him a way of defining the importance of a coherent architecture in terms intelligible to those who know nothing about it. In 1977, Stein and Doshi and the Indian Jai Rattan Bhalla founded the architectural firm of Stein, Doshi, and Bhalla, with offices in Delhi and Ahmedabad—a partnership lasting until Stein's death in October 2001. Stein frequently talked about planning for two Indias—for the wealthy, who live expansively, and for the disenfranchised poor, whose movements are propelled by misery.

Ahmedabad in the 1950s and 1960s had turned into a microcosm of the architectural world, reflected in the founding in 1962 of the School of Architecture at the Centre for Environmental Planning and Technology (CEPT), of which Doshi became a codirector with the French-born, American-educated Bernard Kohn. Several other Western architects, both well-known and less-known, passed through Ahmedabad and left their imprint on the city: Harry Weese, Christopher Benninger, Christopher Alexander, Ray Eames, and others. A few Gujaratis from the upper-middle class, like Hasmukh Patel, trained in the United States in the 1950s and returned to set up offices in Ahmedabad.

If ever an architect was summoned to his subject by divine design it was Louis Kahn and his call to the IIM complex—a work that would stand as a counterpoint to Le Corbusier's Chandigarh capitol complex (Kahn admitted to boyish admiration in his younger years for the French master). The IIM complex would also serve as an enduring reminder to the crime of architecture that would be committed in Gandhinagar. Like Le Corbusier, Kahn arrived in India in his early sixties, by which time he had worked out an independent path for himself. From the account Alexandra Tyng[20] has given of her father in her biography of Kahn and from the descriptions that have been provided of Kahn by his friends and associates, particularly by Doshi,[21] his collaborator in Ahmedabad, Kahn emerges as a person who was deeply spiritual—contemplative, simple, and reclusive—and singularly devoted to architecture. Kahn searched for "beginnings" in architectural designs to achieve "order" and "form," and his architectural quest was linked to city planning and urban renewal; by the 1960s, he had come to nuance his ideas, like his personal life, by "silence and light"—all of these various elements making up his personal philosophy and the basis of his profession, rendering him far more complex than he appeared in person, in part because he used these terms so idiosyncratically.

Kahn was born in 1901 on the Baltic island of Ösel (modern Saaremaa), to a Jewish family of mixed Slavic, German, Scandinavian, and Persian blood, and he was still an infant when his family migrated to Philadelphia in 1905 on the crest of the industrial revolution that was sweeping Europe and the United States. He thus grew up in the throes of Western urban transformation that witnessed cities swelling all over the world. In northern Europe, the urban population decidedly outnumbered the rural; and in the United States, the urban population had outpaced the rural by the 1930s. Growing up in these tumultuous times meant growing up in inequity, although scholars continue to argue over how well or how badly the industrial wealth was distributed among the classes.

Philadelphia, which traces its origins to when the Algonquian Indian tribes—Delaware and Shawnee—lived in villages in the region before the first Europeans arrived, is situated near the North-South divide of the United States, which must have allowed the young Kahn to view his adopted country from both sides of the Mason-Dixon line. Kahn was to grow up in an era in which long-standing racialism in the United States had been legalized in the Jim Crow laws. American cities and states also enacted laws closing stores on Sundays, prohibiting the sale of alcohol on Sundays, and making English the language of public schools—all in an effort to standardize social behavior, control the habits of new immigrants, and accelerate their assimilation into the American melting pot.

It was a Dutch navigator who sighted the land in 1615. The modern city of Philadelphia started as a Dutch trading post and stockade in 1623. Several treaties with the Indian tribes to sell their land followed, until the Quaker William Penn received the title to Pennsylvania in a land grant from Charles II, the Stuart king, in 1681. Penn picked Philadelphia as the capital because of its frontage on the Delaware River, establishing the city in 1682 on a rectangular grid pattern on twelve hundred acres between the Delaware and Schuylkill Rivers. Penn's plan consisted of a block grid pattern (22 by 8), a building and housing layout, and potential for the city to grow. Penn provided an innovative city plan by creating four public squares (now parks) and a town square (now City Hall); and his plan would influence the future growth of Philadelphia as well as set the urban planning pattern in most later American cities. In its long history, Philadelphia has been home to many immigrant groups, among them the Dutch, Swedes, Finns, English, Germans, Scots, Irish, and Italians; the city has served as the capital of the colony of Pennsylvania, as a trading and manufacturing center, a military, economic, and political center, a railroad center, and from 1776 to 1800 the seat of national government—although not without interruption. By the time the Kahn family moved to Philadelphia in 1905, the city had outgrown itself; unplanned growth continued unabated in the first half of the twentieth century, resulting in congestion and overcrowding. The 1950s witnessed the flight by the wealthy to the suburbs, with resulting economic stifling downtown. For Louis Kahn, Philadelphia proved an urban laboratory wherein he watched the city's future swing in different directions. He also took live lessons in planning and architecture.

The fluctuating fortunes of the city created economic hardship for Kahn and his two siblings: Kahn's father, Leopold, unsuccessfully tried his hand at construction jobs and small business; his mother, Bertha, kept the family financially afloat by working as a seamstress. Bertha also kept the trappings of European culture alive in the house "by reading Goethe and singing Schubert songs," which must have inspired Kahn to learn the piano. Later, as a teenager, he played the organ in movie houses to augment the family income.[22]

The Kahn parents had mapped out different careers for their eldest child: his father wanted Louis to become an artist, his mother wanted him to be a musician. In the New World working-class life that they felt trapped in, both were projecting their Old World dreams of becoming respectable members of the literati onto their son. Louis chose to become an architect, however. He started out at the Philadelphia-based, free Fleischer School of Art, moving on to finish secondary education at Philadelphia's Central High School and completing his architectural degree at the University of Pennsylvania, where he would later return to become a faculty member. In school, Kahn had been exposed to the prevailing theory of the Beaux Arts, with its deep roots in classicism. When Kahn entered the Department of Architecture at the University of Pennsylvania in 1920, it was the most respected Beaux Arts school in the United States; when he finished in the mid-1920s, modernism, with its "international style," was gaining attention, albeit slowly.

The modern movement formally made its debut in America at an exhibition entitled "Modern Architecture—International Exhibition" at the Museum of Modern Art, New York, in 1932. Soon thereafter, Walter Gropius and Mies van der Rohe, two of the three masters of the modern movement, fled fascist Europe for the freewheeling United States, taking with them the modernist message that art must serve technology in order to improve society. Le Corbusier, the third master, was attracting attention by employing industrially produced materials for his projects in France, which drew students from all around the world to his atelier, and Norman Rice became the first American to study the new vocabulary of modernism under Le Corbusier.

Kahn's introduction to modernism came through his partner, Oskar Stonorov, and the young architect could not resist the liberating influence of the international style in the middle-class, race-conscious America that prevented the full integration of blacks, Italians, Irish, Jews, and other minorities into the social system. He also befriended George Howe, who, along with his partner, William Lescaze (from Zurich), built the Philadelphia Savings Fund Society Building (1929–32), displaying the tenants of the international style, applied to both the exterior and the interior of the building. Richard Neutra and Rudolf Schindler's projects in California also drew attention to modernism. Working in the depression years in Philadelphia's Public Works Department, Kahn was exposed to the depth and scale of the city's poor, far worse than he had known in his youth, and he saw in the sociopolitical principles of the international style the promise of reshaping society, in much the same way that some others, in many countries, including India, looked to the international style for the modernizing of their social systems. What made modernism truly universal was both its neutral cultural stance and a promise of unlimited possibilities and a better life through good design and planning. It was for reasons like these that Kahn organized and directed the Architectural Research Group, a group of thirty-odd unemployed architects and engineers who discussed city planning, slum redevelopment, new concepts for housing and construction, and so on.

Kahn and many other young architects were in their late twenties when they came under the influence of the international style. Kahn became a "faithful admirer" of Le Corbusier; but after World War II, Europe was beginning to grow disillusioned with the modern movement, and both in Europe and the United States the new tendency was "toward the humanizing of the mechanistic approach."[23] Tyng has suggested that in the 1950s her father was influenced by the Columbia University architect Talbot Hamlin, who published his *Forms and Functions of Twentieth Century Architecture*, a powerful reappraisal of Beaux Arts style in the context of the modern movement, restoring the importance of beauty and permanence with function.[24] In the 1950s, Kahn also developed interest in Carl Gustav Jung and his psychology of spirituality. He was also exposed to the ideas of Jaap

Kunst, a Dutch musicologist who in 1950 invented the term *Ethnomusicology*, started the ethnomusicology program at the University of California, Los Angeles, and advanced the theory that "there is a psychic order as well as a physical order. . . . The opposite end of the poles of Affective and Intellective is art and science. Somewhere in the middle lodges religion and philosophy. All these facets of our behavior or conduct are natural and inevitable and the cross insemination of these manifestations of the nature is what makes man a complex individual."[25] Nearing his mid-fifties, Kahn was looking to ways in which to unify various strands of his life and to weave them into a cohesive personal architectural philosophy. In 1954, he wrote to Anne G. Tyng, his confidante: "I must not forget . . . that the training I had in other relative fields made it possible to emerge from a thoroughly misguided start to one of a relatively realistic direction."[26] Soon thereafter, he declared that "the 'new architecture' was beyond functionalism because it was concerned with the psychological effect of the space. He also believed that the measurable design process in the end produced the unmeasurable work of art."[27] In order to evaluate where he stood in the present and where he would go next, he was returning to his "beginning," just as he would do with his building projects. The "new architecture" he helped to define was a dialectical synthesis between the Beaux Arts vision of history and the functionalism of the modern movement.

By the time Doshi wrote Kahn in 1962 asking him to design the Indian Institute of Management, Kahn had drawn urban renewal schemes for Central City, Philadelphia, for northeast Philadelphia, and for Mill Creek; he had designed several private homes and many public and institutional buildings, including the Trenton Bath House in New Jersey, the Yale University Art Gallery, dormitories at Bryn Mawr, the Richards Medical Research Building at the University of Pennsylvania, the Salk Institute at La Jolla, and the American consulate at Luanda in Portuguese Angola (the project was never implemented). He had also served as the consultant architect to the United States Department of Housing and Urban Development and to the city of Philadelphia; and he had taught architecture at several prestigious schools, including Yale University, ultimately joining the faculty of his alma mater in Philadelphia, the University of Pennsylvania. In 1959, he had delivered the closing remarks at the tenth meeting of CIAM (Congrès Internationaux d'Architecture Moderne) in Otterlo, in the Netherlands, where he complained about the loss of public spaces for civic assembly and other social and cultural activities; he also synthesized his form-order-design idea—conceiving buildings from their archetypal essence to finished products. The same year, he implemented these ideas in the First Unitarian Church in Rochester, New York. It had been a difficult journey to finding his place privately and professionally, however.

Although Kahn was merely an infant when his family moved to the United States, and he shared his mother's optimism that America was a country of infinite possibilities, his East European Jewish origins might have made him feel like an outsider. His daughter, Tyng, provides an insight: "[His wife] Esther Kahn's parents, unlike his, were not recent immigrants; they had received higher formal education and permitted only English to be spoken in their home. . . . To him, his wife's family was fully American; what they had intrinsically, he felt he had to acquire. His involvement with city planning and redevelopment was based on a respect for American ideals that came from having adopted the culture rather than taking it for granted."[28] This sense of "otherness" might have propelled him to search for a universal language, which led him to declare: "Art is the language of God. The only language of man is art."[29] It became necessary for him to explain the meaning of his architecture in a language that would strike a common cord in all people; hence, he chose the mediums of philosophy and religion to express systems of thought and feeling that transcended cultures in multiracial America; and he also developed an aesthetic vocabulary that gave poetic discipline to his architecture: *form, order, silence, light,* the *measurable* and the *unmeasurable, presence* and *existence,* the *psyche, commonality,* and *servant* and *served* spaces.

Kahn's use of poetry to convey his ideas provided the license he needed to build without reference to a particular movement or stylistic nuance, thereby freeing modernism of its sterile cant. The Kahnian poetry of architecture rested upon what he called Order and Form, the phenomenal and the psychic in a mystical union. According to Tyng, Kahn, like Albert Einstein, viewed order as "the basic, immutable law that governs the organization of natural structures;" and his "understanding of form closely resembles Jung's definition of archetypes."[30] Kahn explained this in poetic imagery as the metamorphoses between silence and light:

> Silence to Light
> Light to Silence
> The threshold of their crossing
> is the Singularity
> is the Inspiration
> (where the desire to express
> meets the possible)
> is the Sanctuary of Art
> is the Treasury of the Shadows
> Material cast shadows,
> shadows belong to light.[31]

Again his daughter has provided a clue to Kahn's responses to silence and light. Kahn derived his meaning of silence from *Les Voix du Silence,* the 1951 work by André Malraux, the French novelist, adventurer, art historian, minister of cultural affairs, and foremost spokesman of Gaullist politics. The book is a well-documented synthesis of the history of art in all countries and all ages. Kahn explained his understanding of silence thus: "By silence I don't mean quiet . . . when you pass the pyramids, you feel that they want to tell you. . . . Not *how* they were made, but what made them *be,* which means what was the force that caused them to be made. . . . These are the voices of silence." Kahn derived his understanding of light from a line in a poem by Pennsylvania-born Wallace Stevens that Kahn paraphrased as, "What slice of the sun does your building have?" To Kahn the poem expressed the way in which the structure of a room is defined by the light entering it. Tyng also mentions that Kahn had "badly burnt" his face and hands in a childhood accident, making him self-conscious because his classmates called him "Scarface"—an added burden to his East European Jewish origins. "His father thought Kahn would be better off dead than disfigured, but [his mother] insisted that he would live and become a great man some day."[32] For a long time, Kahn wore a soft Italian hat pulled low over his ears to shade his scarred face, which must have sensitized him to the interplay of light and shadow. His self-consciousness, born of his Jewish immigrant origins and physical handicap, made him search for external validation, which he found in the writings of Kunst, Jung, Stevens, Malraux, Einstein, and others; and it was his genius to turn his "otherness" as well as ideas from others into his personal and professional advantage.

In the end, what drew Doshi and Kahn together when the two first met in Philadelphia in 1958 was Kahn's elemental humanity and his essential regard for continuity that only a respect for history can provide. By inviting Kahn to Ahmedabad (and he would also try very hard to get Kahn the commission for the planning and architectural detailing of Gandhinagar), Doshi was only acknowledging his debt to the Beaux Art teacher Batley and the modernist master Le Corbusier, the two influences that Kahn had united in his aesthetics. For Doshi, identification with Kahn meant reinterpreting his past in a modernist tradition— a long journey back to rediscovering his roots. Doshi explained the differences between Le Corbusier, with whom he had an existing relationship, and Kahn, with whom he was starting a new relationship:

> Kahn and Le Corbusier can be compared to Mughal and Hindu architecture. Now in India we had the same craftsmen working on both, but if they were building a mosque it would be very simple, clear, and pure and the geometry would be very explicit. In the temple, on the other hand, things would twist and turn, go up and down, in apparent disorder. Like Le Corbusier who delighted in pure geometry which he would then destroy.
>
> In general, I think Lou [Kahn] would accept the constraints while Le Corbusier would not. He would rise above, and that is why he could create those fantastic unfolding spaces, those marvelous changes of light. Lou's buildings are for meditation[;] Le Corbusier's buildings "sing."

Doshi also commented on their temperaments:

Oh, they had totally different temperaments. Take food habits. While he was in India Lou would just eat boiled fish and boiled potatoes—nothing else. Whereas in Delhi Le Corbusier took me straight to Moti Mahal, ordered tandoori chicken and all kinds of Mughlai dishes and enjoyed enormously. [Lou] was like a Quaker. [Ostensibly, Doshi was referring to Philadelphia's German-Jewish and Quaker traditions, although Kahn as an East European Jew did not grow up in the manner of the *haute bourgeois* of the 1920s.] Le Corbusier's home reflected his personality[:] it was full of things, paintings, prints, objects d'art from many countries. Lou was a different man because when Gira Sarabhai asked him, 'What is architecture?' He [*sic*] hesitated, then said, 'Is it all right if I tell you tomorrow?' And next morning he came with a little note that said, 'If you were to ask me what architecture is, I do not know the answer because it is in the spirit of what it wants to be.' Now Le Corbusier has defined architecture many[,] many times in his voluminous writings. To select just one sentence at random: 'Architecture is forms, volumes, colours, acoustics, music. Light and shadow are the loudspeakers of his architecture of truth.'[33]

Notwithstanding their differences, Kahn always felt deep devotion for Le Corbusier, and on his (Le Corbusier's) death in August 1965 reportedly stated: "But who shall I work for now?"[34] For his part, Doshi saw in Kahn's Alfred Newton Richards Medical Research Building, the University of Pennsylvania, "images of the new world, the new idiom of a modern skyscraper." Only in his early thirties, he was overwhelmed by the stark contrast between the stoic brick towers and the transparency, reflections and details of glass windows, visualizing "in this project the future of our [Indian] cities and towns." In March 1991, thirty years later when he received the commission for the Bharat Diamond Bourse, Bombay, he admitted that he was "trying to express" Kahn's ideas.[35] Doshi was equally impressed by the Salk Institute, La Jolla, California, majestically overlooking the expansive Pacific Ocean, transcending modernism's irrational devotion to structure and technology. Kahn had proposed in the Salk Institute (1959–65) a spatial division of functions—for studios, laboratories, meeting rooms, and so on—rendering the service aspects of the program clear and clean while "at once celebrating the site and his virtuoso treatment of reinforced concrete."[36]

When Doshi returned in 1960 to Philadelphia to lecture on Le Corbusier's work at the invitation of Holmes Perkins, dean of the University of Pennsylvania's School of Arts, Kahn was detailing the Salk Institute. "What struck me the most during my visit," Doshi noted, "was the eerie look of the institute, almost like being in outer space. The big plaza between the blocks created an ideal abode for the moon and the sun making the two buildings receptor[s]. It is very unusual." What Doshi saw in the Salk Institute was the diversity of space and liveliness of traditional materials in architecture that were beginning to emerge by the late 1950s in response to the tiered standardization that had animated some segments of the modern movement. "I was also impressed by the impact of the geometry and the rigour with which the institute is designed," Doshi noted. "But here the order exalts. The angular projections with their repetitions visually create Beethoven's March of Athens. Concrete which I always took as not so good a material, becomes as exquisite as marble. And lastly, the centrally located water channel and transparent, simultaneously still and flowing fountain[s], create the essence of Lou's philosophy, the hearing of silence and its contact with the psyche."[37]

Starting in 1962, Doshi became a regular visiting lecturer at the University of Pennsylvania, and he continued to visit Philadelphia every year until Kahn's death in 1974.[38] He learned to question Corbusian pedagogy from Kahn, who saw his own work as a theoretical response to the modern movement in general and to Le Corbusier in particular. Doshi's extended visits to the United States provided him with the window to witness the dislocation between modernism as a historical movement and modernity as the contemporary condition—while residence in the School of Arts at the University of Pennsylvania served as a seminar to debate the fruits of industrial production and its ideal of shared economic growth.

As the middle class fled the inner city for the comforts and safety of suburbia in the 1950s and the 1960s, low costs and speedier and spectacular construction popularized modernist buildings in America as a panacea for revitalizing decaying cities in which lower-income groups, always made up of racial and ethnic minorities, remained marginalized. The 1970s saw the rejection of unity of form and the canonization of diversity of style, quaintly called postmodernism—a meaningless term because the scholarly community has no unanimity of agreement on what it really implies, other than being a reactionary movement to modernism. Doshi cogitated on the American urban scene and searched for viable contemporary alternatives for addressing architectural and urban issues in pluralistic, poor India. In India itself, heterogeneity of cultures and urban neighborhoods had made it impossible to implement the CIAM-dictated modernist aesthetics, with the debatable exception of Chandigarh, where first Le Corbusier and later his cousin Pierre Jeanneret, with the political backing of Prime Minister Nehru, could control construction and zoning. In the end, polytheistic India remained uncomfortable with the monotheistic modern movement and its creed of technological determinism. On the other hand, Kahn, with his growing contradictory interests in humanism and regionalism (meaning respect for local culture, tradition, history), which he had seemingly reconciled in his metaphysical "existence will," introduced a new language to modern architecture.

Doshi must have reported his observations of the American urban scene and the prevailing architectural ideas to his patrons in Ahmedabad, and his recommendation of Kahn for the IIM project was accepted without opposition. So, was it Kahn's aesthetics or his mysticism or his disregard for money that drew the cotton plutocrats to him? Doshi provided the answer:

> I saw in Lou an Indian yogi. A yogi is one who constantly tries to search his real self because in it he believes lies the harmony and the dynamic balance of the entire cosmic world. . . .
>
> Incidentally, Kahn agreed to undertake this assignment on my advice and it did not make [a] difference to him where we worked as long as I was responsible for getting his ideas executed as per his wish[es]. . . . His commitment to me and to architecture made him visit Ahmedabad and do some of the initial drawings in Philadelphia. Even though we had foreign exchange problems, he agreed to accommodate to almost everything that we suggested. And I must say, we in India have always respected his work and did all that he wanted so that this great architect would be proud of his work. Luckily, he was. . . .
>
> It is neither philosophy nor architecture [which made us invite Kahn to Ahmedabad]. It was the sensibility, values and concerns, that prompted us to invite Lou. My clients were very much affected by Lou's teachings, thoughts, approach. Once impressed, they gave Lou a free hand . . . [and] no one even asked a single question about his design[s].
>
> . . . he confided to me one of the most important secrets of architectural practice[:] 'Get the client in total confidence, let him understand your values, your philosophy, your approach. Once convinced, he will back you far beyond the completion of the project.' . . . And this is why his buildings have turned out to be masterpieces.
>
> However, he conveyed all his concepts for the IIM designs through philosophical statements which were akin to the way our saints talk. . . .
>
> As an architect[,] I think, Lou showed us another direction. Personally, for me and my family, his three to four trips a year, from 1962 to 1974, reinforced my values acquired from my parents. His observations on Le Corbusier and his works in India made me more aware of my first Guru. For example, I still remember Lou's describing Le Corbusier's Assembly [in Chandigarh] as 'the frozen dream.' I owe to Lou my sensitivity and the design of the School of Architecture building which I designed in 1964. His ideas of the class room under the tree in the open, interconnected classrooms and multidimensional education has influenced my professional and teaching career. In fact[,] after almost 30 years of the School's existence one can still feel his presence in some of these concepts.[39]

A dozen years after P. N. Thapar and P. L. Verma, the representatives of the Punjab government, had proposed to Le Corbusier at his atelier in Paris that he plan and design Chandigarh, Doshi, with the approval of the cotton barons of Ahmedabad, wrote to Kahn in 1962 in Philadelphia, inviting him to visit Ahmedabad for the planning and designing of the IIM complex. Meanwhile, between March 1960, when Gandhinagar was designated as the capital of Gujarat, and July 1964, when the no-objection-to-build certificate was issued, the construction in Gandhinagar remained moribund. The reason was the oil exploration at the site by the National Oil and Gas Commission,[40] which kept the future of the capital site hanging in the balance. Would the capital have shifted to another location had the site yielded a gushing oil well? Probably not. In July 1964, the commission cleared the way for the construction work to begin by issuing a no-objection certificate to the New Capital Project Circle, to the relief of everyone. By the time the no-objection certificate was issued, Kahn and Doshi had started work on IIM in Ahmedabad. Le Corbusier had turned Chandigarh into a training school for Indian architects and planners; Kahn would make Ahmedabad and the neighboring Gandhinagar sites into a graduate seminar in architecture and planning. The Ahmedabad mill owners "wanted the National Institute of Design to be the project office [for IIM] with me [Doshi] as their [mill owners] consultant and Kahn as the architect," Doshi explained. "The project team was hired by NID through me and we worked from NID. . . . The advantage of NID's association was to get the students of NID involved with the philosophy of Louis Kahn and his method of working."[41] Subsequently, the project office was moved to the IIM campus, which is where it remains today to monitor and maintain Kahn's work. After Kahn's death in 1974, Doshi and Anant Raje, another protégé of Kahn who apprenticed in Kahn's Philadelphia office, and, like Doshi, a graduate of J. J. School of Art, jointly took over the IIM project: however, Raje became, and remains, the principal architect for the rest of Kahn's work at IIM.

When the Indian government invited Le Corbusier to Chandigarh, he was a "disappointed" man in his early sixties: several of his recent projects had not materialized. "Men are so stupid that I'm glad I'm going to die, he had declared in 1947. "All my life people have tried to crush me. . . . Luckily, I've always had an iron will."[42] Likewise, Kahn was a "disappointed" man of sixty-something when he started work in Ahmedabad and, soon thereafter, on the National Assembly complex in Dhaka, East Pakistan (now Bangladesh). To his bitter disappointment, the U.S. government had shelved his designs for the U.S. consulate at Luanda, and the prospect for building monumental public spaces looked bleak. In a letter to Irving Litvag, director of special events at Washington University, Kahn noted the irony of "not receiving a direct commission from [his home] city of Philadelphia, but hav[ing] been asked to design the Second Capital of Pakistan." He remained optimistic, however. "Someday I hope to build a building for Philadelphia and one for the U.S. Government."[43]

In the March 1958 issue of *Architectural Forum*, Kahn had declared the city center to be the cathedral of the city.[44] He worried about growing suburbanization, which he equated to the decline of democracy in cities. He traced this trend to the erosion of public spaces where communal, and hence democratic, interaction occurs. He felt mass culture and consumerism were destroying individualism; orthodox modernism itself had been co-opted by the corporate culture, complained architects like Alvar Aalto, Kevin Lynch, and the English husband-and-wife team of Peter and Alison Smithson. These concerns had been raised earlier by Britain's Maxwell Fry and, to a lesser degree, by his wife Jane Drew, who talked about linking the individual to community, house, and family, even before they had collaborated with Le Corbusier in Chandigarh. Kahn hoped to recover individualism and restore democracy by building public spaces that will "evoke a way of life" in accordance with typology, not function. Understandably, because Kahn viewed his own work in direct response to Corbusian orthodoxy, he felt betrayed when Le Corbusier died in 1965.

Both Le Corbusier and Kahn faced personal contradictions in the subcontinent. It was ironic that democratic India should have assigned the designing of monumental symbols of independence to Le Corbusier, who possessed no faith in democracy and who credulously believed Western colonization to be a "*force morale*" for development.[45] It was no less tragic that Kahn, a Jewish American, who wanted to build public spaces that would "evoke" democracy and humanism, should design the second National Assembly for Pakistan, a country that has lived under military rule for most of its history. Actually, Pakistan had approached Le Corbusier and Alvar Aalto about designing the Dhaka assembly, albeit unsuccessfully. Kahn's arrival in Ahmedabad opened up the possibility for the Pakistan government to recruit him for the Dhaka project, just as it opened up the opportunity for the mill owners to enlist him for Gandhinagar. In the end, both men resolved their moral dilemma—Kahn more than Le Corbusier—by serving their personal ambitions.

In cleverly crafted apologies for both Kahn and his Pakistani client General Muhammad Ayub Khan, Sarah Ksiazek has suggested that "Sher-e-Banglanagar [lit., the city of the Bengal tiger, the name given to the National Assembly complex] was 'a place of transcendence'" for Kahn, and that Kahn was representing "American ideals" to the world through his "architectural work in Pakistan." On his client's insistence, Kahn had been forced to incorporate the mosque into the capitol, thereby blurring secular and religious spheres and negating the post-Reformation Western ideal of the separation of church and state. "In spite of Kahn's claims that he wove a mosque into the capitol to express the transcendent nature of assembly," Ksiazek has reasoned, "in his handling of the program Kahn effected a symbolic separation of church and state."[46] This has to be the most disingenuous argument, considering that Islam does not recognize any separation between the temporal and the religious worlds.

Ksiazek offers an equally incredulous account of General Ayub Khan. "Although President Ayub Khan engineered a military coup overthrowing the parliamentary government in 1958," she explains, "he was elected president the following year and advocated a representative system he called 'strong democracy.'"[47] Writing twenty-some years after the event, she should know the history. Born primarily out of a separatist religious sentiment, Pakistan from the beginning floundered on waves of provincial conflict and ideological disagreement. Even before Pakistan was able to recover from the death of Quaid-i-Azam (Great leader) Mohammad Ali Jinnah in September 1948, Liaquat Ali Khan, the first prime minister who dared espouse a secular position, was assassinated by the orthodox faction in October 1951. Until 1958, Pakistan drifted from one crisis to another under an inefficient and corrupt administration that failed to resolve the fundamental constitutional questions of how politically to satisfy East Bengal's majority population without estranging western Punjabi and Sindi national leadership and how to build a "modern" state without antagonizing the popular orthodox Islamic leadership.

Political failure produced the military coup of 1958, placing Sandhurst-trained Pathan General Muhammad Ayub Khan in control of a balkanized Pakistan. Ayub quickly legitimized his position by declaring himself prime minister, self-appointed president, and field marshal of Pakistan, setting an example for future generals, precluding any possibility for return to a legitimate representative government. Ayub maneuvered to placate the restive East Bengali majority by building the Parthenon of the East in Dhaka—this with the help of Louis Kahn, with whom he signed a contract in November 1962, just as he had earlier successfully finagled generous U.S. aid in return for Pakistan's support of John Foster Dulles's network of military alliances to "contain" Communism.

Ksiazek's failure to question Ayub's message to the U.S. Congress in 1961 that "our aim always was and always has been and always shall be to have representative institutions"[48] speaks as much of her historical fatigue as of Kahn's naive belief that architecture will transcend politics in Sher-e-Banglanagar—originally named Ayub Nagar,[49] after the military dictator; it acquired its present name after Bangladesh emerged from the ruins of East Pakistan as an independent nation in 1971.

Did Kahn fail to notice the "silent" winds of the independence movement that blew across the delta country from 1964 to 1970? Perhaps not. But because he viewed his work in personal terms, Kahn felt that he understood his client's needs better than the client himself. Also, those who have reviewed Kahn's work in Dhaka have generally ignored the political history of Bangladesh and examined the capitol complex in the terms in which Kahn defined it (Lawrence Vale is one of the few exceptions). Scant attention has been paid to the unfurling of the green, red, and gold banner of Bangladesh at the new National Assembly by East Bengalis after the Pakistani army surrendered to Indian General Sam Manekshaw on December 15, 1971, on which occasion Indira Gandhi, the Indian prime minister, declared that "Dacca is now the free capital of a free country." Pakistan paid rupees

500,000 to Kahn for the assembly complex, of which rupees 400,000 was paid in U.S. dollars. At completion, the assembly costs had accelerated to a staggering $150 million. Bangladesh's history itself after its birth in 1971 would test Kahn's notions of transcendent architecture and democracy.

Meanwhile, the whispers of a plot grew louder in the Kasturbhai-Sarabhai-Doshi discussion group: how to recruit Kahn for the Gandhinagar project? Indian architects frequently attending these discussions included Charles Correa, Anant Raje, and Kulbhushan Jain. They talked in low tones among themselves about how to persuade the Indian government to provide American dollars to pay Kahn. Although the Gujarat government had prepared a preliminary plan, there was still no architect-planner to formalize and implement it. By his work at IIM, Kahn had already "brought order to Indian architecture in style, plan, climate, and materials" —so reflected Raje on the early Kahn years in the 1960s. "He brought the system of layering light—i.e. Indian light is intense, and he cut the light by layering it so that it wouldn't be blinding."[50]

Inspired by Harvard in its curriculum and following the new architectural aesthetics of Kahn, the IIM complex was beginning to take shape and provide a future vision. How could the industrial-mercantilist community of Gujarat allow predominantly agricultural Punjab to have a modern capital—at least, not with Kasturbhai Lalbhai sitting on the Capital Project board? "As you are aware, the Government machinery has its own short comings and for the time being they are asking three or four architects to give their terms," Kasturbhai wrote Kahn on March 2, 1964. "I have no doubt however in my own mind that ultimately I shall succeed in getting you the appointment," he reassured him. "I hope you will be able to design the ideal city that we aspire to build."[51]

What Kasturbhai and the other Ahmedabad mill owners aspired to was modernist architecture that would define their institutions and cities. As early as 1945, Kasturbhai and the Ahmedabad Education Society had questioned the New Delhi –based architectural firm of Master, Sathe, and Bhuta on the Buddhist-inspired sketches for the Science College, Ahmedabad, instructing the architectural firm to produce "a more imposing façade."

In March 1964, Doshi, too, wrote Kahn, urging him to accept the Gandhinagar project: "The Government, as a part of their formalities have written to 5 architects. Nonetheless, I have a strong feeling that Shri Kasturbhai Lalbhai and a few members are decided on awarding you the work. I hope that all this materialises." He added, "They will take decision sometime in April or May [1964]." In the same letter drawing Kahn's attention to his slowly shaping IIM buildings, Doshi speculated on the possibility of linking the IIM project with Gandhinagar. "Your visit to Ahmedabad at your earliest will be useful for both these projects [IIM and Gandhinagar],"[52] Doshi tellingly concluded. It could not have occurred to either Kasturbhai or to Doshi that in offering Kahn the Gandhinagar project they were providing the best illustration of the traditional *jajmani* system (the traditional Indian patronage system of barter on which the village economy was based) in modern India.

Approaching his mid-sixties, Kahn was becoming increasingly aware of the limited time available to him to realize his burning ambition of planning a city and building public monuments of democracy that would rival his idol Le Corbusier's work in Chandigarh. "I should be singularly honored to be the architect of the Capital of Gujarat at Gandhinagar,"[53] Kahn had confided to Kasturbhai in one of his letters. It seems likely from the correspondence that the Kasturbhai-Doshi team had hired Kahn for the IIM project in 1962 with a view to Kahn planning and designing Gandhinagar. That the Oil and Gas Commission was so slow in issuing the no-objection certificate for construction to begin at Gandhinagar worked to the advantage of the Kasturbhai-Sarabhai-Doshi team to hammer out a contract with Kahn. Unfortunately for them, the negotiations involved the Gujarat government, where Kasturbhai carried political weight, and the Indian government, where national concerns superseded regional needs in matters involving foreign exchange. And foreign exchange in the end would break down negotiations with Kahn, just as it had broken down negotiations with Albert Mayer in Chandigarh nearly fifteen years earlier.

Doshi first discussed in detail with Kahn the capital city project in the fall of 1963 in Philadelphia. He mentioned the Gujarat government's decision "to commission an architect for its planning and buildings." In that meeting, Doshi informed Kahn that he had been instructed by Kasturbhai to request that Kahn write Kasturbhai concerning the "working arrangements" he would require for "this assignment of architectural and national importance." In his requirements, Kahn asked for architectural-planning offices in Gandhinagar and Philadelphia; rupees and dollars to pay for consultants in India and America for working architectural drawings of the site and buildings; and living arrangements for Kahn's American staff in India and for the Indian staff to work in his Philadelphia office "to facilitate flow of communication between the two offices." Already aware of the constraints of foreign exchange in India, he was willing to do much of the work in India, which he felt would be "most feasible during the working drawing and construction phase of the work." Work would continue in his Philadelphia office "at all times whether in a full or limited way, especially when I am [in India]." To help the Indians with writing a contract, Kahn mailed a copy of his contract with the Pakistan government negotiated in November 1962 for the National Assembly in Dhaka, and he promised to send soon "a few photographs of the preliminary sketch models for the Second Capital of Pakistan at Dacca [modern Dhaka]." He also promised to take a few days off from his impending visit to Pakistan in December 1963 and "meet you [Kasturbhai] about the 27th or 28th of December to talk about this wonderful project and about agreement of services. Also, I should like to tour the site."[54]

Kahn's terms and conditions for undertaking the Gandhinagar project were very similar to the ones that the Indian government had negotiated first with Mayer and later with Le Corbusier in Chandigarh, with the exception of having Indian staff in his Philadelphia office, which he might have included to assist his three Indian protégés: Doshi would receive a visiting lectureship at the University of Pennsylvania; Raje would be sponsored by Kahn to work in his Philadelphia office; and Kulbhushan Jain would complete his master's degree in architecture at the University of Pennsylvania in 1968 and return to India to start architectural practice in Ahmedabad with his wife, Minakshi, also a graduate of the University of Pennsylvania (1966). In fact, Kahn informed Kasturbhai that he was willing "to work under a contract patterned after Le Corbusier's," which gave Le Corbusier "sufficient financial and physical resources to do his important work." He even expressed his understanding of "the restrictions which will not permit you to pay an architect in dollars."[55] Kahn and Kasturbhai even tried to formulate a scheme to raise the much-needed dollars in the United States—a scheme Kahn was to explore with various American foundations to support his work in India. He even offered to collaborate with the Indian ambassador to the United States in applying to the U.S. government under the foreign-aid program "for dollar support in the planning and building of Gandhinagar, the Capital of Gujarat."[56] Over the next three years, the financial negotiations between Kahn and the Gujarat government looked more like vaudeville acts, with foreign exchange as the central theme.

In early March 1964, K. M. Kantawala, the chief engineer for roads and building and joint secretary to the Gujarat government, informed Kahn about his responsibilities:

a. Advise and actively assist in the preparation of the Master Plan of the new Capital of Gandhinagar[,] including the location of various zones, formation of sectors, placing of various administrative, cultural, marketing, commercial, trade and industrial units and any other items required in the Township at their proper places and elaborating details for each sector. Also advise on the system of communications, landscaping, cultural and recreation[al] spots to be located in the Township.

b. Advise and actively assist in the determination of the general style of architecture to be adopted for the new capital town.

c. Guide, lead and supervise the work of the team of Town Planners and Architects, [Drafting] office and the Drawing Branch which may be employed by the Government of Gujarat for handling the detailing work of the Master Plan and for preparing detailed plans of various buildings.

d. Advise and actively assist in the preparation of the designs of the principal buildings and in this connection even to furnish the sketch studies for some of them.

e. Advise and actively assist in the laying down of the architectural treatment and control of the prominent features of the new town such as important roads, street squares, public gardens and water features.

f. Advise and actively assist in the work connected with the landscaping of public places in the new town and its surrounding area.

g. Advise and actively assist in the development and detailing of the Master Plan.

h. Advise and actively assist in the working out of the programme of work for the town planning and architectural branch.[57]

Kahn was expected to achieve the stated program in three years, spend at least two months a year in India, and was to be assisted by Indian planners and architects employed by the Gujarat government. Kantawala in his letter ominously added that there was great difficulty of foreign exchange in India, which made it impossible for the Gujarat government to pay fees in foreign exchange; he requested that Kahn accept fees in Indian rupees. "It would not be possible to make payment in any other currency," he informed Kahn.[58] The Gujarat government offered to buy Kahn a return air ticket to Ahmedabad so that he could visit the site and "quickly" complete the preliminaries of the agreement.

It is not surprising that Kantawala saw no contradiction between suggesting to Kahn—and presumably to other architects—that the Gujarat government had decided to have the master plan and principal buildings designed by a planner-architect of "international reputation" and insisting to pay the fee in rupees. The shortage of foreign exchange in the 1960s was a serious issue, especially after the Indo-China war of 1962, which had made national defense the top priority. Military rule under General Ayub Kahn in neighboring Pakistan had made war imminent: Indo-Pakistani sparring started in early 1965, as the army general attempted to test the newly supplied U.S. Patton tanks in the Rann of Kutch, bordering Gujarat, and also use the conflict with India to divert popular attention away from growing regional problems. Neither Nehru nor his successor Lal Bahadur Shastri, who took over the prime ministership after his mentor's death on May 27, 1964, could ignore national defense. Shastri died a few hours after signing the peace accord with Ayub in Tashkent, the Soviet Union, in January 1966, leaving Nehru's daughter Indira Gandhi, who succeeded him, to deal with the specter of national famine resulting from monsoon failure of 1965. In the mid-1960s, for the Indian government using the scarce American dollars to pay for large quantities of American grain to feed the Indian population outweighed the importance of hiring the services of an American architect. Of course, Le Corbusier and his European team in Chandigarh and Kahn himself in the IIM project had themselves demonstrated that they were artists seeking immortality through their work, rather than coveting wealth to pay for their creature comforts.

Meanwhile, Kahn reported to Kasturbhai that his visit to the site confirmed "the vision that led to its choice as a place that could be inspiring to the sponsors and planners of the capital. The Sabarmati [River], the character or the land's contours, the groves and trees are there as age-old points of departure to the creative acts composing land and building, and I look forward to this wonderful challenge to my talents and beliefs." Kahn noted that he felt "assured by my personal experiences in India of the sincere appreciation and love that people of India have for the arts and architecture. My present arrangement with the young architects in the Design Institute under the direction of Mr. Balkrishna Doshi has shown that my role as teacher and architect has enriched my own principles and ideas." He said his Indian students and colleagues had taught him "the ways of India, and I have in turn discovered greater clarity of principles and ideas through their participation in design. I therefore know that I can establish an inspired and efficient office in India. I would visit India at regular intervals. I would have sketches and drawings from my home office which would be developed into working documents in the Indian Office."[59]

For the Indian office, which had not yet been created, Kahn insisted that the initial appointments must include the architects he had met and come to know in Ahmedabad: Achyut Kanvinde, Maharastra-born and Harvard-educated; Charles Correa, Hyderabad-born and MIT-educated; Balkrishna V. Doshi, Poona-born and Corbusier-trained; and A. R. Prabhawalker, Maharastra-born and educated at the J. J. School of Art. Because Prabhawalker had served as a planner under Le Corbusier in Chandigarh, Kahn felt him to be the "best qualified to be in-charge of the office and [he] should be appointed immediately . . . in order [to] appoint the junior staff needed." Kahn was willing to let Chief Engineer Kantawala "select experienced engineers [who would be] inclined to appreciate the principles behind site engineering." Perhaps learning from his Ahmedabad experience about the adversarial positions between the office of architecture and the office of civil engineering in the Indian Public Works Department, Kahn emphasized that the "collaboration of architects and engineers is most necessary . . . in the exchange of realizations and critical review of accepted practices." Kahn expressed his sentiment to the Indians: "Designers, both architects and engineers, working toward and with well conceived directions would be inspired to create true and appropriate designs that would stimulate the building of the modern new city in good time."[60]

Kahn envisioned Gandhinagar to "be the seat of an Institution in memory of Gandhi."[61] In the Sher-e-Banglanagar designs, Kahn had tried metaphysically to discipline bucolic Bengal with modern geometry: a composition of brick, concrete, marble, arches, cylinders, triangles, circles, and plazas that defines his subcontinental oeuvre, including the IIM in Ahmedabad. On his last visit to Dhaka, Kahn reportedly looked at the arches under construction and remarked, "Look at them, how beautiful they are. These people sure know how to make them right."[62] The arches with which Kahn "felt such a spiritual kinship," noted a local architect, "in reality borrowed their strength from thick layers of reinforced concrete poured in the middle, not seen from outside. The brick wanted to be arched but could not make it on its own until concrete and steel helped out."[63] Kahn originally wanted to use concrete in the Dhaka capitol complex, but he reluctantly changed his mind because of the unsuitability of the material to the climate and its high cost. Arguing that the "poet in him prevailed over the architect," a critic of Kahn's Dhaka composition has noted that the Bangladesh capital is like "a brown necklace with an octagonal gray pendant. Institutions, including the mosque, rub shoulders, giving the composition a spiritual rigor. Louis Kahn seems to say that man's institutions are innately ethnocentric and must remain true to their original desires"; Kahn rejects the "Western" distance between buildings as seen in Le Corbusier's capitol complex in Chandigarh. "In Dhaka, the Highcourt [sic], the Secretariat and the Assembly enjoy the shared experience of intimacy found in a joint family." Without allowing the institutions to dissolve in a total ethnocentric integration, Kahn leaves them "in a stage of 'anguished co-existence' as implied by the subtle defiance of the mosque. The mosque aligns with the western axis, its geometry singularly tense in its twist towards Mecca."[64] For Kahn, "Form never follows function: it guides its direction for it holds the relation of its elements."[65] In the end, Kahn's aesthetic in Dhaka succeeded neither in reconciling form and function nor in achieving a balance between the two Pakistans.

Just as Kahn had been guided by the symbols of Islamic civilization in Dhaka, he proposed, along with his disciple Doshi, to compose Gandhinagar in the contradictory idioms of the Mahatma's passion for village India and his benefactor Kasturbhai's zeal for industry. "In talking this over with Doshi, he [Doshi] suggested the Institution of Village Culture and Industry." Kahn flattered Kasturbhai by suggesting that "the program for this Institution should really be written by you."[66] In Dhaka, Kahn had tried to reconcile the temporal with the spiritual; and in Gandhinagar he proposed to unite the village with industry. Unlike Le Corbusier, who, while acknowledging India's great agricultural civilization unabashedly proposed in Chandigarh architecture suited "for modern civilization,"[67] Kahn in his thinking on Gandhinagar disturbingly equivocated between ethnocentric symbols and modern metaphors. Nehru, the cosmopolitan client, wanted Chandigarh to be "unfettered by the traditions of the past" and unhesitatingly declared, "We want to urbanize the village."[68] The cotton plutocrats of Gujarat remained shackled in their taste by social conventions and religious traditions. They also remained fiscally disadvantaged by lack of the U.S. dollars that Kahn needed to pay his American staff in Philadelphia, making negotiations with Kahn increasingly opaque.

On August 11, 1964, K. M. Kantawala, the chief engineer, cabled Kahn with mixed news. The Indian government had approved an honorarium of $10,000 per annum for Kahn to prepare the master plan and also approved $85 in per diem, not to exceed $9,000 annually. But the Indian government declined Kahn's request for a commission of 3 percent for the capitol buildings, insisting that "this work to be done by Indian Architects."[69] The next day, Kantawala wrote to Kahn clarifying that both the honorarium and the daily allowance were to be paid in "Indian Currency . . . only and not in any other Currency."[70] Doshi interjected himself into the negotiations in an effort to break the impasse. "I met Kantawala this morning and have suggested him to invite you here to discuss the implications of the Indian Government's decision [not to engage you for designing the capitol buildings] and to find out the possibility of your designing the major buildings," Doshi wrote from Ahmedabad to Kahn in Philadelphia. "Mr. Kantawala and the Gujarat Government must realise the importance of your doing the works," he told his new teacher. He advised Kahn to request that Kasturbhai "write to the [Gujarat] Government from London" (Kasturbhai was visiting London on a business trip in late summer 1964).[71] Doshi also wrote to Kasturbhai at the Mayfair Hotel in London, informing him about the Indian government's directive to engage "Prof. Kahn only for the Master Plan. The major Government buildings and other buildings, the [Indian] Government suggested, should be designed by Indian architects." He added, "I personally do not see the reasoning behind this suggestion since the expenses on account of fees in either case would be the same." He emphasized Kahn's sentiment that "it is not possible for an architect to work on master plan alone since his ideas without the buildings can not be fully expressed."[72]

Predictably, Kahn responded by shooting cables to Kantawala, Kasturbhai, and Doshi, "regretfully declining the commission which offers me to establish the master plan of Gandhinagar but excludes me the opportunity to express its meaning architecturally by the actual design of certain buildings." He maneuvered with Kasturbhai by adding, "I understand that you will be away from Ahmedabad the beginning of October. I should like to plan my next visit to India when you are there."[73] Kahn got the desired result. "It is with great difficulty that the Government of Gujarat have been able to persuade the Government of India[,] and Chief Minister [Jivraj Mehta] took special interest in getting at least some building work for you for the new Capital Project of Gandhinagar," Kantawala wrote back to Kahn. "Government of India have agreed to allow Rs. 1,00,000/- [100,00] or equivalent amount in Dollars as your lump sum fees for any major building which you may select. I think you will thus have an opportunity of designing one principal building of your choice." He exasperatingly added, "I am sure this will enable you to accept the offer and I would request you to come to Ahmedabad early and finalise the Agreement and start your work on the master plan."[74]

Doshi also wrote to Kahn, buttressing the offer: "The Government of Gujarat tried their best and they have at least got the permission to allow you to design any major building. The only condition is with regards to money. They agree to pay you a lumpsum [sic] of Rupees One Hundred Thousand or its equivalent in dollars." He tried to soothe Kahn by suggesting that he could, through the Capital Office, "design the remaining major buildings and have them built as you wish. This way you won't have any financial burden." He impressed upon Kahn, "There is no other way possible. As I see, the Government of Gujarat is too anxious to decide the appointment and go ahead." He tried to reassure Kahn, "I know that they [the Gujarat government] are really helpless in this, but I know for certain that Shri Kasturbhai Lalbhai when he comes back will try to do whatever he can." He pleaded, "Please do consider and then reply." Adding, "I suggest you contact Shri Kasturbhai at . . . c/o Dolder Grand Hotel, Zurich (Switzerland)."[75]

The intuitive Kahn had not learned the ways of India, his assertions to the contrary notwithstanding. Artistic ambition had usurped the mystic in him. Kahn, responding to Kantawala, gave his reasons for declining the commission. Thanking the Indians for placing the confidence in him to design Gandhinagar, he noted:

An unusual opportunity for the emergence of work of art is present when a new city is planned. An approach to design which considers city planning and building planning one unified art could produce an inspiring example to be followed by a city in its subsequent development.

I have long considered the planning of a city and its services to be inseparable from the design of its buildings. There is an architecture of highways, streets, waterways, bridges, parks, gardens, and utilities, as well as an architecture of buildings. Each can bring out its own rules of design and each should be answerable to the other and to the whole. I thought that in Gandhinagar, as in no new city so far, this unity could be accomplished [obviously, neglecting to note Chandigarh]. I thought of the land, the services and the buildings as one architecture and I felt that there could be developed an order and exemplary buildings which would influence all work toward the city's maturity in time. A city of good buildings reflecting design principles that are understood and followed in subsequent construction grows in beauty and importance. Individual designs belong to the artist but the principles leading to the design belong to everyone.

Such architectural conceptions as a source of inspiration towards the singularity of Gandhinagar are not realizable if the plan on paper conceived by the planner is left entirely to others to bring out the mental images that lead to the making of the plan. There will be created a love for certain buildings in the mind of the architect-planner which will inspire the plan itself. Not to be allowed to express this love by the acts of designing and building is to present this architect with the unacceptable conditions of planning for his own disappointments.

I am fully aware that my explanation here of my refusal of such an important commission is far from adequate. I want you to know that my decision is not based on any considerations of remuneration or the considerable financial loss when away from my office, but solely on my principles as an architect. It is also based on the need for the assurance of funds to pay for the engineering and drafting services required when I am preparing principles of planning and design in Philadelphia. I would be obliged to pay for these services in dollars which I accept and which I thought would be restored by fees of my commissions in rupees. This preparatory work must be constantly active during the entire period of study, design and building in India and in America. Because of my tendencies in work, I cannot act merely as a traveling designer concerned with construction and work on a problem only at specified times.

In conclusion, your proposal will not provide me with the scope of expression in actual building, nor the funds for study. I considered the privilege of expressing my art thru buildings as the true compensation. I feel I owe it to you and to the Government of India to try to better explain my position when next I am in India.[76]

A couple of millennia ago, the Greeks recognized that what all artists have in common is, as Aristophanes noted in his play *Clouds*, "the longing for applause." Kahn was Schiller's sentimental artist, the one who is always self-consciously struggling to reconcile his longing for perfection with the imperfections of the real world. That struggle dictated to Kahn that he design the capitol complex if he was going to prepare the plan. Kahn's emotionally charged letter to Kantawala was designed not so much to close doors on the capital city project as to initiate new thinking on the contract. He was defining the artist's position, which, in the mid-1960s, was clearly at variance with the national priorities. The haggling continued until the summer of 1966, when Kahn presented a new set of conditions in which he was willing to forego payments in American dollars and accept architectural work to be entrusted to Indian architects in return for Doshi and Charles Correa directing the work of the Gandhinagar commission in India. Kahn's new manifesto of demands, worked out after several meetings in the living room of Kasturbhai in Ahmedabad and rethinking in Philadelphia, stated:

1. That the architect be given a contract in line with the one entered into with Le Corbusier for Chandigarh, except that the architect will accept Rupee payment and that no agreement is entered into in regard to the development of the Master Plan of Gandhinagar. All other payments and conditions of the Chandigarh contract shall be retained except as otherwise noted.

2. The architect is to be commissioned to design the Capital Buildings: The Secretariat, Legislative Assembly, High Court, Governor's Palace, and other related buildings of the Capital group, and be responsible for the Master Plan of the Capitol site.

The complete ensemble of the Capital group gives the architect a broader base for the employment of a comprehensive aesthetic unity of appropriate architectural motives, sympathetic materials of construction and inspiring interior and exterior space character.

The complete building ensemble will relate itself to the approaches, plazas, gardens, pools and fountains, sculpture, and general landscaping. . . . The landscaping of the site shall be in keeping with the Town plan landscaping premises and plans.

3. The architect is to receive 3% on the total cost of the Capital Buildings and site design payable in Rupees. All engineering—structural, mechanical, electrical, acoustical, site and service engineering—shall be provided and paid for by the Public Works Department of the Government of Gujarat. The engineers are to be made available to the architect for all stages of his required performance. The continued consultation during these stages is essential in order to evolve toward a full integration of structure and services with the architecture.

4. The architect for this fee will staff an office and pay the services of his consulting architects, Mr. Doshi and Mr. Correa, who will direct the work of this commission in India.

(The architect would appreciate a place in the P.W.D. office where the project can be on exhibit and discussions of the project can take place with the P.W.D. staff.)

5. The architect explained that he should be permitted frequent and unlimited number of trips to Ahmedabad to criticize design and to integrate engineering. This will be necessary since he will be unable to employ men in his United States office for continued study. Dollar funds that may be made available would be used for the purpose of United States study.

6. The architect's trips and the expenses of the stays will be entirely paid by the clients. The length of stay in India will be at the discretion of the architect. If it is mutually agreed upon that a man is required to be deputed from his office, the clients would bear the cost for his transportation and stay. It would be advisable to arrange that some personnel from India come to the United States to intensify study in the office during the absence of the architect from India.

7. The architect should be exempted from taxes. Persons volunteering from his office to work in India on this project should also be exempted from taxes and helped in the exemption of import taxes on necessary living conveniences.

8. The Chief secretary inquired of the architect whether he would like to revise his fees in light of the devaluation of Rupee. Mr. Kahn said that since he was not able to transfer the Rupees into dollars, and since he will be paying his establishment in Rupees, he would not press the point but would leave it to the

clients to decide appropriate increase in the fees if the dollar value becomes necessary in the proper exercise of this work.

9. Talking of the cost and nature of appropriate construction, the architect explained that he would certainly work toward an expressive architecture and the use of economic materials. The final cost of the building will be based on the architectural interpretation of space needs and its architectural conception, which will become the true arenas and appropriate type of construction.

10. Mr. Kahn suggested that the Government of Gujarat should immediately start preparation for the setting up of a brick factory to realise the finer standards of construction.

11. Mr. Kahn offered to stop in Germany or Holland on his way to India during his visits to inquire about brick molding machinery, as in his opinion these two countries were the most advanced in brick-making and they knew the chemistry of bricks very well.

I believe these points are the most salient.[77]

So what made Kahn change his position and accept his fees in Indian rupees? In the murky world of Gujarat politics and banking, Kasturbhai had brokered the agreement by offering to pay Kahn $100,000 over the four-year period. "I appreciate your generosity and personal interest in providing $100,000.00 payable to me over a four-year period in Philadelphia for study of the [Capitol] Buildings," Kahn wrote Kasturbhai. "I am also grateful for your mention of the necessary further effort to acquire additional funds in dollars from Foundations in the United States. Probably I could work with your Ambassador in the presentation of objectives to the United States institutions or authorities for dollar support in the planning and building of Gandhinagar, the Capital of Gujarat."[78] The mystic had turned into the entrepreneur.

By the end of 1966, however, Doshi was to write disappointedly to Kahn that there had been no news on his new conditions "either from the Gujarat Government or from Shri Kasturbhai Sheth [Seth]." Meanwhile, in January 1965, the Gujarat government had appointed H. K. Mewada as the chief town planner and architectural adviser for the New Capital Project. Doshi informed Kahn that "Mewada of the Capital [City] project has already started laying the roads on the capital site and I hear that very soon they shall be building a large amount of quarters for their staff. At the moment I am not very much hopeful about this job." The bureaucratic battles and haggling over fees had left everyone exhausted, and Doshi told Kahn he wanted to visit the United States for six weeks "to clean the rust from my brain pipe." He requested that Kahn "speak either to Dean [Holmes] Perkins or to Mr. [Ronaldo] Giurgola [who designed Parliament House, Canberra]" to arrange a visiting lectureship. "Even a stay at Columbia will not be very far from your office,"[79] he ingratiatingly told his mentor.

As for the Gujarat government, nearly two decades after Indian independence it felt confident it could find a swadeshi solution for its capital. The Indian Institute of Technology campuses modeled after the Massachusetts Institute of Technology and the Indian Institute of Management campuses modeled after the Harvard Business School were beginning to turn out the technically trained graduates that Prime Minister Nehru had said India needed in "hundreds of thousands." Meanwhile, the slow progress of the IIM project at Ahmedabad caused as much by shortages of materials as by Kahn's countless revisions of his drawings was making Kahn's strongest supporter, Kasturbhai, impatient. "While the Institute is very grateful to you and is very appreciative of your efforts in building a model campus," Kasturbhai wrote early in summer 1969 to Kahn, "it is very much concerned over the slow progress that has been made so far compared to our commitment to the Government to finalize it in 1966."[80]

Gautam Sarabhai, chairman of the National Institute of Design, delivered the news to Kahn that he was being replaced by his protégé Doshi as the project architect for IIM. The time had come for the IIM project also to be placed into the hands of a local architect, just as the capital city project had been. "The first phase in the IIM Project is over," Gautam Sarabhai explained, "and on reviewing the needs of the second phase, Shri Kasturbhai, Doshi and we all agreed that for expeditious . . . execution, it would be in the best interests of everyone concerned that the Project should henceforth be handled by Shri Doshi. NID's association on the IIM Project will therefore end on 1st June [1969]." He politely added, "May I take this opportunity of thanking you for accepting to be our Architectural-Design-Consultant on this project and for giving us your support."[81] The Kahn seminar in Ahmedabad was ending.

4

The Plan and Architecture

WHEN THE AHMEDABAD daily newspaper *Prabhat* editorialized on June 24, 1964, that "a backward country like Morocco [has shown] more efficiency and planning" in developing its capital at Agadir than had the Gujarat government "in the construction of our Capital [at Gandhinagar]," it was following the tradition of the Indian press—always acerbic and never trusting of government.[1] The government had "not made any progress," said the paper. The editorial may be deemed facile rhetoric, given India's own economic backwardness, but it may also be viewed as India's growing sense of confidence almost a generation after independence, made possible by steadily increasing numbers of technically trained graduates in the country. As far as inefficiency in government was concerned, that was, as it remains today, an old theme with many variations. More than four years after being declared the capital, M. D. Patel, the Capital Project Circle superintendent engineer, admitted that "the Master Plan for Gandhinagar is not yet finalised."[2]

The editorial had the desired result on the media-sensitive Gujarat government, however. In January 1965, Cornell-educated H. K. Mewada, who had worked in Chandigarh with Le Corbusier, was appointed chief town planner and architectural adviser for the new capital city project, as well as made head of the newly created (Capital) Town Planning and Architectural Department. In keeping with the practice of creating competing urban authorities that was followed in the development of Chandigarh and Bhubaneswar, and that continues to be followed unquestioned throughout India, the Gandhinagar Capital Project itself was placed under the administrative control of the superintendent engineer of the State Public Works Department. In other words, Mewada was reporting to the chief engineer in the State Public Works Department. In little over a year, however (in April 1966), the master plan had been prepared and approved by the Gujarat government.[3]

Mewada wrote to his former colleague from Chandigarh, Jugal Kishore Chow-dhury, a graduate of London University and the University of Tennessee, who had worked with Antonin Raymond in New York as well as with the State Planning Commission, Tennessee, before returning to India to work with Le Corbusier in Chandigarh and later serving as chief architect for the Punjab government: "I agree that it is a rare opportunity in the life of any Planner [to build a new city]. In fact this very consideration prompted me to accept the new assignment. We are also trying to get more technical assistance from the United Nations."[4] Although Mewada had not been as close to Le Corbusier as Doshi or even as close as Ulie Chowdhury had been to the Frenchman in Chandigarh, the French master must have felt a measure of satisfaction at the end of his life to learn of the upset caused by one of his trainees in the contest for the planning and designing of Gandhinagar: Corbusian pedagogy in Indian planning would perpetuate itself through his students after his death on August 27, 1965.

Hargovind Kalidas Mewada was born on January 23, 1921. The Mewada family traces its origins to Benap village in the agricultural district of Mehsana, north Gujarat, about 150 kilometers from the Rajasthan border. The Mewadas are the highest members of the Suthar (or Suttars) caste, claiming brahmanical status. Mewada's father, Kalidas K. Suthar, was a carpenter by trade, earning twenty-five paisas (a monetary unit of India, Pakistan, and Burma equal to one-sixteenth of the former anna; an anna was one-sixteenth of a rupee; since India's adoption of the decimal system, one hundred paisas has equaled one rupee) a day, which must have prompted him to encourage his eldest of five sons to pursue education to better himself and help the family. Mewada matriculated in 1940 from a school seventeen miles away in the village of Visnagar, passing the Bombay board examination. From his father, he inherited interest in arts and crafts, which led him to study architecture at Kala Bhavan Technical Institute, Baroda, established by Maharaja Sayajirao Gaekwad on the models of the Bauhaus and Tuskegee. In 1947, while waiting to hear from the Bombay government about his application for a scholarship to study in the United States, he was granted a scholarship to pursue advanced studies in that country by the ruler of Kishangarh (Rajasthan), and on that basis he secured admission to Cornell University, at Ithaca, New York.[5] Soon after arriving in the United States, the provenance of his scholarship was changed to the Bombay government, which obliged him to sign a bond to work for a year for the government after completing his studies. Records at Cornell indicate that he completed both his bachelor's and his master's degrees in architecture in 1949. He then moved to the University of Illinois to study city planning, completing his master's there in 1950.

Mewada's Cornell training was not in accord with the new direction of the American architectural thought of the 1940s, which had definitely tilted in favor of the modern movement after the arrival of Gropius and Mies in America in late

1937 and 1938. In planning, he was certainly exposed to the community benefits of Arthur Perry's neighborhood unit, popularized in the United States by Clarence Stein, the influential American planning theorist who would collaborate with Mayer in Chandigarh.[6] Although Andrew Dickson White, the first president of Cornell University, had established a new program to provide formal academic training in architecture in 1877, a decade after MIT had established America's first formal program in architecture, Cornell, like so many other second-tier American institutions of architecture, was slow in responding to modernism, perhaps because of the college's geographic isolation and rural setting in upstate New York. From its beginnings, Cornell pedagogy displayed a sense of the importance of cultural history, offering an opportunity to study in Europe, which served as architectural laboratory for the enduring Eurocentric curriculum in American institutions. Soon, classes in drawing, painting, and sculpture were added, and a program in urban and regional planning was started in 1935. The College of Architecture, Art, and Planning officially acquired its present name in 1967.

That the Beaux Arts tradition would be established as the ruling orthodoxy of the Cornell architectural curriculum had been insured by the appointment of Dean Alexander Trowbridge in 1896; and the Beaux Arts tradition was faithfully maintained by John V. Van Pelt, one of the few Americans to receive a degree at the Ecole des Beaux-Arts, when Van Pelt succeeded Trowbridge as dean in 1902. A brochure produced on the 125th anniversary of the College of Architecture in 1996 noted that in the first half of the twentieth century "the curriculum resembled that of an art school, with nine hours weekly of freehand drawing and sketching in the first two years, plus six hours of water color. Beginning with the sophomore year, design dominated the curriculum. Junior year courses included clay modeling and rendering, while seniors took life class."[7]

During Mewada's time at Cornell in the late 1940s, urban planning remained neglected even though the New York State regents had approved the formal master's degree program in planning in 1941. In the 1950s, the architectural and planning program at Cornell experienced expansion in a new direction under the leadership of Thomas W. Mackesey, who had taught Mewada and about whom he wrote: "I have followed his academic progress carefully. He is competent, energetic and cooperative and stood high in his class. . . . Seldom has a foreign student in this College showed more ability to assimilate new ideas and more rapid progress." Mackesey prophesied that Mewada would "become a distinguished architect in his native land."[8] Under Mackesey's guidance, Mewada was exposed to interdisciplinary research in housing and urban development through the Center for Housing and Environmental Studies, an experience that would prove invaluable to him upon his return to an India crowded with refugees because of Partition. Through Mackesey, Mewada also came to define architecture as purely professional, as opposed to art, and came to see the architect in his medieval role—that of a multitalented person who combined artistic ability with engineering training and administrative aptness to coordinate the work of experts in many fields. Mackesey emphasized the architect's obligation to society as well as to the client. Mewada mastered his teachers' eclectic ideas and later successfully applied them in India. In architectural and planning circles in Ahmedabad, Mewada is still remembered for his dexterity in handling politicians as well as his staff, suggesting that his "people skills" more than his architectural talent had won him the Gandhinagar project.

At the University of Illinois, Mewada came under the influence of the prolific Karl B. Lohmann (1887–1963), professor of landscape architecture (1921–48) and city and regional planning (1948–55), whose seminal books *Principles of City Planning* (1931) and *Landscape Architecture in the Modern World* (1941) continue to generate discussion. Lohmann's diverse interests led him to reflect on a variety of interrelated subjects: landscape architecture; city planning; regional and rural planning; campus recreation; schools; smoke; streets; traffic; water and zoning. He also wrote *The Municipalities of Illinois* (1945) and produced a manuscript on the history of city planning and landscape architecture at Illinois (1954). Lohmann was closely connected with thinkers and social activists from multiple fields, including Carol Aronovici, Harland Bartholomew, Joseph C. Blair, Charles DeTurk, Henry V. Hubbard, Evert Kincaid, John Nolen, James S. Pray, Hideo Sasaki, Stanley White, and Henry Wright. The collective focus of these people in the 1930s and 1940s was on the social and physical form of the emerging twentieth-century metropolis, with considerable influence from the English experience of the preceding several decades. They advocated interdisciplinary and collaborative approaches to urban and architectural problems.

Lohmann served as Mewada's adviser and teacher at the University of Illinois, and many of Lohmann's ideas were expressed by Mewada in his planning of Gandhinagar. Mewada "has not only shown special talent in research, design and in other aspects of the planning field," Lohmann wrote in a testimonial for his Indian student, "but he has demonstrated an unusual capacity for hard and creative work. Moreover, he has displayed a charming pleasantness to those about him to the point where we shall not know what we miss him for most, as a scholar or as a friend."[9] It was Mewada's social skills that helped him with K. M. Kantawala, the chief engineer and joint secretary at the Public Works Department in Gujarat who wanted to appoint the American-trained Balkrishna Doshi, Charles Correa, Bernard Kohn, and Hasmukh Patel as architects for the principal buildings of Gandhinagar after negotiations with Kahn had broken down.[10] Inducting Mewada in the government employment at rupees 3,000 a month in the mid-1960s was certainly a more economical decision than contracting with private architects on a commission basis.

That Mewada was obsequious and U.S.-trained were additional attractive qualities. Attractive also was his one-year (1950–51) experience with Le Corbusier in Chandigarh (that period satisfied his obligation to the government, due because of his scholarship to the United States). In 1951 he left Chandigarh for Lucknow, the capital of Uttar Pradesh and the heartland of Hinduism, to become architect-planner for the state government. The peripatetic Mewada soon left Lucknow for the rain forests of the northeastern state of Assam, where he served as architect –town planner from 1955 to 1959, moving again to become the chief town planner and architectural adviser for the arid Rajasthan, in western India. He was thus placed in the right position when the position of chief town planner and architectural adviser became available in neighboring Gujarat.

The ease with which Mewada was able to crisscross the country, changing jobs, in the 1950s and 1960s suggests both the shortage of technically trained personnel in India and his easy manner with people. After returning from the United States, he had acquired considerable experience in government: he knew his way around the corridors of bureaucracy and had worked on large architectural and planning projects. The lessons learned from Mackesey and Lohmann in America had served him well in India, and the maharaja of Kishangarh, who had provided the initial scholarship for Mewada's American education, testified to this in a letter: "Mr. Mewada designed works of various magnitudes, [including] the Mittra Nivas Palace at Kishangarh, costing about [rupees] eight lakhs, the Kishangarh Club, the remodeling of the Manjhela Country House, etc." The testimonial speaks to Mewada's ability to fit "the new into the old" and to his "quickness to understand the requirements and his application and industry"—qualities that had been noted by Mewada's American teachers. The testimonial added: "The people who worked with Mr. Mewada were happy with him, and he always seemed more interested in the work than what he received in payment for it."[11] Because he had not been involved in the Kahn negotiations and because unlike many local architects he had not jockeyed for architectural contracts, he appeared to be the least-controversial, yet with substantial experience in planning and architecture.

Mewada was not above protecting his self-interest, however. When the Bombay-based architect Raghav L. Patel submitted a pilot master plan to the Gujarat government in the hope of securing the Gandhinagar project, Mewada was quick to discredit it as "a heterogeneous mixture of principles of city planning as practiced during [the] 17th and 18th century [sic], the axial planning adopted for imperial cities like New Delhi, and adoption of the basic plan of Versailles gardens near Paris." In Mewada's view, the Patel master plan was "an example of imperial or grand planning"; at best, it could "be called Utopian in its approach to the problems of planning for a city in a democratic state." In postcolonial India, describing the Patel plan as "imperial" and undemocratic and equating it with New Delhi was the equivalent of declaring it politically incorrect. Both by Indian instinct and American training he had learned the art of political polemics for self-advocacy without projecting himself into the picture. "In the literature accompanying the plans," he argued, "various provisions like headquarters for Army, Navy and Air Force, offices for Atomic Energy, etc. have been made which clearly indicate that the plan probably provides for a national capital rather than a modest state capital."[12]

From the efforts of the Kasturbhai-Sarabhai-Doshi team to negotiate a contract with Kahn, it certainly cannot be concluded that the Gujarat government was looking to build "a modest" or even a swadeshi capital. In fact, Mewada himself castigated Patel for trying "to relate his plan with the figure of . . . God Ganesh, which is probably the most irrelevant description that one can come across. . . . Unless the plan is basically sound, provides for the efficient functioning of the main purpose . . . comfortable and good living accommodation to the people, no purpose is served in going into [its] . . . minor details." He concluded that "the plan as submitted by [Patel] could have been adjudged as a good scheme if it were to be adopted years back in past."[13]

Mewada clearly did not see any contradiction in his criticism of the Patel plan; nor did he see the irrelevance of equating the Patel plan with the Versailles Gardens, in France, and (another example that he cited) Karlsruhe, in Germany. References to the West and wallowing in historicism is a running theme in Indian intellectual and artistic thought. "From the sketches enclosed it can be clearly seen that the [Patel] plan . . . is a very clever adaptation of [the] plan of [the] Versailles gardens and [the] plan of [the] city of Karsruhue [sic]." It is not clear whether Mewada here intended to parody Patel or muddy the discussion. The reference to the suburban capital of Versailles,[14] which had originally started as a hunting lodge and had grown to be the official residence of the kings of France (from 1682 until 1790), was intended to evoke the gluttonous age of imperial power in which people were divorced from rulers. Louis XIV used the Versailles Palace as a secret refuge for his amorous trysts with the lovely Louise de la Valliere, building a fairy-tale park around it. Planned by Jules Hardouin Mansart, the king's principal architect, and representing the French classical architecture that was complemented by extensive gardens, Versailles became the center of French power from which the destiny of Europe was decided for more than a century. But in the end, it generated so much discontent among the French middle classes that on July 14, 1789, it was besieged by the people. Had not Gandhi built in Ahmedabad his Sabarmati Ashram and from it launched his national campaign of satyagraha against the British raj, built on mercantilist greed?

Mewada's comparison of the Patel plan to Karlsruhe was designed to suggest the placid, backwater German constitutional city and university town near the French border, and it was also designed to discredit Patel's proposal by giving it a certain French flair for self-indulgence. That Karlsruhe is a quiet town is true: the many civil servants and court employees who live and work in Karlsruhe contribute to the city's placid atmosphere, just as many civil servants who live in Gandhinagar contribute to the capital's bland flavor. But it must scarcely have occurred to

Mewada that the German *ruhe* means tranquility—a quality that Gandhi so fervently sought for volatile, multireligious India, torn by communal strife. In time, Karlsruhe would acquire an international reputation as a center for natural sciences and engineering, but especially for new technologies, which today Gandhinagar is aspiring to acquire for itself by building a technology park just outside the capital. According to legend, the idea to establish Karlsruhe in 1715 came to Margrave Carl Wilhelm while he was taking a nap after a strenuous day's hunting. He dreamed of his own city; hence, Carls-Ruhe, or Carl's Rest. Wilhelm also influenced the city's unusual architecture, wanting all its main streets to radiate like the sun's rays from the central baroque castle. Its thirty-two streets, in star formation, were later to be supplemented by two ring roads. The clear, geometric structure of the city allows its almost three hundred thousand inhabitants to find their way easily around. The city is lavishly constructed—both the city center and the surrounding districts. But Mewada argued that "the system of radial roads as adopted in the old city planning methods is highly unsuitable for the heavy and fast [moving] traffic which has developed since . . . the industrial revolution." To Mewada, no matter that in Europe the automobile did not make its debut until the beginning of the twentieth century and that in India the automobile revolution would not occur until the end of that century (and then be limited to the middle class). Mewada would instead introduce the neighborhood idea in his plan for the capital, as it had been introduced in Chandigarh and Bhubaneswar, on the basis of safeguarding the pedestrian from the automobile. Moreover, modern principles of planning made it possible for him "to orient . . . roads and buildings in such a way as to avoid direct[ly] facing [the] sun."[15] Mewada's criticisms notwithstanding, many ideas from Karlsruhe would show up in Gandhinagar, particularly in the assembly building.

The detailing of the Gandhinagar plan was done by Mewada with the assistance of his senior town planner, P. M. Apte, in consultation with the Capital Project Circle's chief engineer, M. D. Patel. Chandigarh served as the inspiration from the beginning, having become the new monist Vedanta of urbanism in postcolonial India, which would be repeated with mantra-like regularity in the construction of the new cities and the replanning of the old—always with idiosyncratic variations to legitimize the enterprise as truly Indian. Through this process of repetition, the Chandigarh plan would be absorbed into the assimilative Indian tradition, just as, for millennia, Hinduism itself had assimilated so many cultural and philosophical influences entering India. "Your experience in the [d]evelopment of Chandigarh would be a great help to us in formulating our own approach and policy [in the development of Gandhinagar]," wrote Secretary M. G. Shah, of the Gujarat Public Works Department, to the Chandigarh chief commissioner, B. P. Bagchi, and the chief architect, M. N. Sharma. Shah proposed that he, the Gandhinagar chief town planner and architectural adviser, the deputy chief engineer, and the administrator visit Chandigarh to see the city and talk with officials there.[16]

Because Gandhinagar was named after the Mahatma, Mewada conceived the plan in the image Gandhi. The master plan "was prepared [by] keeping in view [the] location for a monument to the Mahatma befitting his stature as a leader of the masses," Mewada explained. "It will be seen from the Master Plan that the State Government offices complex[,] including the main buildings of [the] Sachivalya [the secretariat], Vidhan Sabha [assembly] and Offices of Heads of Departments are located on a north-west, south-east axis. The complex is approachable from either directions [sic]. The river Sabarmati is to the south-east. A grand vista with beautiful lawns and green area has been planned from the Sachivalya complex towards the river. The river itself will take the shape of a beautiful lake, full of water throughout the year, as there is a proposal to build a barrage across the river near Indroda."[17]

Because Gandhi's ashram was located downstream on the banks of the Sabarmati, Mewada placed the monument near the river, overlooking the Sachivalya complex, on the main axis. "The monument would overlook the great expanse of the lake and the park and [the] recreational area along [the Sabarmati] bank[s] and also the capitol complex. It would be seen from almost anywhere in the town because of its location and . . . size." Mewada noted that the Gandhi monument should be abstract in form. In support of his idea he cited the examples of Western and Indian cities. He argued that several "outstanding monuments dedicated to the memories of great personalities in the world have taken the shape of abstract forms rather than statutes." Pointing to the Gandhi Samadhi at Rajghat, New Delhi, which was built as the memorial to the Mahatma, and to the Eiffel Tower in Paris, and the Washington Memorial in Washington, D.C., he argued that in Gandhinagar the monument to the Mahatma "should [also] take an abstract form" and that no representational Gandhi statute be allowed in the capital.[18] Nearly twenty years earlier, the German planner Otto Koenigsberger had made the same suggestion in Bhubaneswar and unsuccessfully furnished the plan for the Gandhi Memorial Pillar inspired by the ruler Asoka Mauraya's pillars and resembling Gandhi's spinning wheel in design.[19] And in Chandigarh, Le Corbusier had successfully opposed statutes.[20]

Mewada strongly felt that the ultimate success of the capital would depend not only on careful city planning and its architectural form but also on the creation of public spaces and civic areas where people could assemble to enjoy the visual pleasures of buildings, adding "vitality" and "attractiveness" to the city. The sentiment was very similar to one expressed by Kahn, who had already begun his work at the Indian Institute of Management in Ahmedabad. Several of Kahn's ideas would flow out to Gandhinagar. Meanwhile, Mewada recommended in Gandhinagar an "extensive" plan, including a potpourri of architectural adornments to unify the public buildings: landscaped lawns, trees, artificial hills, large pools "to complement and set off the buildings," sculptures, murals, mosaics, reliefs, paintings, and "fountains in public places and in important public buildings." He felt that these elements would "greatly help to unite various separate buildings and plazas." In a historical vein, he wrote: "Our state has [a] rich heritage of art and architecture which [found] fusion in the hands of former rulers who understood and encouraged architects, artists, sculptors, craft[smen]. Today also we have many artists, sculptors, architects who have either studied here or abroad." He reasoned that the capital would "be the right place to give expression to the aspirations of these gifted people and thus help to create an environment in the city which is fresh, attractive, full of vitality." Without noting the contradiction in his declared purpose of building an unpretentious state capital that would memorialize Gandhi, the apostle of swadeshi and swaraj, Mewada drew on universal experience and his Cornell education to support his position: "Art history of the world is full of examples of cities and towns [with] . . . such expression[s of] artists, architects, sculptors, planners, engineers [that] are today . . . as in [the] past, places of world interest. . . . [P]laces like Rome, Florence, Venice in Italy, St. Paul's Precincts in London, Paris, [Chartres] in France, Amsterdam, Rotterdam in Holland, City Center in Oslo, Norway, Tokyo, Japan[,] and nearer home at Chandigarh and New Delhi."[21] Such clashes between those drawing from the Indian past and those searching in the Western tradition have been especially visible in national matters of architectural importance in India. In Gandhinagar, Mewada wanted the government to allocate "at least one percent" of the cost of every building for work to be done by local artists; these artists would build a potpourri of architectural adornments in the capital.

Capitalizing on the lessons learned in America and the experience gained from Chandigarh and Bhubaneswar, Mewada in his plan for Gandhinagar considered regional setting, site condition, and the dominant city function. "The new city is predominantly the administrative centre of the State and consequently may acquire many [other] important cultural, civic and allied functions [to make the city a living organism]," declared the planning document.[22] Because the state government was to be the principal employer, the city design was based on the government employment structure. Planned initially for a population of 150,000, the population projections were raised to 300,000 by the beginning of the 1980s. In 2001, the capital, or the Gandhinagar Notified Area (GNA), registered a population of 196,925, which is projected to stabilize at about 300,000 by 2011; and the Gandhinagar Urban Development Area (GUDA) registered a regional population of 381,821, which is expected to level off at 500,000 by 2011.[23]

The total area to be developed was estimated to be seven thousand acres, with an additional twenty-five hundred acres along the river to be developed as an elongated botanical park. The main pattern of the roads was to be a grid, except that the road along the river would follow the natural features, forming a crescent and thus breaking the monotony of straight roads, while linking the capitol complex, the Governor's House, the ministers' bungalows, and the quarters for members of the legislative assembly (MLAs). As in Chandigarh, the city was divided into rectangular neighborhood blocks (sectors) by the main roads. The area of each sector in Gandhinagar was 185 square acres (250 square acres in Chandigarh). The sector size was one kilometer by three-fourths of a kilometer. The residential sectors were divided into zones, with distributor roads skirting their perimeters, but not passing through them. The average residential zone could be traversed only on bicycle paths. Each sector was planned as a self-contained neighborhood, with a shopping strip, a community center, a medical clinic, schools, and so on, all located within the limits of distributor roads so that pedestrians would not have to cross a road to reach the neighborhood community centers. Roads were designed to run not parallel to the boundaries of the capital, but 30 degrees northwest-southeast and 60 degrees northeast-southwest to protect motorists from the direct glare of the afternoon sun—clearly an influence coming from Kahn, who had been discussing his ideas of "silence" and "light" in Ahmedabad. The main roads would be forty-five meters wide, the road in front of the secretariat one hundred meters wide, to accommodate heavy traffic, and all peripheral and shopping streets sixty-five meters wide. Following the Chandigarh example, provision was made for bicycle paths that would not cross a road available to motor vehicles except by underpass.[24] There were to be two communication links with Ahmedabad—one with the airport, which is located between the capital and Ahmedabad, and the other with the city center.

Most of the land was reserved for housing: it was estimated that, on average, each self-contained sector would have a population of seven thousand and a density of forty persons per acre, although residential sectors for government officials and wealthy private individuals were designed for lower density. In the planning of housing within a sector, it was assumed that the automobile would remain out of reach for most residents—an assumption that, with the benefit of the hindsight, is now seen to have been erroneous. In accordance with the Indian realities prevailing in the late 1960s, the basic plan was to have clusters of houses built around open spaces. Architecturally, attempts were made to maintain flexibility in housing design, avoiding rigid rows, encouraging staggered clustering around central areas, and having buildings of varying heights. The use of paint was avoided by relying on exposed brick, concrete, and natural building materials, clearly in response to Kahn's influence. The lowest-ranking government employee was provided 450 square feet of covered area, excluding verandas or balconies. Each low-income, double-storied house was to contain two rooms plus kitchen, bathroom, and lavatory, a substantial open space for lounging at the rear on the ground floor, and a terrace on the first floor. Flooring was mosaic tile or Kota stone. Each house was provided with ample storage space and two electric ceiling fans, the latter being essential to the Indian lifestyle and in the local climate.

In order to avoid criticism for building segregated residential areas for public employees on the basis of rank and salary as happened in Chandigarh and Bhubaneswar, in Gandhinagar a muted effort was made within the sectors to provide housing that mixed the classes. Each category was grouped around its own central open space to avoid social conflict. Still, in sector 24, in the northwest corner, low-income housing was segregated. Elsewhere, private housing had been provided along with government housing, thereby eliminating exclusive government colonies, which Koenigsberger had so strongly objected to in Bhubaneswar. "A bureaucrat who sees only other bureaucrats soon develops all the vices of in-breeding," one supporter of the plan noted, adding: "Gujarat is attempting to avoid this."[25]

Such enthusiasm for Gandhi's sarvodaya notwithstanding, the planning document admitted that while "intermixing of different economic classes of society is desirable, at the same time it is also necessary to ensure that the contrast between one category of residential [section] and the other is not too much. Gradual integration of various economic groups is therefore envisaged." Nevertheless, private housing today is concentrated in the western and southern sections of the capital, in sectors 1, 2, 3, 4, 5, 14, 25, 26, and a part of 8. Housing for ministers and senior government officers is located east of the capitol complex in sectors 9, 19, and 20, fronting the river, and has been generously provided with servant quarters, parking, sprawling lawns, courtyards, and wide verandas. In architectural styling, the archetypical bungalow has been the major influence. Still, the planning document insisted that "a healthy community should have the ingredients from different social, economic and cultural background." To achieve this, Mewada suggested the inclusion of "some [state and national] educational and research institutions,"[26] an idea that had been emphasized by both Kahn and Koenigsberger and that was finally beginning to enter into the thought of Indian planners.

Major work areas were placed in the center of the capital, while subsidiary work areas were well distributed along principal roads in an effort to distribute traffic during peak hours. The central commercial district, which was to occupy an area of 185 acres in sectors 11 and 17, housed major civic, cultural, and business facilities, as well as the city administration, the main post office, a regional bus terminal, the Pathik Ashram (guest house), regional offices, and a newspaper complex. Four district commercial centers were placed in sectors 5, 8, 21, and 24 to serve the four corners of the capital, while each neighborhood had its own market. Mimicking Chandigarh, the plan provided for small-scale and light industries to minimize pollution from manufacturing. The industrial estate was located to the northwest of the capital, originally occupying about four hundred acres, to which another three hundred acres was added later. The plan provided for residential sectors in the industrial estate so that workers would have short commutes, as well as easy access to technical institutions to attend training classes.

As time passed, however, the administrative city slowly turned into a technology park. This came about with the establishment of the Gujarat government-sponsored InfoCity on the Gandhinagar-Ahmedabad highway, about twenty kilometers away from Ahmedabad International Airport and twenty-five kilometers from the Ahmedabad city center. The project, which is being funded through private-sector participation, occupies nearly 150 acres that are being developed by the Florida-based Creative Choice (the contract was won in international competition). InfoCity is intended to be more than a working technology park; it is billed as a complete city, with social infrastructure, residential areas, a commercial center with hotels and clubs, hospitals, schools, utilities, and other amenities. It is even being considered to license the area for alcohol, which is otherwise prohibited in Gujarat in deference to the Mahatma. None of this had been envisioned by Mewada; it is capitalizing on India's information-technology revolution of the 1990s. The Compaq division of Hewlett-Packard, the American computer giant, has plans to set up regional headquarters in Gandhinagar, in stark antithesis to Gandhi's emphasis on cottage industry and swadeshi. Former Chief Minister Shankersinh Vaghela (of the right-wing Rashtriya Janata Party), in a political statement, claimed that, unlike the rest of India, which remains a Third World nation, Gujarat was becoming as developed as advanced countries like the United States and Japan.[27]

In contrast to the Chandigarh capitol complex, which Le Corbusier had placed in the northeast corner to take advantage of the Shivalik Hills in the background, Mewada placed government buildings in sector 10, the heart of the city. The 370-acre complex was to house the assembly, the secretariat, the Raj Bhavan (the governor's residence), the circuit house, offices for the central government, and the high court—except, of course, that the high court eventually had to be built in Ahmedabad because the lawyers and judges refused to move to Gandhinagar, arguing that it was impracticable to relocate the courts to the capital when their clients were concentrated in Ahmedabad. Whereas the Chandigarh capitol resembles an acropolis of monuments dominating the city, the Gandhinagar capitol appears as a disembodied ensemble of government buildings attesting to the Public Works Department's plucky attempt at creating monumentality. The question of disjunction insistently nags the observer at the Gandhinagar capitol, the buildings having dichotomous or schizoid profiles. The assembly entrance, for example, resembles the entrance to an Indian cinema hall, and the chamber seems suited for a dance recital, rather than constitutional deliberation.

Judged on some very important criteria of monumentality and accessibility, the Gandhinagar capitol is an outright failure, while on others it serves the functions for which it was designed. The contrast between the Chandigarh and Gandhinagar capitols, even though the latter was modeled after the former, stems from their different pedigree and the intensity of the convictions held by the architects. Le Corbusier served the profligate Punjab government backed by the cosmopolitan, urbane Nehru, at a time when the whole world seemed under reconstruction after World War II; when the avatars of modernism were proclaiming a new era that would be the culmination of human evolution as a species—an era in which houses and furniture and even clothes would be logical, functional, and efficient, and people would be high-minded and happy as a result; and when Le Corbusier had torn down the "wall" that had been obstructing India's and Nehru's view of the future. Mewada, by way of contrast, served the stiff and ungainly Gujarat government, and at a different time—a time when India was embattled with border wars with neighboring Pakistan and China; when a famine was looming large on the national horizon; and when modernism itself was under attack and when even Indian architects who had been consumed by it were beginning to question the French master.

Indians sounded their discordant voices about modernism in a seminar entitled "The Architect and the Community," held in New Delhi in February 1965, a little more than a month after Mewada had been hired to draw the master plan and execute architectural designs for Gandhinagar. The Gandhinagar enterprise was to cost rupees 29.54 crore [U.S.$29.54 million] in the first phase, and another rupees 16.23 crore [U.S.$16.23 million] in the second phase. There were several other government and corporate building projects across the country. Despite so much construction and building work in India, architects remained marginal. Clearly, the state and central governments and major corporations had emerged as the new patrons of architecture in postcolonial India, as elsewhere. Witnessing lucrative government projects executed by public works departments was discouraging to architects in private practice, particularly to those who had studied in the West at considerable personal expense and now viewed themselves as legitimate successors to both the English architects of the late colonial period and to the Western architects who had built in India in the fifteen years following independence.

On the one hand, modernism's salutary message—modernize your house, and your life will follow—had not worked in India. For one thing, the country's large population, indolent bureaucracy, and socialist economic policies just could not produce new materials to meet a growing demand. "Take the case of cement," thundered C. D. Desmukh, the distinguished economist and vice chancellor of Delhi University, at the 1965 seminar. "How do you have 5 or 6 [storied buildings] when the nation is 50 [percent] short of cement?" He also blamed the architects and builders, as well as the government, for failing the community in building low-cost housing.[28] On the other hand, because of high illiteracy, India remained strongly tied to tradition and religion, prompting several leading architects to retreat into history to advance their practice, producing soulless monuments, dreary housing, and gloomy new towns—seemingly made livable by a profusion of colors and ornamentation. It was professionally practical and economically prudent to take refuge in the past, rather than try to make better modern architecture that expressed its own era.

"What are the ethics and tasks of an architect in emerging nations?" asked the distinguished Charles Correa, rhetorically, at the 1965 New Delhi conference. "Projects which waste resources are irresponsible," he added. "Does this stand as a condemnation of the enormous volumes of concrete used in, say, the capitol complex at Chandigarh? In other words, should we avoid spectacular and heroic architecture and concentrate on achieving a great efficiency within a more modest but precise discipline?" Correa was making a case against the monumental buildings to which architects are drawn because they are far more glamorous and lucrative than low-cost housing. "Witness Chandigarh where the master plan looks fine on paper (in fact[,] makes an excellent wall-hanging) but not much else,"[29] said Correa, neglecting to note the French master's concern with collective housing, not just monuments. This was the first open attack on Chandigarh by an Indian architect who had been a faithful follower of modernism. What was lost in the international seminar in New Delhi, and has remained lost in Indian architecture generally, is the realization that what is celebrated as modernism, the movement, is simply modernity, a state of mind. Promoting modernity was, and remains, impossible in a country with a large population and a 53 percent illiteracy rate,[30] the combination of which allows religion and tradition to dominate social behavior. Modernism was about breaking with the past in order to create possibilities for the future.

A visitor to Gandhinagar does not have to pass through a place that reflects history or geography: for that, there is Ahmedabad. Gandhinagar's impact has been more on consciousness than on a particular parcel of land. Still, people are actually living history in Gandhinagar, punctuated by periodic violence that spills over from Ahmedabad, as happened after the Hindu-Muslim communal conflict erupted in the spring of 2002. But Gandhinagar is Mewada's critique of Le Corbusier's Chandigarh, which has made the city a mecca for students of architecture and planning, as well as for administrators interested in new towns. Just as, earlier, Mewada and his team had studied Chandigarh, the iconoclastic M. N. Buch felt obliged to study Gandhinagar. Buch, who as administrator-cum-deputy-secretary to the Madhya Pradesh government supervised the development of his state's new capital at T. T. Nagar as an extension of historic Bhopal (Bhopal was famous for producing begams who once ruled the city and the late bandit-queen-turned-politician Phoolan Devi, who only a decade earlier terrorized it), wrote Buch to Mewada after his visit to Gandhinagar, "My discussions with you have been an education for me." He further exulted, "What I have seen of the Capital of Gujarat has revealed to me a genius, a master builder. You and your team of planners and builders can take pride in having created a city of the 21st Century, but in a wholly Indian-setting."[31] Such hyperbolism, not uncommon in Indian planning and architectural circles, was very common with the impetuous Buch, who had earlier scathingly criticized Koenigsberger's Bhubaneswar plan for neglecting to integrate the

Lingaraja temple and other religious monuments within it.[32] "I have . . . written a note . . . [to] our Chief Secretary [of Madhaya Pradesh government], giving my impressions of my visit. . . . You have, however, reason to be proud of what you have achieved and we as Indians can share your pride, if only by virtue of living in the same country." He assured Mewada that "I shall watch the development of Gandhinagar with very great interest indeed."[33]

In time, Buch would resign from the security of the prestigious Indian Administrative Service, reincarnate himself as a social and urban activist, and become a leading critic of the government's policies and urban management. In fact, his Gandhinagar report to the chief secretary of Madhya Pradesh is more a diatribe of how the Gandhinagar administration is organizationally superior to the capital city project administration of Madhya Pradesh than an insightful discussion of the "Indianness" of the Gujarat capital. Intending to show the flaws of T. T. Nagar by comparing it to Gandhinagar, the Buch report noted, "The Chief Architect [of Gandhinagar] has had a completely free-hand [sic], comparable to the free hand given to Le Corbusier in Chandigarh, in preparing the town plan, in determining the location of important [buildings], in determining building admixtures category-wise in sectors and in preparing the type designs of every single building. Shri Mewada told me that there had been absolutely no interference at any level with his discretion." The report declared that the "results are spectacular" in Gandhinagar. His other point was that, while both Gandhinagar and T. T. Nagar were "within the area of influence of existing metropolitan centres, Bhopal and Ahmedabad, respectively," the capital at Bhopal was built as an extension "of the existing city, so that the new capital has not acquired a character or identity of its own. . . . Gandhinagar is separated from Ahmedabad by 18 miles of open land, so that while remaining within the tidal pull of the great metropolis of Ahmedabad, the capital has still a character of its own and is free of the more noxious aspects of Ahmedabad's development."[34]

Buch's report was misleading in many important ways, and may have been designed to gain greater freedom from the state government for the Madhya Pradesh capital city project office and even to encourage politicians to stop interfering in planning and architectural matters in his state. He neglected to mention the political pressure that had caused the high court to be retained in Ahmedabad. Then there was the case of one Mr. Sompura, who had demanded that the new capital should have an entrance gate "in ancient Indian style."[35] Under political pressure, Mewada had also been forced to expand the area for industry. Mewada himself admitted that "after spending all these years in various Town Planning [Departments], I am becoming rather pessimistic about the results of the Master Plans." He noted that although statutory master plans "have been prepared for a number of . . . towns, those have not been followed," causing "great hardship to the people whose properties fall within [them]"; and master plans "quite often have proved to be a source of public exploitation and even corruption."[36] Sure enough, Ratilal K. Patel, a former member of the legislative assembly in Ahmedabad had complained to the chief minister about the Public Works Department's "malpractice and irregularities committed on a large scale in the construction of the Gandhinagar structures." The complaint was investigated by the vigilance commission, which concluded that "the allegations of irregularities in construction and favouritism to contractors can not be established." Nor could the commission determine examples of poor workmanship, although it did identify some "minor defects" in construction. In the end, the commission concluded that "no prima facie case against any public [servant] or Government Officer" could be established.[37]

Some private businessmen, too, did not share Buch's enthusiasm about Gandhinagar. Mandeep Kumar, from Bombay, who wrote to the Gujarat chief minister to say he had visited Gandhinagar with a view to starting a business venture there, said he concluded that the capital lacked the necessary infrastructure to support business. He complained that land values were too high, loan facilities for private construction were absent, and communication and transportation infrastructure was missing; the city was also sorely lacking in entertainment and sanitary conditions: "I had actually been given to understand that Gandhinagar had been planned along the lines . . . of 'Chandigarh' . . . which is regarded as an ultra modern city in India—well planned and beautifully executed," he complained. He expressed his disappointment that, whereas Chandigarh had become a tourist attraction for both domestic and international travelers, Gandhinagar was a dull city.[38] Predictably, Kumar's complaint produced a lengthy government response. Drafted by senior town planner Apte, the essence of the reply was that "there are certain basic differences between the character of . . . Gandhinagar and Chandigarh. . . . [Chandigarh] was planned not only as the administrative seat of [Punjab] but also as a business, commercial, industrial and educational centre":[39] Chandigarh was a city with multiple functions and therefore differed from single-function Gandhinagar, Apte reasoned; many Western capitals such as Washington, D.C. were single-function cities. Since Chandigarh was in fact planned principally as an administrative town,[40] Apte either was not familiar with Chandigarh or he was being duplicitous; he also apparently was not familiar with the thriving cultural and educational life in Washington. It was more to the point when he argued that Gandhinagar was only a year old and that it was therefore "unjust to expect it to provide everything which a city like Ahmedabad may provide."[41]

Buch's commending Mewada for creating a city of the twenty-first century in an Indian idiom is both emblematic of the thinking that prevailed in government circles, and that to a degree continues to prevail there, and problematic as a nationalistic expression of identity. Perhaps no nation more than India, with the possible exception of Germany, is more attuned to the political manipulation of built imagery. Every conquering people of India wielded the power of the architecture of capital cities, to awe, to alienate, to inspire, and to intimidate: Delhi itself underwent many mutations from the Hindu Indraprastha to the Mughal Delhi to the British New Delhi. At some subconscious level, this experience may be the source of the tribal fetish for manipulating images and texts, though based in fact, for recapturing the "dazzling" past, going as far as to inserting the image into this already inflated omnium gatherum future. After a generation of being tutored by Western masters, the choice of Mewada as the architect-planner was itself a symbolic gesture of self-reliance, just as the decision to site the capital in bucolic Gandhinagar was a demonstrated desire for a new start.

Mewada was far more adept as a civic functionary than as a path-breaking artist, and his understanding of how public architecture gets to be assigned and built was not the least of his noteworthy talents. Feeling out of his depth in Gandhinagar, building on an order of magnitude that even the practical Doshi would have envied, Mewada marshaled international assistance from the British academic Vernon Z. Newcombe, arranged by the Gujarat government under the United Nations program of technical cooperation. After visiting Chandigarh and examining the Gandhinagar plan, Newcombe concluded that the "general grid and land-use pattern appeared to be an adequate basis for the development of the new city." Agreeing to accept the plan "as a working basis," he decided "to direct [the Gujarat government's] attention towards its further development."[42] Newcombe did not favor architectural control, however, because it "can easily lead to dull uniformity. . . . Within the housing areas, interest should be sought in the contrast formed by the greater uniformity of the Government housing areas and the greater diversity of the public housing areas." He was prepared to let private housing be subject to general controls for town planning like height, density, location, and so on. He also saw no need for architectural controls for the industrial area, but he supported them for the capitol complex, as well as for the commercial center. He reasoned that "a sufficient degree of architectural coordination "is attained by insisting on a uniform facing for a group of buildings."

Newcombe considered the capitol complex to pose the most "outstanding problem" of architectural design because the Gujarat government wanted the buildings and monuments to be of "outstanding quality—as regards both design and construction." To achieve the desired architectural style he said there were several choices: (1) the Gujarat government could hold a public competition; (2) or it could hold a limited competition; (3) or it could set up a jury of peers to select architects; (4) or it could invite foreign consultants to design the capitol; (5) or it could have the designs done by the public works department. Newcombe himself preferred the jury selection process, thereby suggesting that Indian architects in private practice be commissioned to design important buildings. "If more than one architect is appointed," he argued, "as it might be (one for each building), the problem of coordination becomes highly important. This would need to be effected efficiently and with imagination by the staff of the [Capitol] Project. Facing materials would have to be specified which would give the whole complex a unified appearance, and individual buildings would have to fit into a general grouping to be determined by the [Capitol] Project Staff."[43] In addition, he recommended that "a travel fellowship lasting two to three months should be granted to Mr. Mewada to enable him to make himself familiar with recent developments in the field of planning in Europe, with special reference to new towns. He has not been abroad since 1950. He might possibly visit Finland, Sweden, Denmark, the United Kingdom, the Netherlands and Yugoslavia."[44]

Realizing how limited in international travel Indians were, Newcombe suggested that Indian architects and planners in the Public Works Department travel to Europe to study new technologies and ideas in order to design their cities and homes in India. It was both a matter of exposure as a source of inspiration for new ideas and a means of reinterpreting the Indian past. Put simply, Newcombe felt that Indians in general were too insulated and that the architectural profession in particular was too isolated. The sentiment was very similar to the one expressed by Le Corbusier in Chandigarh, by Koenigsberger in Bhubaneswar, and by Kahn in Ahmedabad. The absence of a critical mass of middle-class Indians with access to new technologies and ideas lay at the very center of the conflict between Indian and Western national thought systems. The reason this debate has gradually abated in recent years is that growing numbers of Indians from the working classes and the middle classes have traveled overseas, returning home to demand the comforts of Western homes and cities, even as they continue to use traditional Indian adornments as part of their aesthetics. The Indian diaspora in Western countries, particularly in North America, has been instrumental in influencing extended family members in India in a quiet but deep way to aspire to many of the same creature comforts and new technologies that are available in the West. The Indian government's post-1985 economic liberalization policies have facilitated social change, albeit for a limited number of people.

By June 1970 "the entire Secretariat Offices and staff [had] shifted to Gandhinagar." By that time, the Gujarat government had also expended rupees 24 crore out of the rupees 29 crore allocated for the first phase of the development. The distribution of the spending included rupees 2 crore for land acquisition, rupees 11 crore for roughly six thousand government residential quarters, rupees 3 crore for the construction of public buildings, rupees 7 crore on infrastructure, and rupees 1 crore on miscellaneous expenses. The completed infrastructure included the main expressways to Gandhinagar from Ahmedabad, main city roads, a sewage-treatment plant, a water-supply plant, supply lines for sewage and water, branch plants for sewage and water supply, and street lighting in ten sectors. The completed public buildings included an office complex, which served as the temporary secretariat, the government printing press, the Pathnik Ashram, a guest house for the MLAs (members of the municipal legislative assembly), colleges, a library serving tem-porarily as the legislative assembly, a hospital, infirmaries (dispensaries), schools, and a police station. In 1970, the capital had a population of twenty-five thousand, principally made up of government employees. Construction of the capitol complex buildings—the assembly, the secretariat, the high court—along with other govern-ment buildings and recreational facilities was to be undertaken in the second phase of the development at an estimated cost of rupees 16 crore.

But private development languished in the capital, notwithstanding creation of the infrastructure. The main reason was that the state government had failed to provide incentives for economic development outside the government sector. "Without appropriate sources of employment and income for all sections of the community," Newcombe had warned in his report, "Gandhinagar will not be able to attract population as planned." He had suggested that the Capital City Project Office cooperate with the Department of Industry, the Gujarat Industrial Develop-ment board, and the Chamber of Commerce to explore ways of diversifying the economic base of the city,[45] as well as recommending "inducements and advan-tages . . . to [business] applicants for sites in the early phase of development." New-combe mentioned a number of inducement measures such as long-term leases, tax abatements, subsidized housing for private sector employees, and so on. "Equally important is the provision of educational facilities for the children," Newcombe argued, "and as far as the middle and higher income groups are concerned, it is par-ticularly important to attract those private educational institutions which are so popular with them in Ahmedabad."[46]

Estimates for the two phases of development had been prepared in 1966, and for the first phase the Capital Project Office stayed under the projected amount of rupees 29 crore. But devaluation of the rupee in the late 1960s escalated the build-ing costs for the second phase. The *Times of India* reported on July 4, 1971, that a former member of parliament belonging to the Congress party, Narendra Singh Mahida (of the Fourth Lok Sabha, March 1963 to December 1970), was demand-ing immediate "scrapping" of the capital city project plan and the shifting of the government to Ahmedabad. Mahida's motives were both selfish and altruistic. Ahmedabad had remained the political power base as well as the economic center of Gujarat; it was closer to his constituency of Anand in the southeast. But he was also echoing the ruling party's concerns about spiraling inflation caused by the India-Pakistan war over Bangladesh in 1971. By September 1971, India was spend-ing nearly $200 million a month to feed its eight million Bangladeshi refugees, compared with the $70 million a month during the 1965 war. The Nixon admin-istration, which was pursuing China diplomacy through Pakistan, was openly an-tagonistic toward Mrs. Gandhi's Congress government, ruling out any assistance from the United States, thus impelling her to sign a twenty-year Treaty of Peace, Friendship, and Cooperation with the Soviet Union. To Mahida and many others, the revised cost of rupees 75 crore for completing the capital by 1982 at an annual debt interest of rupees 8 crore for the next decade must have appeared extravagant at a time when the Indian nation was facing economic emergency at home and when war with Pakistan appeared to be imminent.

"First of all it is necessary to comprehend that the construction of a New Capital City does not mean establishment of a housing colony," the Gujarat government sarcastically responded to Congressman Mahida in its position paper on the capital city, pointedly observing that "those who contend that . . . residential accommodation could be built in Ahmedabad [in order for that city to serve as the capital] very conveniently forget the fact that the existing socio-cultural facilities in Ahmedabad (Schools, Hospitals, Playgrounds, Gardens, Transportation[,] etc.) are inadequate even to cater to the present population of the city and ultimately these facilities will have to be provided to the growing population either by the local authority or by the State Government." The paper further noted that the cost of updating facilities in Ahmedabad would be higher than in Gandhinagar, and the new capital's construction costs "have to be seen in this background." Moreover, Gandhinagar was seen as relieving the population burden on Ahmedabad. Enumerating the benefits of low costs, modern infrastructural facilities, and plenty of land, the paper concluded that "no one in his right senses can oppose creation of a good social, cultural and physical environment for a people by its government."[47]

The minutes of a meeting held on March 18, 1973, that was presided over by the minister for public works speak of the construction of the capital becoming swamped with disputes between private contractors and the Public Works Department, corruption charges against public servants and officials, and shortages of construction materials,[48] all of which delayed the completion of the capitol complex. In the end, the capitol complex was completed in July 1982, covering 370 acres. It housed the secretariat and the assembly, as well as state government offices to the north of the capitol complex and Indian government offices to the south. In the heart of sector 10, the capitol complex is a grouping of buildings housing the legislature and government offices. Well laid out, it is reached by a short walk from the neighboring residential sectors. The assembly and the secretariat are named after the famous Patel brothers: the Vithalbhai Patel Bhavan Assembly, after Sardar Vithalbhai Patel, the lawyer-turned-nationalist; and the Sardar Patel Bhavan Secretariat, after Sardar Vallabhbhai Patel, the iron man of India who negotiated accession settlements with most of the princely states in favor of India in return for a measure of autonomy in domestic affairs after independence.

Sardar Patel Bhavan, or the secretariat, is a grouping of seven blocks raised on concrete columns to provide parking and pedestrian movement at ground level. Of the seven, two (blocks 3 and 6) are parallel to CH Road. These blocks are smaller, two stories high, resting on two-story columns. Four blocks are nine stories high and rest on one-story columns—the ground floor thus being open on all sides, except on the side where the expansive entrance contains a generous hallway, equipped with elevators and a staircase. The central block (block 1), which is designed exclusively for ministers and their staff, is on the ground level, ten stories high, and contains the main entrance for the entire group of seven. Because this building is exclusively reserved for elected officials, it has twelve elevators, two of which are reserved for ministers, two for service, and eight for the staff and general public. The top two floors (9 and 10) have a double-storied auditorium and conference hall. Ministers' chambers and their staff offices are located on the sixth, seventh, and eighth floors; the chief minister's chamber and offices is on the fifth floor; two committee rooms are on the fourth floor, and the chief secretary's (chief administrator's) office and the cabinet room are adjacent to each other on the third floor. There are some additional offices for ministers in block 2 on the third, fourth, and fifth floors. The ministers' and the chief secretary's chambers have attached anterooms and bathrooms.

The secretariat departments are located in four blocks—2, 4, 5, and 7—that each have a separate but subsidiary entrance hall with its own elevators and staircases. Each building has also been provided with an underground basement for document storage (old records, etc.). Lighting and ventilation into the basement is by means of skylights that are protected from the weather. Because of the high cost of electrical energy, only the ministers' and senior administrators' offices have central air-conditioning. A cafeteria, lounge, and other facilities are in two blocks (blocks 3 and 6) that are not as tall as the four for the secretariat. While connection between buildings is allowed for, the independence of individual blocks has been preserved. Mewada's office explained in a document, "This kind of grouping of the seven blocks affords us with two vast open-to-sky paved quadrangles enclosed by blocks on all four sides but, at the same time[,] giving a sense of openness and freedom of movement at the ground level." These quadrangles have underground parking for "two-wheel vehicles" [motor scooters] and are connected to the central block, block 1, by staircase. "This group of seven blocks known as . . . Sardar Patel Bhavan is, in fact, a part of the entire Assembly-Sachivalya [assembly-secretariat] Complex with the dominating Assembly building in the centre as the focal point."[49]

On the east-west axis of the assembly building is the main boulevard—Road No. 4—coming from the railway station to the west and terminating at the proposed Gandhi Memorial on the banks of the river to the east. The north-south axis of the assembly building is coincident with the central block of the Sardar Bhavan (secretariat) to the north and the central block of another group of seven identical blocks to the south. The seven southern blocks house the heads of departments of the secretariat. The entire complex is approached from CH Road to the west and subsidiary approaches from CHH Road to the east.

The assembly building appropriates stylistic features of a Hindu temple, which typically stands on a high base, with a circumbulatory passage around the internal sanctum, which is almost always enclosed by a single rectangular wall. In Gandhinagar, Mewada and his team of government architects raised the assembly complex by 1.5 meters, using earth fillings to create a downward-sloping berm and thus giving the assembly building "a more commanding view from far and near." The central block of the assembly complex stands on a podium, 4.5 meters high by 133 square meters, "giving the impression of a . . . crowned King sitting on his throne." Evidently, Mewada had the Acropolis in mind, but the reference to kingship missed the irony involved for Gandhi's political descendants in Gujarat. The area under the podium has been naturally lighted and ventilated by eight square openings in the concrete slab. It is accessible from four corners, chamfered for this purpose, through wide, segmentally arched gateways, possibly inspired by the more decorative gateways at Jhinjhavada and Dabhoi, near Baroda, where Mewada started his education in architecture. A circular moat filled with water, reminiscent of temple tanks, canals, and sluices with bathing steps and shrines, surrounds the podium, channeling access to the four archways over short bridges. The chief architect's office described the body of water as breathing "life" into the assembly complex and providing "a sense of constant mobility."[50]

Wide steps in front and back of the central block lead up to the podium, where a pedestal (90 meters by 90 meters) sits in the middle. From the center of the pedestal rises the domed main assembly hall, and around it, rising to four stories, are rooms for related functions. "All this inspires a feeling of awe in a person climbing these steps and gives an impression of entering a temple," Mewada's office proudly noted, "and a temple it is, with the domed octagonal Assembly hall rising three stories . . . as its 'Sanctum sanctorium [sic].'" Forgotten in this religiously inspired architectural monument was India's commitment to secularism, just as Gandhi, his best efforts notwithstanding, could not avoid making reference to religion in order to galvanize Indians for his satyagraha marches. While for the large Muslim population of Gujarat the assembly building must have appeared in another light, for the Hindu architects "the light filtering down through the . . . skylight in the dome's apex [gave] this hall an air of mystic sanctity."[51]

The front and back entry doors to the assembly are framed in granite. The ground level (the podium level) houses a library, post office, bank, and other facilities. In the vestibule stands an imposing central column, rising two stories and branching out at the top into radial beams that form a pattern in the ceiling— "giving the impression of a gigantic lotus [Lord Vishnu's resting bed] out of which springs the main Assembly Hall above."[52] Other features of the assembly include modern sanitary fittings, a central duct system, elevators, escalators, and staircases for vertical movement, concealed electrical wires and plumbing pipes in concrete columns, wood-paneled walls inside the hall, and an electronically controlled public-announcement system. The assembly hall itself rises three stories to its dome, which is eight meters high, its interior surface finished in teakwood, its paneling forming radial patterns.

The Central Assembly Building—the Vithalbhai Bhavan—is connected by a bridge on two sides to the central blocks of the Sardar Bhavan (the secretariat) and the Narmada Bhavan, which houses the offices of the heads of departments. The cantilever design renders the bridge visually free of the structures it connects. The bridge was designed to connect legislative and executive facilities, but because of fear of terrorism and because it is so long, no one uses it.

In all, the assembly complex is 17,700 square meters in size. All the mis-givings and lapses notwithstanding, it was inaugurated by Sharda Mukerjee, the Gujarat governor, on July 8, 1982. In Chandigarh, Le Corbusier had questioned the significance "of Indian style in the world if you accept machines, trousers and democracy,"[53] and the same problem of finding the Indian style had been debated in the building of Bhubaneswar. In Gandhinagar, that question seems to have been answered, however unsatisfactorily. The assembly building won the best-building design in 1985 from the Guild of Practicing Architects of India. In voting for the Gujarat assembly, the jury was affirming that historicism and modernity can co-exist, even if awkwardly. The capitol complex designs in Gandhinagar did not come from an interweaving of secular and religious spheres; rather, they sprang from the ability of the planners to resist that interweaving, while making use of it. The Hindu identity has often hinged on the capacity to assimilate—to find a place to stand and to have the freedom to do so. The assembly dome, for better or worse, is a modern stage on which the zenith and nadirs of Gujarat's history continue to play themselves out.

5

Conclusions

NEVER FORGET. A good axiom. But there is a great deal more to remember than British rule, even though the debate over the universal impact of colonialism has been narrowly framed into an ideological wrangling between the bogus historicism of the postmodern, neoconservative defense of colonial rule made by Dinesh D'Souza, who, like Le Corbusier, views it as a *force morale* for development,[1] and the abandoned angst of the deconstructionism of the late Edward Said, Gayatri Spivak, and others, who, like Frantz Fanon, have viewed it as inherently evil. True, at the beginning of the twentieth century, power and autocracy interacted to produce the aesthetics of imperial authority in New Delhi, where colonial life was sanitized in the spacious symphony of Garden City greenery and imperial power was celebrated in "the grouping of public buildings in a monumental center as well as radiating axial vistas, terminating in polygons, ovals, and circles of open space which enthroned monuments and buildings as imposing visual accents."[2] But there is also indigenous creativity: the blazing talent of twentieth-century Indians, the inspiration of a people held in subjugation for more than two centuries, but not bowed.

And there is remembrance itself—the capacity of a culture to bring itself to mind and to assimilate old with new. The stories of Chandigarh, Bhubaneswar, and Gandhinagar in the second half of the twentieth century represent an interplay between memory and creativity for a promising, although not perfect, future. The linkage of these two ideas in architecture and planning is the cornerstone of the making of the modern Indian state. Building on the idea that the power to create is stronger than the will to subjugate, the three state capitals as well as scores of new towns and redesigned neighborhoods in old cities testify to the stunning proposition that the twentieth century has been arguably nothing less than a golden age of Indian architectural achievement.

The point is beyond argument. In 1947, there were fewer than two hundred registered architects in India, even though the British had implemented the mega-project of New Delhi (1911) and scores of other building projects; consequently, Chandigarh's development had to be entrusted first to the American Albert Mayer and, later, to the Frenchman Le Corbusier; and in Bhubaneswar, the German Otto Koenigsberger drew the plan. Building Gandhinagar nearly a generation after independence, the Indians remained tentative about their talent and tried unsuccessfully to recruit the American Louis Kahn to plan and design the capital. But today, Indian architects compete globally. Besides Charles Correa and Balkrishna Doshi, their ranks include, among others, Raj Rewal, Uttam Jain, Kulbushan Jain, Ranjit Sabikhi, Hasmukh Patel, Kuldip Singh. Rewal, for example, recently completed the Agha Khan Centre in Lisbon, and Correa is building the Center for Brain Research at the Massachusetts Institute of Technology. Aesthetically and ideologically, this group spans a spectrum that ranges from the boldly inventive forms of Correa to the intellectually inquisitive designs of Doshi to the evolutionary approach to modern architecture of Rewal.

But the story of city building in India has been fraught with controversy. This stems from the fact that efforts at building by both the British and Indians have never been singular in purpose. When the British built New Delhi, the images from both Garden City and City Beautiful clashed. On the one hand, the British called for a tightly knit, high-density city that evoked broad boulevards and the high-rise buildings of the Champs Elysées or Bombay; on the other hand, the British felt that in hot and humid India they must have space, greenery, and low-density because "we could not breathe with a Champs Elysées."[3] Crouching bungalows on spacious parcels of land ensured distance between the English and the Indians, which had become the objective of British policy under Crown rule following the Mutiny (1857). Similarly, the desire to build something that would reflect and exalt British "achievement" and also acknowledge Indian tradition as a concession to the Indians produced mixed results in New Delhi.

New Delhi remains the most ostentatious expression of the raj. Shortly after independence, Jawaharlal Nehru, the cosmopolitan prime minister, derided New Delhi as "most un-Indian."[4] Nehru's nationalist remark, made at the outset of the building of Chandigarh, was to set the terms of national debate on the character of new cities and national architectural style in postcolonial India. Nehru felt that the average American or English town planner could not understand the social background of India. Still, he realized that modern India could not be built without Western technology, and consequently he supported creating the Indian Institutes of Technology and the Indian Institutes of Management (modeled after the Massachusetts Institute of Technology and Harvard Business School, respectively). But Western technology had to be fused with Indian cultural traditions, just as he had fused political ideologies of Communism and democracy to create democratic socialism as a means for leading India on the path of planned economic development.

India today, as in the past, continues to straddle two very different cultures. This has been evident whether India was attempting to abolish the dreadful custom of *sati* (the immolation of a Hindu widow on the funeral pyre of her husband) or fighting the grim practice of caste untouchability; whether opposing the raj or demanding swaraj (self-rule); whether resisting laissez-faire policies of the British or promoting swadeshi (indigenous good); it has been evident in the debates between Western education and the vernacular tradition, between the communal and the secular. It is precisely this dual identity, this two-headed Janus quality, that ensures India's ability to invent, to create, now as before. Just as the British were torn between two worlds in deciding the character of New Delhi, so would be the Indians in building state capitals in Chandigarh, Bhubaneswar, and Gandhinagar. Prevailing international ideas in planning and architecture were to influence the British as well as the Indians, the respective rhetorics, imperial and nationalist, notwithstanding.

To a degree, the British, too, were influenced by the ideas of Beaux Arts city planning, American style, which tended to group monumental public buildings in the center, leaving the rest of the city to green spaces. What Nehru was objecting to in New Delhi was not the "leafy capital" per se—for that resembled bucolic India; he was objecting to the overmonumentality of its official buildings decorated with classicism as the urban centerpiece attesting to British rule of India. As the British art critic Sir George Birdwood declared, "It is not a cantonment we have to lay out at Delhi, but an Imperial City—the symbol of the British Raj in India—and it must like Rome be built for eternity."[5] It therefore followed that in postcolonial India, a new paradigm of planning and architectural style had to be invented for capital cities. Prime Minister Nehru provided the imaginative shape to the new capital at Chandigarh: "Let this be a new town symbolic of the freedom of India, unfettered by the traditions of the past . . . an expression of the nation's faith in the future."[6] Arguably, Nehru's greatest gift was his ability to bring to the surface, through his historical vision, images that fused traditional India with the modern world. He thus introduced a modernist discourse for the making of a nation-state—a discourse that was to encourage his countrymen to live with a more encompassing sense of what constituted their world.

The imaginative shape that Nehru had provided for India's urban future at Chandigarh was fervently embraced by India's political leaders, and it was variously interpreted in the building of Bhubaneswar in Orissa and Gandhinagar in Gujarat, as well as in the many other new urban communities that sprang up in postcolonial India. In Chandigarh, the elegant and quick-witted careerwoman Rajkumari Amrit Kaur, India's minister of health, declared, "As a Punjabi I want the new capital of the Punjab to be the last word in beauty, in simplicity and in standards of such comfort as it is our duty to provide to every human-being." Chief Minister Gopichand Bhargava hoped that Chandigarh would be "the world's most charming capital."[7] In Bhubaneswar, Nehru sought a more equitable urban solution when he declared that the new capital would not "be a city of big buildings . . . and it would accord with our idea of reducing differences between the rich and the poor."[8] In Gujarat, while the young visionary Balkrishna Doshi tried to visualize the future of Indian cities in the "images of the new world" by Louis Kahn and his new interpretation of the modern skyscraper, the political leadership of the state agonized about building its new capital at Gandhinagar to memorialize the Mahatma and his ideals.

In both colonial and postcolonial India, the urban debate and architectural discourse was never particularly local; it was energetically universal. The ruler of a princely state and regional politicians were always eager to draw from the global experience in city planning and architectural styling. On the other hand, the pressure from the nationalists to search in the national past for the "Indian city" only inflamed censure of Western ideas. Within the Indian political establishment, architectural ambitions and tastes broke along ideological and cultural lines. Progressives with wide exposure to Western values were prepared to accept ideas from the West in order to modernize India. Conservatives steeped in tradition argued fervently for a grander, visible echo of the past that would restore national greatness, a sense of being "somebody again." This naturally produced contradiction in purpose —a debate that government architect Julius Vaz clarified in Bhubaneswar:

> The tendency [in postindependence Indian] architecture is to accept the glamorous experiments in architectural innovation of "novelty" and "stunts" borrowed from . . . European and American [cities] . . . without discriminating their use and relevancy in our case. The result is what we generally see today in some of our larger cities[,] "a mongrel style" . . . correctly termed by the Prime Minister of India.
> . . . What is the architectural character to which we in India should aspire for our . . . buildings? Some of us are in favour of the strict revival of the Indian Traditional forms [in] architecture; others feel that an international style would automatically be the outcome due to the tremendous impact of [the] world civilization in India; and . . . still [others] pray for an evolution of a new character by accepting all the ideas the world has to offer us and [assimilating] the new forms [into] our aesthetic traditions. I belong to the last [latter] school of thought.[9]

Vaz demanded meaning from what he observed, not merely a feeling of the grandeur of architecture. In the wake of independence, Prime Minister Nehru felt that political sovereignty without economic progress was empty. Just as Anglophile Indian princes in colonial India had been attracted to Western education and technology as necessary tools for modernization, in postcolonial India dependence on the West for modernization continued, quite apart from the nationalistic rhetoric that was issued from the electoral hustings.

At least since the time when the Bengali brahman Rammohan Roy (1772–1833) launched the Bengal Renaissance by revitalizing Hindu philosophic religious dogma and challenging archaic traditional customs on the basis of reason and rationality in thought, a platform had existed from which to view prevailing social customs from a modernist position. By embracing the best in British education while retaining his Bengali brahman roots, the social reformer Roy was a pioneer in illuminating the phenomenon of "Western" and "Indian" histories in India. Spending much of his career trying to dislodge Indian history from its religious moorings, he emerged as the first portent of cross-cultural identity, though it took more than a century after his death in Bristol for full fruition of that promise. In his writings in several Calcutta publications, many of them started by Roy himself, he was not merely challenging old religious dogmas and traditional practices: he was promoting the new ideas and syncretic cultural concepts that blossomed in India's urban soil and that influenced generations of Indians from Rabindranath Tagore to Satyajit Ray to Arundhati Roy. He believed that such syncretism could only enrich Indian history. He came to see himself as a historical outsider in India, but one who could use his Indian duality, the famous double consciousness (the competing identities of being Indian and Western-educated) as a lens through which to observe and interrogate the nation's history.

Nehru, himself a product of this modernist tradition, was fully familiar with the urban utopias in city planning of the late nineteenth and early twentieth centuries. He recognized their potential for improving old Indian cities and building new. In various ways in several of his speeches and writings, Nehru asserted that the pluralistic Indian experience stood at the center of national history, at least for those who cared to look at conflict, rather than only continuity, to view irony, rather than pleasing myth. Nehru seemed to be saying: Specters haunt, and Indian memory is haunted. India's collective memory awaited new voices, new ideas, and new storytellers who might peer into its contradictions and make irony the lifeblood of the story, rather than merely the unseen background. At the very least, such an approach might change the national landscape.

New Delhi itself stood as an example of imperial arrogance and contradictory ideas. In New Delhi, Edwin Lutyens had called for a more tightly knit, high-density city. When a voice was raised in favor of the City Beautiful, which would allow heroic architecture, he approvingly wrote to his wife, Lady Emily, "Now they want, apparently, a town rather than a Garden City. I agree to this and am glad if they do it."[10] With its emphasis on classicism, belief in urbanism, and faith in the Beaux Arts tradition, the City Beautiful movement marked a watershed between the passing of agrarian life and the emergence of industrial promise in the Gilded

Age of American history. With its abiding faith in urbanism and uncritical belief in the city as the means to the 'good life' beyond mere survival, the movement aimed at rectifying the problems of tenements, overcrowding, and corruption in municipal government that scarred the city in the 1890s. The movement was supported by left-leaning, middle-class and upper-middle-class liberals who, in the face of a growing urban poor population, were increasingly fearful about their own fate and who hoped to cure city ills and control social behavior through beautification of the decaying cities. The idiom the movement leaders used in their ideal civic centers was the Beaux Arts style, named for the famous Ecole des Beaux-Arts in Paris, which called for order, dignity, and harmony in cities by introducing the concept of a monumental core, or civic center—an arrangement of buildings intended to inspire the fleeing middle classes back into the fold of the city. In summer 1893, the ideals of the City Beautiful were showcased at the World's Columbian Exposition in Chicago. Later they were incorporated into the 1901 plan for Washington, D.C., by Daniel Burnham, the director of construction for the Chicago fair. To be sure, given European prescriptions for American urban ills, there were skeptics. Notable was the influential Chicago-based architect Louis Sullivan, who complained that the reliance on European ideas and the monumental idiom set indigenous American architecture back decades. Although trained in the Beaux Arts tradition at MIT and the Ecole des Beaux-Arts, Sullivan ultimately rejected the standard classical ornamentation of the day; he replaced it with highly original, organic architectural details inspired by nature—and thereby created a definite American architectural identity.

Nehru, the future architect of modern India, while exhibiting an embracingly cross-cultural notion of what architecture should be, shared Sullivan's rejection of European classicism as expressed in the City Beautiful. Having spent his childhood in the religious city of Allahabad, where the Ganges and the Jamuna, India's holiest rivers, come into confluence, and having received his education in industrial England, where he witnessed urban blight and decay, Nehru had wide knowledge of Western modernism. The ideas that appealed to his disciplined, speculative nature are easy to spot. Just as he had fused Western democracy and socialism to create democratic socialism, he approved of a fusion of the Garden City and its neighborhood block with the promise of modernism and saw it as the best planning-architectural paradigm for the Indian city. At an architectural seminar in New Delhi in 1959, he defined the direction for the Indian city:

> Architecture to a large extent is a product of the age. It cannot isolate itself
> from the social conditions. . . . The static condition in regard to architecture
> in India in the last 200 or 300 years . . . really was a reflection of the static con-
> dition of the Indian mind or Indian conditions. In fact, India has been static,
> architecturally considered, for the last few hundred years. The great buildings

which we admire date back to an earlier period. we were static even before the British came. In fact, the British came because we were static. A society which ceases to go ahead necessarily becomes weak. . . .

. . . Today I believe very good work is being done all over the world by creative architects. It is a delight to see plans and designs and pictures of this new work being done. We should not be afraid of innovation.

Nehru then focused on Chandigarh:

I have welcomed very greatly one experiment in India, Chandigarh. Many people argue about it, and some dislike it. It is the biggest example in India of experimental architecture. It hits you on the head, and makes you think. You may squirm at the impact but it has made you think and imbibe new ideas, and the one thing which India requires in many fields is being hit on the head so that it may think. I do not like every building in Chandigarh. I like some of them very much. I like the general conception of the township very much but, above all, I like the creative approach, not being tied down to what has been done by our forefathers but thinking in new terms, of light and air and ground and water and human beings. Therefore, Chandigarh is of enormous importance. There is no doubt that Le Corbusier is a man with a powerful and creative type of mind.[11]

This was the most emphatic endorsement of the Garden City and modernism by Nehru. In the early twentieth century, the Englishman Ebenezer Howard, the American Frank Lloyd Wright, and the Frenchman Le Corbusier had postulated their ideal city in response to the prevailing urban ills of their age.[12] In his *Vers une architecture*, Le Corbusier glorified the centralized metropolis, inspired by science and technology. Although in Chandigarh Le Corbusier essentially ended up implementing a Garden City plan, after some modifications, which had been drawn earlier by Albert Mayer, he remained convinced to the end of his life that the harsher side of industrialization had to be tamed by confronting the machine age rather than by building leafy green cities. Wright, in his Broadacare City, postulated "a city without walls, spiritual or material, which would nonetheless be a stable community": in his ideal city there would be "organic" reconciliation between man and nature, to be achieved through radical decentralization and in which a citizen would find his individuality in the family, the building block of Wright's new society.[13] Although it is doubtful whether Wright had any abiding faith in the stability of the family, his purported belief in the institution certainly resonated with Indian values. But his emphasis on the decentralization of power must have sounded suspicious to the political leadership of communally divided India.

The *Times* hailed Howard's *To-morrow: A Peaceful Path to Real Reform* as "ingenious," but it also declared the Garden City difficult to create.[14] Howard proposed to build his ideal society by building the Garden City, a tightly organized urban center surrounded by a "green belt" of farms and parks. The Garden City would contain "quiet residential neighborhoods and facilities for a full range of commercial, industrial, and cultural activities." The Garden City was not intended to be a "satellite" town serving a great metropolis; rather, it was to replace the metropolis as people changed one way of life for another. "My proposal is that there should be an earnest attempt made to organise a migratory movement of population from our overcrowded centres to sparsely-settled rural districts; that the mind of the public should not be confused, or the efforts of organisers wasted in a premature attempt to accomplish this work on a national scale, but that great thought and attention shall be first concentrated on a single movement yet one sufficiently large to be at once attractive and resourceful."[15]

With the conviction of a missionary, Howard had declared that town and country must be married, which would produce a new civilization. Howard's ideas resonated with Nehru, who had served as the mayor of his native Allahabad and who was only too familiar with decaying, overcrowded Indian cities. "We want to urbanize the village, not take away the people from the villages to the towns. However well we may deal with the towns, the problem of the villages of India will remain for a long time and any social standards that we seek to introduce will be judged ultimately not by what happened in Delhi but in the villages of India,"[16] declared Nehru. By modernizing rural India, Nehru was proposing to improve urban India, and the Garden City plan, with its anti-urban bias, provided the best solution. It also conformed to Indian conditions and sounded politically correct after the imperial rhetoric of New Delhi that had dominated Indian urban thought in the first half of the twentieth century.

Deriding New Delhi for its "over-scale sterility and stiltedness" and blaming Washington, D.C. for its monumentality, Mayer, who in his anti-urban aesthetic drew inspiration from the Radburn plan (1929) and the American Greenbelt towns of the 1930s, declared his purpose in Chandigarh:

> We want to create a beautiful city. . . . Since the City Beautiful concept was thrown out fifty years ago, and the functionalists and sociologists took over, the concept of a large and compelling and beautiful unity has not been enriched by these important later additional and integral concepts, but has rather been replaced. . . . We have creatively fused them, but we are unabashedly seeking beauty. . . .
>
> Can anybody who has studied our proposed new civic centers [in America]— such as for example Foley Square in New York, or the Chicago Civic Center, seriously claim that they have an abiding harmony or sense of scale or humanity. . . . We have turned to some of the great exemplars—to the Concorde in Paris, the Piazza San Marco, St. Peter's, and studied them . . . to extract the essence.

Our basic purpose [in Chandigarh] is to create a sense of pride in the citizen, not only in this his own city, but in India, its past and its potential imminent future. . . . We are seeking symbols, to restore or to create pride and confidence in [the Indian] himself and in his country.[17]

The centerpiece of Mayer's Garden City plan was to be a residential neighborhood unit, or superblock, a planning device from the 1920s, the city developing from the multiplication of such units, rather than from a single dominant formal concept. Mayer believed that "the neighborhood concept is . . . even more [valuable] in India where so many people are villagers at heart." He felt that the "nature of our neighborhood is intimate. The local shopping centre preserves, as far as we can [be] consistent with orderly development to do so, the excitement and gaiety of the bazaar—the people undisturbed by traffic in their social preoccupation with shopping and visiting."[18] Mayer was acting on Nehru's instructions, who had told him "to build up community life on a higher scale without breaking up . . . [India's] old foundations." The eclectic Nehru wanted "to utilize [Western technology] and fit it into Indian resources and Indian conditions."[19]

In the end, the man who would deliver Nehru his dream was the Frenchman Le Corbusier, whose vision of the urban future outpaced the age in which he lived. By bringing down old walls that imprisoned India and defying ancient prejudices that shackled Indians, Le Corbusier opened the doors to modernism's golden age, which stretched from the 1920s through the 1960s, promising to make the world a better place through design. This was to be achieved, according to the menu of early modernism, by providing plenty of unadorned open space, abundant natural light through large expanses of glass, and an intimate connection with the outdoors. The advocates of this optimistic age—they ranged from pioneers of the international style like Mies, Gropius, and Le Corbusier to more organic modernists like Frank Lloyd Wright and the Viennese native Richard Neutra and postwar innovators like George Nelson and the husband-and-wife team Charles and Ray Eames—began working with new forms, new materials, and new manufacturing methods, promising to transform society through design.

These ideas were available in India, at least to the upper classes. The late distinguished writer and editor of MARG (Bombay) was validating Rammohan Roy's rationalism when he observed that Indian "architecture of the future will . . . be a humanistic creative activity, not only in terms of human beings as they are today—but as they may become under the conditions of the free societies released by the urges incipient in the Asiatic and African world today."[20] It is easy to imagine how animated Nehru, who worried so much that the nation's inexcusable religious anachronism might ruin the world's greatest experiment in democracy and secularism, would have felt about the notion that life would imitate design. He was even prepared to allow excesses to the architectural demigod Le Corbusier in the hope that modernism would modernize India. Le Corbusier "may produce extravagances occasionally," Nehru would say in justification, "but it is better to be extravagant than to be a person with no mind at all."[21] But modern design was also about distillation—the act of boiling elements down to their essence and eliminating the unnecessary, while keeping what delighted the eye. Modernist masters were not so much reinventing the wheel; rather, with modern materials and manufacturing methods, they were reinterpreting it. This, too, was appealing to Nehru in those early years after independence when he was drawing the blueprints for the young Indian nation.

In a photograph from 1964, Le Corbusier stands at Nehru's side—the two men who had boldly taken the future of Indian urban life into their hands. The old architect is reported to have said, "I am 77 years old, and my moral philosophy can be reduced to this: in life it is necessary above all to act and by that I mean, to act in a spirit of modesty with exactitude, with precision. The only possible atmosphere in which to carry on creative work is one in which these qualities prevail: regularity, modesty, continuity, perseverance."[22] Meeting at the end of their lives (Nehru died on May 27, 1964; Le Corbusier on August 27, 1965), they could view the miracle of the modernist experiment in India that they had brought about. If Nehru had provided opportunity to the Frenchman to experiment with his ideas without restraints, Le Corbusier had helped the Indian prime minister embrace the machine age and its aesthetic potential that would transcend time. Acknowledging Le Corbusier to be the father of modern architecture in India, the art critic William Curtis has noted:

> Modern architecture was adopted during the Nehru period as a suitable vehicle for the technological and social programmes of rapid modernisation. After independence, it was necessary to make a clean break with the cultural forms of the Raj: modernism had some of the right associations with "progress" and "liberalism." But Gandhian admiration for the supposed moral integrity of the village was never totally displaced by the progressive ethos. Even today, craft and industry have a special alliance in India and this allows the use of computer and intensive manual labour in the same project. Many different societies and stages of development coexist, and the tension between country and city is continual. Some artists try to bridge the gap, combining modernity with the lessons of the rural vernacular. The Modern Movement's dream of harmony with nature is reinvigorated by an older philosophical framework placing man and community in a natural and spiritual order.[23]

In the 1960s, the experiment in modernism was expanded by Louis Kahn in his seminal work on the Indian Institute of Management (1962–74), Ahmedabad. But unlike Le Corbusier, Kahn was diffident, and, while he had the backing of Ahmedabad's cotton plutocrats, he lacked the support of a patron with Nehru's stature or his facility with cross-cultural ideas. Moreover, while Kahn had the attention of young Indian architects, he did not have their "unconditional" devotion. Kahn's metaphysical ideas found a natural synergy with Indian classical traditions, although his penchant for abstract geometric and parallel structures predisposed him to Islamic architecture, particularly Mughal examples, but unlike Le Corbusier, he was not able to conjure a vision for India's future. Kahn had gained international attention for his work, but he had not revolutionized the profession—something that Le Corbusier did do. Still, Kahn helped to diversify the architectural discourse in India, restored the dignity of the vernacular brick in architectural form, and provided a counterpoint to Le Corbusier's work, leaving young Indians to reconcile the positions of the two masters.

One reason for modernism's gaining quick currency in technologically stilted and economically underdeveloped India was that it was never monolithic in its emphasis. Technological innovation and aesthetic self-expression were seen as the twin forces in design that could solve housing and other social problems. Even though the leading principles of the modern movement had been obscured by modernity interpreted as a monumental classicism in politically and economically torn Europe and America in the 1930s, the postwar building boom gave modernism a mythical importance. Modernist buildings became popular with developers because of low costs and quicker construction. The miracle of modernism to meet a surging housing demand, to revitalize decaying cities in postwar Europe, was not lost on India, which itself was burdened with refugees in the north and the east as a result of the partition of the subcontinent. Modernism, with its social and technological imperatives, appeared to be the natural answer and one that would facilitate a reconciliation of both modern technology and indigenous methods. Modernism was free of the encumbrances of imperialism and was therefore acceptable for adaptation to an invented national identity. As Curtis observed:

> The search for "roots" takes place within the structure of a modern state. A secular democracy, India contains deeply embedded religious strata. The task is one of revival but without overt reference to the imagery of particular communal groups. With a perspective that was not available to his pre-Raj ancestors, the contemporary Indian architect is able to look back over millennia of Buddhist, Hindu, Islamic, vernacular and colonial inventions and to seek out common themes. . . . But the architect also needs schemata relevant to the problems and technologies of today, and that is where the more recent inheritance of Modernism is relevant.[24]

The application of modernism in Chandigarh, Bhubaneswar, Gandhinagar, and elsewhere in India produced different results in the hands of different architects, however. Le Corbusier's own influence was not even on Indian architects, as is visible in the architectural treatment in the three capital cities, as well as in other cities. "The facile imitators erred in the direction of pastiches using concrete scoops and ugly *pilotis;* the more discriminating grasped his manner and analysis and extended [Le Corbusier's] principles."[25] That is where the rub is: what separated the "imitators" from the "discriminating" architects was, and is, social class. Those young men and a limited number of women who belonged to elite families were able to buttress their education by international studies and travel; those who could not afford the luxury of international travel remained limited in their vision. Recognizing the stakes involved in struggles over rival versions of the Indian city and architecture between the public works department and private practitioners, the United Nations consultant Vernon Newcombe suggested that the government architects who were building in Gandhinagar travel to Europe to gain information on new technologies and ideas. It was a matter of exposure as a source of inspiration for new ideas and a means of reinterpreting the Indian past. At the time of Gandhinagar's construction in the mid-1960s, Doshi recognized the limited impact of modernism in shaping the vision of the architect when he noted:

> The scientists visualize that by the twenty-first century we shall have command of extreme climatic conditions, widespread use of telecommunications, transportation facilities, and the general use of electronic instruments. We shall have medicine to reduce fatigue and increase our capacity to work and prolong our life span. . . .
>
> What image does the architect have, that matches this authority.
>
> It is perhaps not surprising that the architect's vision is so small by comparison, since, unlike the economists and scientists, he has no real power to change the world. In spite of his boasts, his buildings do not really change the face of the earth. . . .
>
> Even people themselves don't really require architects; except in so far as modern fashion tells them to. They can live anywhere, because they can adapt themselves to almost any condition. . . .
>
> In fact even architects don't believe that the principles of modern architecture are essential to modern life. Many of them prefer to live in old houses.
>
> Of all the design problems in the man-made environment, the only one where everybody likes to consult architects is that of monument design. . . .
>
> Yet, in spite of this, architects talk complacently of designing entire cities, and occasionally, as in the case of Brasilia or Chandigarh, actually manage to implement their designs. . . .
>
> The statisticians say that in the year 2000 India will have 500 million people [India's population in fact topped the billion mark by that date], which means that we would have either many more cities or the actual cities with five to ten times the present population. As architects, if we accept this fact, we will have to reconsider an entire attitude towards design of the environment so that the

change in economic and social conditions will not continuously disturb the basic structure of the city.

The Indian architect today should design for the present with the experience of other countries and the changes anticipated in the future.[26]

The question of the stakes involved in the struggles over rival visions of a nation's future not only leads to the political and social meanings of what architects build but also provides an angle of understanding about the confluence of history and memory for intellectuals and for larger societies. Partitioned India demonstrated two competing versions of history and ideology: Gandhi's vexed, sometimes mystical, attachment to villages as a source of ideals for building a new India competed with Nehru's inclination for cities. Gandhi had tirelessly campaigned in the hope that his life might help mediate the nation's treacherous journey between memory and expectation about villages, about religious violence and about the untouchables. Nehru, on the other hand, was illuminating the phenomenon of "alternative" histories of India, especially with reference to the city and religion. He spent much of his career as an intellectual and a political leader trying to confront traditional India, and his Western training placed him in an oppositional —and sometimes advantageous—position to comment on the struggle over memory in Indian society. In Nehru's writings and speeches, he was portraying a historical vision for India in which urbanism flourished, where villages became citified and where modern industry thrived. Modernism in India would serve two separate masters who had different ideologies, which explains the constrictions it felt and the tensions it generated in the careers of architects like Doshi, Correa, and others who came under its spell.

India's experiment in modernism and social urban planning was also severely restricted because of shortages of materials. With the exception of brick and, to a limited extent, concrete and plaster, until recently wood, glass, steel, and aluminum remained in short supply. But this disadvantage of a scarcity of materials was turned into an advantage by the more imaginative architects. Charles Correa sagely noted:

Architecture is a complex thing involving, at one and the same time, the pragmatic problem of construction and function; philosophical consideration of systems and concepts; and the painter-sculptor's world of visual form. It is totally irresponsible to divorce the problem of visual form from the other two which are the roots and guts of architecture. Without them, architecture is reduced to a mere matter of photogenic "styling." But an architect can extract a high degree of "efficiency" from the materials he is using *through his visual sense*—if he can put the simplest and crudest materials to work in the pursuit of meaningful forms.

Correa added that "the real incentive one has for working in India is that you always feel a new series of answers will help you break through into a new landscape—of course you never really do: but the hope somehow keeps Indian architecture going."[27] Restricting modernism further was what Kenneth Frampton has called "Critical Regionalism": the particularities of a place, such as air, wind, water, topography.[28]

To a great extent, the importance of a particular building or quadrangle is not quantifiable. Pedagogy is intimately tied to the sense of place. The question is, How does architecture most effectively work the tension between tradition and the modern, between the particular and the universal? After independence, India was in the throws of a love affair with modernism and was gripped by its promise that design, when freed from the strictures of the past and empowered with new forms, materials, and manufacturing methods, seemed capable of making the world a better place. But conformity is not, and it never was, a popular practicing virtue in India, and Indians could never, alas, live up to the purist ideal of Le Corbusier's Sarabhai House (1955) or his Maisons Jaoul (1956). After its first impact, modernism lost its way, resulting in idiosyncratic building designs that architect Gautam Bhatia has sardonically called "Chandni Chowk Chippendale, Tamil Tiffany, Maratha Chauvinism, Bengali Asceticism, Akali Folly, Marwari Pragmatism, Punjabi Baroque, Bania Gothic, Bhaiyya Eclectic, Brahmin Medievalism, Parsi Propriety and Anglo-Indian Rococo."[29]

Still, along with the presumptuous architecture that would make an orthodox modernist cringe, the best Indian architecture, which represented the thoughtful synthesis of old and new, the fusing of regional and universal, and the blending of local craft with modern technology, would evolve after the masters of modernism had been consigned to history. Partly as icons of a refurbished Indian identity, partly just as old men searching for their more active and noble youth, and partly as symbols of changelessness in a rapidly industrializing India, veterans like Correa, Doshi, and Rewal discovered a heroic nostalgia in architecture. In their idealistic youth they had so fervently sought answers from the masters of modernism to build a new India; they now truly belong in a society that is building monuments for the future and rapidly forgetting the burden of colonial rule and the deep religious and communal roots of the partition. But without modernism's pedagogy, that story would have turned out very differently—a story that deserves to be told another time.

NOTES

CHAPTER 1. The Making of the Gujarat State

1. *History of Gujarat*, ed., James M. Campbell (reprint; New Delhi: Vintage Press, 1989), 1. Originally published as *Gazetteer of the Bombay Presidency: History of Gujarat*, vol. 1, part 1 (hereafter, *Gazetteer*) (Bombay: Government Central Press, 1896).

2. Ibid., 1–2.

3. M. R. Majumdar, *Cultural History of Gujarat* (New York: New York Humanities Press, 1966), ix.

4. *Gazetteer*, 79.

5. Majumdar, *Cultural History of Gujarat*, 95.

6. See Ravi Kalia, *Bhubaneswar: From a Temple Town to a Capital City* (Carbondale: Southern Illinois University Press, 1994).

7. Majumdar, *Cultural History of Gujarat*, 97–99.

8. Stanley Wolpert, *A New History of India*, 4th ed. (New York: Oxford University Press, 1993), 105–7.

9. Philip Ward, *Gujarat, Daman, Diu: A Travel Guide* (Cambridge, U.K.: Oleander Press, 1994), 204; see also *Gazetteer*, 521.

10. *Gazetteer*, 522.

11. Ward, *Gujarat, Daman, Diu*, 205.

12. Majumdar, *Cultural History of Gujarat*, 106. Also see D. B. Diskalkar's essay "An Outline of the Religious History of Gujarat," in *The Gujarat Parishad Proceedings*, 1924.

13. *Gazetteer*, 530. For a good account of Arab sources on India, see Sir Henry M. Elliot and John Dowson, eds., *The History of India as Told by Its Own Historians: The Muhammadan Period*, 31 vols. (Calcutta: Susil Gupta, 1952–59).

14. *Gazetteer*, 530.

15. Ibid., 530.

16. Ibid., 531.

17. Ibid., 429.

18. For a good history of the Marathas, see G. S. Sardesai, *New History of the Marathas*, 3 vols. (2nd imp.; Bombay: Phoenix Publications, 1957). For a study on the Maratha agrarian policies, see André Wink, *Land and Sovereignty in India: Agrarian Society and Politics under the Eighteenth-Century Maratha Svarajya* (New York: Cambridge University Press, 1986).

19. *Gazetteer*, 385.

20. Wolpert, *A New History*, 143.

21. Ibid., 144.

22. Ibid., 145.

23. R. D. Choksey, *Economic Life in the Bombay Gujarat, 1800–1939* (Bombay: Asia Publishing House, 1968), 10.

24. The British followed a similar policy later in Orissa. For details, see Kalia, *Bhubaneswar*, 28–29.

25. Cited by Choksey, *Economic Life*, 10.

26. *Gazetteer*, 435–36.

27. Wolpert, *A New History*, 204.

28. *Survey and Settlement into Broach Taluka*, 1874, 6–9.

29. C. A. Bayly, "From Company to Crown: Nineteenth Century India and the Visual Representation," in *An Illustrated History of Modern India, 1600–1947*, ed. C. A. Bayly (New Delhi: Oxford University Press, 1991), 130.

30. Wolpert, *A New History*, 205.

31. *Gazetteer*, 430.

32. Ibid., 433–37.

33. Choksey, *Economic Life*, 22, 66–67.

34. For a good discussion on British Orientalism, see David Kopf, *British Orientalism and the Bengal Renaissance: The Dynamics of Indian Modernization, 1773–1834* (Berkeley: University of California Press, 1969).

35. Wolpert, *A New History*, 209.

36. R. L. Raval, *Socio-Religious Reform Movements in Gujarat during the Nineteenth Century* (New Delhi: Ess Ess Publications, 1987), 42. Also see K. M. Jhaveri, *Further Milestones in Gujarati Literature*, 2nd ed. (Bombay: Forbes Gujarati Sabha, 1956), 4–5.

37. R. L. Raval, "Cultural Perspectives of the Emerging Nationalism in the Nineteenth Century Gujarat," in *Regional Roots of Indian Nationalism*, ed. Markand Mehta (New Delhi: Criterion Publications, 1990), 19.

38. Biographers of Mahatma Gandhi have so far lamentably ignored exploring these early ideas and their impact on him.

39. For comparison of the Gujarat political situation with Assam and Orissa, see Sudhir Chandra, "From Gujaratni Asmita to Gujaratni Rashtriye Asmita," in *Regional Roots*, 28–38. For fuller discussion on the Oriya movement, see Ravi Kalia, *Bhubaneswar*, 27–63.

40. See Kalia, *Bhubaneswar*, 46–48.

41. Ibid., 51.

42. For a full discussion of the integration of Indian states, see V. P. Menon, *The Story of the Integration of Indian States* (New Delhi: Sangam Books, 1979).

43. Cited in Nagindas Sanghvi, *Gujarat: A Political Analysis* (Surat: Centre for Social Studies, 1996), 137.

44. Ibid., 141.

45. Ibid., 149.

CHAPTER 2. The Politics of Site

1. Govt. of Gujarat, Public Works Dept., Capital Project Circle, "Preliminary Report on Gandhinagar, the Capital of Gujarat," Ahmedabad, 1961, 1. Another document from

the Public Works Department (undated) gives March 1, 1960, as the date on which Dr. Jivraj Mehta declared Gandhinagar as the site for the new capital; however, the government literature overwhelmingly puts the date as March 19, 1960.

2. Ibid.

3. For a full discussion on Chandigarh and Bhubaneswar, see Ravi Kalia's *Chandigarh: The Making of an Indian City* (New Delhi: Oxford University Press, 1999), and *Bhubaneswar: From a Temple Town to a Capital City* (Carbondale: Southern Illinois University Press, and New Delhi: Oxford University Press, 1994).

4. Gulam Mohammed Sheikh, ed., *Contemporary Art in Baroda* (New Delhi: Tulika, 1997), 17. The book was sponsored by Indian Petrochemical Corporation, Vadodara, India.

5. There is a controversy over Sayajirao's date of birth. Some accounts place it as March 17, 1863, others as March 17, 1862. Since he ascended to the throne on Dec. 3, 1881, at the age of eighteen, the birth date of 1862 is widely accepted. Fatesingh Rao P. Gaekwad (*Sayajirao of Baroda: The Prince and the Man* [Bombay: Popular Prakashan, 1989]) puts his grandfather's date of accession as 1875; however, Murali Lal Nagar, in his *Shri Sayajirao Gaekwad, Maharaja of Baroda: The Prime Promoter of Public Libraries* (Columbia, Mo.: International Library Center, 1992), places the accession as being on December 3, 1881.

6. Gaekwad, *Sayajirao of Baroda*, 1.

7. Ibid., vii.

8. Stanley Rice, *Life of Sayajirao III, Maharaja of Baroda*, 2 vols. (London: Oxford University Press, 1913). Also see Philip Walsingham Sergeant, *The Ruler of Baroda: An Account of the Life and Work of the Maharaja Gaekwad* (London: J. Murray, 1928).

9. Rev. Edward St. Clair Weeden, *A Year with the Gaekwar of Baroda* (Boston: Dana Estes, 1913), 41.

10. Gaekwad, *Sayajirao*, 53.

11. Diwan Mirza Ismail of Mysore was responsible in bringing the German Jew Otto Koenigsberger to beautify Mysore and Bangalore in the 1930s. Koenigsberger played a major role in resettling refugees and building and redesigning cities in independent India. See Kalia, *Bhubaneswar*.

12. Cited in Murari Lal Nagar, *Shri Sayaji Rao Gaekwad*, 15.

13. Sergeant, *The Ruler of Baroda*, 118.

14. For a good discussion on industry in Baroda, see Howard L. Erdman, *Political Attitudes of Indian Industry: A Case Study of the Baroda Business Elite* (originally published by Athlone Press, University of London; reprint, New York: Oxford University Press, 1971).

15. Cited by Nagar in *Shri Sayaji Rao*, 54–55.

16. Quoted in Gaekwad, *Sayajirao*, 342.

17. Ibid., 331.

18. Ibid., 307–8.

19. Weeden, *A Year with the Gaekwar of Baroda*, 48–50, 290.

20. Thomas Pantham, *Political Parties and Democratic Consensus: A Study of Party Organisations in an Indian City* (New Delhi: Macmillan of India, 1976), 2.

21. Ibid., 22–23.

22. Erdman, *Political Attitudes of Indian Industry*, 7.

23. Ibid., 7 and 50.

24. G. W. Forrest, *Cities of India: Past and Present* (English ed. reprint; Mumbai, 1999), 64. This was originally printed in London in 1903, under the same title.

25. Kenneth L. Gillion, *Ahmedabad: A Study in Indian Urban History* (Berkeley: University of California Press, 1968), 7. There are several books on Ahmedabad. Gillion's account of the city remains one of the best.

26. Ibid., 40–41.

27. Sujata Patel, *The Making of Industrial Relations: The Ahmedabad Textile Industry, 1918–1939* (New Delhi: Oxford University Press, 1987), 17–18.

28. See Gillion, *Ahmedabad*, for a full discussion of Runchhodlal. Also see M. J. Mehta, "Runchhodlal Chottalal and the Ahmedabad Cotton Textile Industry—a Study in Entrepreneurial History" (unpublished doctoral thesis, Gujarat University, 1979).

29. Gillion, *Ahmedabad*, 56.

30. Weeden, 51.

31. Patel, *Making of Industrial Relations*, 37.

32. See Gillion, *Ahmedabad*, and Patel, *Making of Industrial Relations*.

33. For a good discussion on the Muslims in Ahmedabad, see Asghar Ali Engineer, *The Muslim Communities of Gujarat: An Exploratory Study of Bohras, Khojas, and Memons*. (New Delhi: Ajanta Publications, 1989); Satish C. Misra, *Muslim Communities in Gujarat: Preliminary Studies in Their History and Social Organization* (New York: Asia Publishing House, 1969).

34. M. K. Gandhi, *The Story of My Experiments with Truth* (Boston: Beacon Press, 1957), 395.

35. Yashodhar Mehta made a career of writing about Gujarat and Gujaratis. His most famous play in Gujarati is *Ranchhodalal and Bija Natko* (Ahmedabad, 1948); it continues to be produced locally. He was also a commentator on All-India Radio, frequently drawing caricatures of Gujarat and Gujaratis. Also see Gillion, *Ahmedabad*.

36. Howard Spodek, "On the Origins of Gandhi's Political Methodology in the Heritage of Kathiawad and Gujarat," *Journal of Asian Studies* 30 (1971): 365–67.

37. Erik H. Erikson, *Gandhi's Truth on the Origins of Militant Nonviolence* (New York: W. W. Norton, 1967), 264; see also 256–59, 413–15; and Gillion, *Ahmedabad*, 156–57, and Stanley Wolpert, *Gandhi's Passion: The Life and Legacy of Mahatma Gandhi* (New York: Oxford University Press, 2001), 17–18, 84.

38. *Collected Works of Mahatma Gandhi* (New Delhi: Govt. of India, Ministry of Information and Broadcasting, 1959–1984), 19:420.

39. On the Champaran campaign, see Jaques Pouchepadass, *Champaran and Gandhi: Planters, Peasants, and Gandhian Politics* (New Delhi: Oxford University Press, 1999).

40. Aparna Basu, *Mridula Sarabhai: Rebel with a Cause* (New Delhi: Oxford University Press, 1996), 14–19.

41. Erikson, *Gandhi's Truth*, 299–301.

42. Patel, *Making of Industrial Relations*, 89.

43. For the section on Kasturbhai Lalbhai, I have relied on Dwijendra Tripathi, *The Dynamics of a Tradition: Kasturbhai Lalbhai and His Entrepreneurship* (New Delhi: Manohar, 1981); and Niranjan Bhagat et al., eds., *Tribute to Ethics: Remembering Kasturbhai Lalbhai* (Ahmedabad: Gujarat Chamber of Commerce and Industry, 1983). I also had several extensive interviews on the family's role in Ahmedabad with Shrenik Kasturbhai Lalbhai in the summers of 1995 and 1996 in Ahmedabad. For other useful sources on Kasturbhai Lalbhai, see Gillion, *Ahmedabad*; Patel, *Making of Industrial Relations*; Kasturbhai Lalbhai Papers in the Nehru Museum and Library, New Delhi; Ahmedabad Textile Mills Associ-

ation records in Ahmedabad; and Ahmedabad Millowners Association Records, Ahmedabad.

44. Cited in Tripathi, *Dynamics*, 99.

45. Quoted in Kalia, *Chandigarh*, 87.

46. Ibid., 26.

47. For labor relations in the textile industry, see Patel, *Making of Industrial Relations*.

48. *Times of India*, March 29, 1926. Also see Tripathi, *Dynamics*, 179.

49. Tripathi, *Dynamics*, 192. Also see Bhagat et al., *Tribute to Ethics*, and Dwijendra Tripathi and Markand Mehta, eds., *Business Houses in Western India: A Study in Entrepreneurial Response, 1850–1956* (New Delhi: Manohar, 1990).

50. Vikram Sarabhai, "My Inspiration," in Bhagat et al., *Tribute to Ethics*, 45.

51. Gandhi, *My Experiments with Truth*.

52. Christopher Tadgell, *The History of Architecture in India: From the Dawn of Civilization to the End of the Raj* (London: Architecture, Design, and Technology Press, 1990), 289.

53. Pantham, *Political Parties and Democratic Consensus*, 21–22.

54. Tripathi, *Dynamics*, 187.

55. See Kalia, *Chandigarh*.

56. See Kalia, *Bhubaneswar*.

57. H. Allen Brooks, ed., *Le Corbusier: Ahmedabad, 1953–1960* (New York: Garland Publishing, 1983), xi–xiii.

58. For collected essays on Indian textiles, consult *Treasures of Indian Textiles: Calico Museum, Ahmedabad* (Bombay: Marg Publications, 1980).

59. Tripathi, "The Lalbhais," in *Business Houses in Western India*, 101.

60. Ibid., 102. Tripathi argues that the Ahmedabad industrialists were prisoners of their cultural conditioning, which restricted them from venturing out of India.

CHAPTER 3. The Kahn Seminar in Ahmedabad

1. "Preliminary Report on Gandhinagar: The Capital of Gujarat," Govt. of Gujarat, Public Works Dept., Capital Project Circle, Ahmedabad, 1961.

2. Ibid., 1–2.

3. See Kalia, *Bhubaneswar*, 142–43.

4. Ibid., 142.

5. For a full discussion of Le Corbusier's ideas, see Kalia, *Chandigarh*, especially 106–9.

6. "Preliminary Report," 156.

7. See Kalia, *Chandigarh*, 108 for the road system in Chandigarh.

8. Otto Koenigsberger, "Tropical Planning Problems," paper delivered on March 23, 1953: Otto Koenigsberger Papers, with Renate Koenigsberger, West Hampstead, London.

9. For a complete and reliable understanding of Wright's ideas, see Robert Twombly, *Frank Lloyd Wright: An Interpretive Biography* (New York: Harper and Row, 1973).

10. Jon Lang, Madhavi Desai, and Miki Desai, *Architecture and Independence: The Search for Identity—1880 to 1980* (New Delhi: Oxford University Press, 1997), 209.

11. Kalia, *Chandigarh*, 106.

12. Cited in Kalia, *Bhubaneswar*, 174. Also see Claude Batley, *The Design Development of Indian Architecture*, 3d ed. (New York: St. Martin's Press, 1973).

13. B. V. Doshi, interview with the author at his office, Sangath, Ahmedabad, July 26, 1996.

14. James Steele, *Architecture Today* (London: Phaidon Press, 2001), 327.

15. B. V. Doshi, *Le Corbusier and Louis Kahn: The Acrobat and the Yogi of Architecture* (Ahmedabad: Vastu-Shilpa Foundation, 1986–1992), 24.

16. Lang, Desai, and Desai, *Architecture and Independence*, 209.

17. Ibid., 220.

18. Tadgell, *History of Architecture in India*, 293.

19. Doshi, interview with the author, Ahmedabad, July 18, 1996. Also see Kathleen James, "Louis Kahn's Indian Institute of Management's Courtyard," *Journal of Architectural Education* 49, no. 1 (September 1995): 38–49; and David B. Brownlee and David G. De Long, eds., *Louis I. Kahn: In the Realm of Architecture* (New York: Rizzoli, 1991).

20. Alexandra Tyng, *Beginnings: Louis I. Kahn's Philosophy of Architecture* (New York: John Wiley and Sons, 1984).

21. Doshi, *Le Corbusier and Louis Kahn*.

22. Tyng, *Beginnings*, 1.

23. Ibid., 15.

24. Ibid.

25. Ibid., 17.

26. Ibid.

27. Ibid., 16.

28. Ibid., 21.

29. Joseph Burton, "Notes from Volume Zero: Louis Kahn and the Language of God," *Perspecta: The Yale Architectural Journal* 20 (1983): 70.

30. Tyng, *Beginnings*, 29–30.

31. Burton, "Notes from Volume Zero," 71.

32. Tyng, *Beginnings*, 23, 25.

33. Doshi, *Le Corbusier and Louis Kahn*, 19.

34. Ibid.

35. Ibid., 22.

36. Diane Ghirardo, *Architecture after Modernism* (London: Thames and Hudson, 1996), 8.

37. Doshi, *Le Corbusier and Louis Kahn*, 23.

38. Ibid.

39. Ibid., 23–25.

40. "Gandhinagar, New Capital of Gujarat—A Short Note," n.d.

41. Doshi, *Le Corbusier and Louis Kahn*, 24.

42. Cited in Kalia, *Chandigarh*, 86. Also see Charles Jencks, *Le Corbusier and the Tragic View of Architecture* (London: Allen Lane, Penguin Books, 1973), 18.

43. Kahn, letter to Irving Litvag, director of special events, Washington University (St. Louis), Apr. 1964, Louis I. Kahn Collection, University of Pennsylvania and Pennsylvania Historical and Museum Commission, Philadelphia (hereafter cited as Kahn Collection). See also Sarah Ksiazek, "Architectural Culture in the Fifties: Louis Kahn and the National Assembly Complex in Dhaka," *Journal of South Asian History* 52 (Dec. 1993): 416–35.

44. Louis Kahn, "Louis Kahn and the Living City," *Architectural Forum* 108 (March 1958): 114–19. Also see Tyng, *Beginnings*, 107; Ksiazek, "Architectural Culture," 418. In the Kahn Collection, this phrase appears in several places.

45. For a full discussion of Le Corbusier's view on democracy and colonization, see Kalia, *Chandigarh*.

46. For a full discussion of the National Assembly, Bangladesh, see Sarah Ksiazek, "Architectural Culture," 416–35.

47. Ibid.

48. Ibid.

49. See "The Agreement between the President of Pakistan and Louis Kahn," March 28, 1968, Kahn Collection. Lawrence J. Vale, in his chapter "The Acropolis of Bangladesh," in *Architecture, Power, and National Identity* (New Haven: Yale University Press, 1992), has correctly noted that Kahn's "buildings were not designed for the Capital of Bangladesh," which he considers to be "far more than a semantic distinction or historical curiosity, given that a civil war was fought against the original client," (237).

50. Anant Raje, interview with the author, Ahmedabad, July 17, 1996.

51. Kasturbhai Lalbhai, letter to Louis Kahn, March 2, 1964, Kahn Collection.

52. Doshi, letter to Kahn, March 24, 1964, Kahn Collection.

53. Kahn, letter to Kasturbhai Lalbhai, Feb. 21, 1964, Kahn Collection.

54. Kahn, letter to Kasturbhai, Nov. 20, 1963, Kahn Collection.

55. Kahn, letter to Kasturbhai, Feb. 21, 1964, Kahn Collection. For the contract between Le Corbusier and the Punjab government, see Kalia, *Chandigarh*; also see the Chandigarh Papers, collected and donated by Ravi Kalia, at the University Research Library, University of California, Los Angeles.

56. Kahn, letter to Kasturbhai, July 20, 1966, Kahn Collection.

57. K. M. Kantawala, letter to Kahn, March 6, 1964, Kahn Collection.

58. Ibid.

59. Kahn, letter to Kasturbhai, Feb. 21, 1964, Kahn Collection.

60. Kahn, letter to Kasturbhai, July 24, 1964, Kahn Collection.

61. Kahn, letter to Kasturbhai, July 20, 1966, Kahn Collection.

62. Kahn, cited in Anupam Banerji, *The Architecture of Corbusier and Kahn in the East: A Philosophical Inquiry* (Lewiston, N.Y.: Edwin Mellen Press, 2001), 43.

63. Ibid.

64. Ibid., 44.

65. Kahn, cited ibid., 44.

66. Kahn, letter to Kasturbhai, July 20, 1966, Kahn Collection.

67. See Kalia, *Chandigarh*, 87.

68. Ibid., 21, 30.

69. Kantawala, cable to Kahn, Aug. 11, 1964, Kahn Collection.

70. Kantawala, letter to Kahn, Aug. 12, 1964, Kahn Collection.

71. Doshi, letter to Kahn, Aug. 20, 1964, Kahn Collection.

72. Doshi, letter to Kasturbhai, Aug. 19, 1964, Kahn Collection.

73. Kahn, cable to Kasturbhai, Aug. 14, 1964. Also see Kahn's cables to Kantawala and Doshi, Aug. 14, 1964, Kahn Collection.

74. Kantawala, letter to Kahn, Sept. 7, 1964, Kahn Collection.

75. Doshi, letter to Kahn, Sept. 7, 1964, Kahn Collection.

76. Kahn, letter to Kantawala, Sept. 18, 1964, Kahn Collection.

77. Kahn, letter to Kantawala, July 20, 1966, Kahn Collection.

78. Kahn, letter to Kasturbhai, July 20, 1966, Kahn Collection.

79. Doshi, letter to Kahn, Dec. 27, 1966, Kahn Collection.

80. Kasturbhai, letter to Kahn, Apr. 18, 1969, Kahn Collection.

81. Gautam Sarabhai, letter to Kahn, May 29, 1969, Kahn Collection.

CHAPTER 4. The Plan and Architecture

1. *Prabhat*, Ahmedabad, June 24, 1964.

2. Superintending Engineer M. D. Patel, letter to the inspector-general of police, Nov. 1964. Unless otherwise noted, all correspondence cited in this chapter is from the Capital City Project Papers, General Administration Department, Gandhinagar, or from the personal papers of H. K. Mewada. Copies of these papers have been deposited with the Louis I. Kahn Collection, University of Pennsylvania and Pennsylvania Historical and Museum Commission, Philadelphia.

3. "Gandhinagar: New Capital of Gujarat—A Short Note," Ahmedabad: Office of the Chief Town Planner and Architectural Advisor, Capital Project, Govt. of Gujarat, n.d. See also *Gandhinagar: New Capital of Gujarat* (Gandhinagar: Building and Communication Dept., Govt. of Gujarat, Jan. 1, 1981); and K. L. Mehta, deputy secretary, Govt. of Gujarat, PWD, memorandum: Master Plan of the Proposed New Capital of Gujarat—Approval, Apr. 27, 1966.

4. M. K. Mewada, letter to J. K. Choudhary, July 27, 1965.

5. The Mewada family has carefully preserved all the degrees and relevant papers relating to H. K. Mewada. The author had several long interviews with Deepak H. Mewada, the son, and J. K. Mewada, the brother, between 1995 and 2000.

6. See Kalia, *Chandigarh*, for details on the neighborhood unit.

7. Brochure (1996) on "The History of Cornell's College of Architecture and Planning, 1871–1996," The exhibition sponsored by Lee S. Jablin on the 125th anniversary of the college.

8. Thomas W. Mackesey, testimonial letter, Sept. 14, 1949, Mewada family papers.

9. Karl B. Lohmann, testimonial letter, May 9, 1950, Mewada family papers.

10. Hansmukh C. Patel, interview with the author, Aug. 12, 1995.

11. Col. M. A. Sharman, private secretary to the maharaja sahib of Kishangarh, testimonial letter, Nov. 3, 1952, Mewada family papers.

12. H. K. Mewada, untitled memorandum, n.d.

13. Ibid.

14. For comparison of Versailles as a capital, see Vale, *Architecture, Power, and National Identity*.

15. H. K. Mewada, untitled memorandum, n.d.

16. Secretary M. G. Shah, Govt. of Gujarat, letter to B. P. Bagchi, chief commissioner, Chandigarh, May 26, 1972.

17. Untitled memorandum, Mewada, July 17, 1968.

18. Ibid.

19. See Ravi Kalia, *Bhubaneswar*, 154–55.

20. See Kalia, *Chandigarh*.

21. Mewada, letter to chief engineer, capital project, May 17, 1969.

22. *Gandhinagar: New Capital of Gujarat* (Ahmedabad: Public Works Dept., Patnagar Yojna Bhavan, 1968), 2.

23. *Draft Development Plan Gandhinagar, 2011* (Gandhinagar: Gandhinagar Urban Development Authority, Jan. 2000), 24.

24. *Fourth Five-Year Plan (1969–70 to 1973–74): Report on Capital Project Programmes, Capital Project* (Bhavnagar, Gujarat: Govt. Press, Apr. 1968).

25. M. N. Buch, "Tour Notes on the Capital Project, Gandhinagar," Feb. 18, 1980.

26. *Fourth Five-Year Plan (1969–70 to 1973–74)*, 45.

27. Shankersinh Vaghela quoted by Privin Sheth (professor, Gujarat Vidyapeeth, Ahmedabad) in his "Medieval Mindset May Harm Gujarat's Development," *India Abroad* (New York), Sept. 12, 1997.

28. Dr. C. D. Deshmukh, president, India International Centre, New Delhi, inaugural speech to the seminar "The Architect and the Community," Feb. 12–20, 1965, at the India International Centre, New Delhi, Feb. 1965.

29. Charles Correa, speech to the seminar "The Architect and the Community," Feb. 12–20, 1965, at the India International Centre, New Delhi, Feb. 1965.

30. See Ravi Kalia, "Education, Business, and Govt.: Empowering the Deprived in Chandigarh," parts 1 and 2, editorial, *Tribune* (Chandigarh), Oct. 8, 9, 1999.

31. M. N. Buch, administrator-cum-deputy secretary, Capital Project Section., Govt. of Madhya Pradesh, letter to Mewada, Feb. 18, 1970.

32. For details, see Kalia, *Bhubaneswar*, 1994, 195–96.

33. Buch, letter to Mewada, Feb. 18, 1970.

34. Buch, "Tour Notes of the Capital Project—Gandhinagar," Feb. 18, 1970, 3.

35. Chief Engineer M. D. Patel, letter to Mewada, Feb. 24, 1969.

36. Mewada, letter to B. Kambo, chief town planner and architectural adviser, Jaipur, Jan. 24, 1974.

37. "A Note on Allegation of Mal-practice in the Construction of Gandhinagar Capital Project, Dec. 9, 1977": Babubhai Jasubhai Patel private papers.

38. Mandeep Kumar, Warawa, Andheri West, Bombay, letter to chief minister, Gujarat, Apr. 1971.

39. P. M. Apte, PWD, Gandhinagar, letter to Mandeep Kumar, May 3, 1971.

40. See Kalia, *Chandigarh.*

41. Apte, letter to Kumar, May 3, 1971.

42. Vernon Z. Newcombe, *Gandhinagar: A New Capital City For the State of Gujarat* (New York: UN Commissioner for Technical Cooperation, Dept. of Economic and Social Affairs, Feb. 8, 1968).

43. Ibid., 47.

44. Ibid., 53.

45. Ibid., 17.

46. Ibid., 42–43.

47. "Notes on Press Report on Gandhinagar Project," n.a., n.d., the Gandhinagar Papers. Also see, *Times of India*, July 4, 1971.

48. M. G. Shah, secretary, PWD, minutes of meeting held by minister of public works, March 21, 1972.

49. "Gandhinagar and Capitol Complex," Office of the Chief Town Planner and Architectural Adviser, n.d., 3.

50. Ibid., 4.

51. Ibid., 5.

52. Ibid.

53. Kalia, *Chandigarh*, 164.

CHAPTER 5. Conclusions

1. Dinesh D'Souza, "Two Cheers for Colonialism," *Chronicle* [*of Higher Education*] *Review*, May 10, 2002, B7–B9.

2. Robert Grant Irving, *Indian Summer: Lutyens, Baker, and Imperial Delhi* (New Haven: Yale University Press, 1981), 88.

3. Sir Harcourt Butler, cited ibid., 89.

4. Kalia, *Chandigarh*, 27.

5. Cited in Irving, *Indian Summer*, 90.

6. Cited in Kalia, *Chandigarh*, 21.

7. Cited ibid., 21.

8. Kalia, *Bhubaneswar*, 191.

9. Cited ibid., 168.

10. Cited in Irving, *Indian Summer*, 88.

11. Cited in Kalia, *Chandigarh*, 28–29.

12. For a good and enduring comparative study of Howard, Wright, and Le Corbusier, see Robert Fishman, *Urban Utopias in the Twentieth Century: Ebenezer Howard, Frank Lloyd Wright, Le Corbusier* (Cambridge: MIT Press, 1999). Also see Kalia, *Chandigarh*, for a discussion on Le Corbusier's work in India.

13. Fishman, *Urban Utopias*, 158.

14. *Times* (London), Oct. 19, 1898.

15. Ebenezer Howard, *Garden Cities of Tomorrow* (London: S. Sonnenschein, 1902; London: Faber and Faber, 1946), 112.

16. Cited in Kalia, *Chandigarh*, 30.

17. Cited ibid., 53–54.

18. Cited ibid., 52.

19. Ibid., 47.

20. Mulk Raj Anand, "The Concept of a Humanistic Architecture," *Indian Architect* 4 (Jan. 1962): 11.

21. Cited in Kalia, *Chandigarh*, 29.

22. Original photograph and picture on display in the Government Museum and Art Gallery, Chandigarh; copy reproduced here by permission.

23. William J. R. Curtis, "Modernism and the Search for Indian Identity," *Architectural Review* 182 (August 1987): 33.

24. Ibid., 33.

25. Ibid.

26. B. V. Doshi and Christopher Alexander, "The Concept of Main Structure," in *World Architecture*, ed. John Donat (London: Studio Vista, 1966), 3:11–12.

27. Charles Correa, "Gun House, Ahmedabad," ibid., 25.

28. Kenneth Frampton, "Towards a Critical Regionalism: Six Points for an Architecture of Resistance," in *The Anti-Aesthetic: Essays on Postmodern Culture*, ed. Hal Foster (Port Townsend, Wash.: Bay Press, 1983).

29. Gautam Bhatia, *Punjabi Baroque and Other Memories of Architecture* (New Delhi: Penguin Books, 1994), 32.

SELECTED BIBLIOGRAPHY

The unpublished sources, government records, and correspondence between officials, planners, and architects, which are cited in notes only, include the personal papers of H. K. Mewada with the Mewada family in Ahmedabad, the Kasturbhai Lalbhai papers with Shrenik Lalbhai, Ahmedabad, the Ambalal Sarabhai papers at the Calico Museum, Ahmedabad, the Chief Minister Babubhai Jasubhai Patel papers, Ahmedabad, and the Louis Kahn Papers, University of Pennsylvania, Philadelphia. In Gandhinagar, I consulted the Capital City Project papers at the General Administration Department and other relevant papers at the Town Planning Office and the Chief Architect's Office, where the early correspondence on the capital project is located. I also consulted the Morarji Desai papers at Gujarat Vidyapith. In New Delhi, I consulted legislative debates on the bifurcation of Bombay at the Parliament Library, the planning papers at the Town and Country Planning Office Library, and relevant personal papers at the Nehru Memorial Museum and Library, which included personal files of Chief Minister Jivraj Mehta, Kasturbhai Lalbhai, Vikram Sarabhai, and other Gujarati leaders. In Bombay, I consulted the Bombay bifurcation papers at the Maharastra State Archives, Elphinstone College; and in London, I received the use of relevant correspondence from the late Otto Koenigsberger. In addition to these sources, I also interviewed several individuals who either had worked in Gandhinagar in the early stages or who have been connected with the capital's later developments. These include: in Ahmedabad and Gandhinagar, Governor Naresh Chandra, Prabodh Rawal, Deepak Mewada, J. K. Mewada, Virendra T. Purohit, Babubhai Jasubhai Patel, Hansmukh Patel, Bimal Patel, Shrenik K. Lalbhai, Surit Sarabhai, L. R. Dalal, I. K. Modi, K. M. Shah, D. A. Kadia, R. K. Pathak, H. M. Shivanand Swamy, S. P. Bhatia, J. H. Tamakuwala, Anant Raje, Miki Desai, Balkrishna Doshi, Barjor E. Mehta, Anjana Vyas, D. G. Pandaya, S. A. Verma, and Ramlal Parikh; in Bombay, P. M. Apte, Rahul Mehrotra, Deepak Raja and Narain Sadhwani; and in Delhi, E. F. N. Ribeiro, S. S. Shafi, D. S. Meshram, K. T. Gurumukhi, the late Achyut Kanvinde, Raj Rewal, and the late Joseph Stein. For data and statistical information, I have relied on the Government of India Census, 1951, 1961, 1971, 1981, 1991, and 2001, the yearly statistical abstracts of the Gujarat government, and the *Gazetteer of the Bombay Presidency* for legislative debates, *Hansard's Parliamentary Debates*, London, and the *Proceedings of the Legislative Council*, Gujarat and Bombay. For news reports I relied on the *Hindustan Times*, the *Statesman*, and the *Times of India*. I also consulted the *Journal of the Institute of Town Planners*,

India, the *Architectural Association Quarterly*, *Architecture + Design*, the *Architectural Review*, *Mimar*, and the *Architects' Journal* for discussions relating to urban and architectural developments in Gujarat. These sources, along with other journal sources, are also generally cited in notes only.

Anand, Mulk Raj. "The Concept of a Humanist Architecture." *Indian Architect* 4 (Jan. 1962): 11.

Architecture in India. Paris: Electa Moniteur, 1985.

Arnold, David. *Gandhi: Profiles in Power.* Harlow, U.K.: Pearson Education, 2001.

Ashraf, Kazi Khaleed, and James Belluardo, eds. *An Architecture of Independence: The Making of South Asia.* New York: Architectural League of New York, 1998.

Banerji, Anupam. *The Architecture of Corbusier and Kahn in the East: A Philosophical Inquiry.* Lewiston, N.Y.: Edwin Mellen Press, 2001.

Basu, Aparna. *Mridula Sarabhai: Rebel with a Cause.* New Delhi: Oxford University Press, 1996.

Batley, Claude. *The Design Development of Indian Architecture.* 3d ed. New York: St. Martin's Press, 1973.

Bayly, C. A. "From Company to Crown: Nineteenth Century India and the Visual Representation." In *An Illustrated History of Modern India, 1600–1947*, edited by C. A. Bayly. New Delhi: Oxford University Press, 1991.

Benjamin, Polk. *Two Americans in the South Asia of Nehru's Time.* Salisbury, U.K.: R. Russell, 1985.

———. *Architecture for South Asia: An Architectural Autobiography.* New Delhi: Abhinav Publications, 1993.

Bhagat, Niranjan, et al., eds. *Tribute to Ethics: Remembering Kasturbhai Lalbhai.* Ahmedabad: Gujarat Chamber of Commerce and Industry, 1983.

Bhatia, Gautam. *Punjabi Baroque and Other Memories of Architecture.* New Delhi: Penguin, 1994.

Bombay Government. *Survey and Settlement into Broach Taluka.* Bombay, 1974.

Brooks, H. Allen, ed. *Le Corbusier: Ahmedabad, 1953–1960.* New York: Garland Publishing; Paris: Foundation Le Corbusier, 1983.

Brownlee, David B., and David G. De Long, eds. *Louis I. Kahn: In the Realm of Architecture.* New York: Rizzoli, 1991.

Burton, Joseph. "Notes from Volume Zero: Louis Kahn and the Language of God." *Perspecta: The Yale Architectural Journal* 20 (1983): 69–90.

Campbell, James M., ed. *History of Gujarat.* Gurgaon, Haryana, India: Vintage Books, 1989. Originally published as *Gazetteer of the Bombay Presidency: History of Gujarat*, vol. 1, part 1 (Bombay: Government Central Press, 1896).

Chandra, Sudhir. "From Gujaratni Asmita to Gujaratni Rashtriye Asmita." In *Regional Roots of Indian Nationalism*, edited by Markand Mehta. New Delhi: Criterion Publications, 1990.

Chatterjee, Ratnabali. *From the Karkhana to the Studio.* New Delhi: Oxford University Press, 1990.

Choksey, R. D. *Economic Life in the Bombay Gujarat, 1800–1939.* Bombay: Asia Publishing House, 1968.

Copland, Ian. *India, 1885–1947: The Unmaking of an Empire.* Harlow, U.K.: Pearson Education, 2001.

Correa, Charles. "Chandigarh: The View from Benares." *Architecture + Design 3,* no. 6 (Sept.–Oct., 1967): 73–75.

————. "India Today: Programmes and Priorities." *Architectural Review* 150, no. 898 (Dec. 1971): 326–31.

————. "New Bombay." *Architectural Review* 150, no. 898 (Dec. 1971): 334–38.

————. "A Place in the Sun." *Royal Society of Arts Journal* 131 (May 1983): 328–40.

————. "The Assembly, Chandigarh." *Architects' Journal* 179 (June 27, 1984): 102–5.

————. *The New Landscape.* Bombay: Strand Books, 1985.

————. *Housing and Urbanisation.* Bombay: Urban Design Research Institute, 1999.

Curtis, William J. R. "Authenticity, Abstraction and the American Scene: Le Corbusier's and Louis Kahn's Ideas of Parliament." *Perspecta: The Yale Architectural Journal* 20 (1983): 181–90.

————. *Modern Architecture since 1900.* Englewood Cliffs, N.J.: Prentice Hall, 1983.

————. *Le Corbusier: Ideas and Forms.* New York: Rizzoli, 1986.

————. "Modernism and the Search for Indian Identity." *Architectural Review* 182 (Aug. 1987): 32–38.

————. *Balkrishna Doshi: An Architecture for India.* New York: Rizzoli, 1988.

Donat, John, ed. *World Architecture.* Vol. 3. London: Studio Vista, 1966.

Doshi, Balkrishna V. "Chandigarh: The View from Benares." *Architecture + Design 3,* no. 6 (Sept.–Oct. 1967): 73–75.

————. "Identity in Architecture: Contemporary Pressure and Tradition in India." *Architectural Association Quarterly* 13, no. 1 (Oct. 1981): 20–22.

————. "Louis Kahn in India." *Architectural Association Quarterly* 13, no. 1 (Oct. 1981): 23–25.

————. *Housing: Balkrishna Doshi.* Ahmedabad: Vastu-Shilpa Foundation, 1983.

————. "Expressing an Architectural Identity: Bohra Houses in Gujarat." *Mimar* 19 (Jan.–Mar. 1986): 34–40.

————. *Le Corbusier and Louis Kahn: The Acrobat and the Yogi of Architecture.* Ahmedabad: Vastu-Shilpa Foundation and Research in Environment Design, 1986–92.

D'Souza, Dinesh. "Two Cheers for Colonialism." *Chronicle [of Higher Education] Review,* May 10, 2002, B7–B9.

Elliot, Sir Henry M., and John Dowson, eds. *The History of India as Told by Its Own Historians: The Muhammadan Period.* 31 vols. Calcutta: Susil Gupta, 1952–59.

Engineer, Asghar Ali. *The Muslim Communities of Gujarat: An Exploratory Study of Bohras, Khojas, and Memons.* New Delhi: Ajanta Publications, 1989.

Erdman, Howard L. *Political Attitudes of Indian Industry: A Case Study of the Baroda Business Elite.* New York: Oxford University Press, 1971.

Erikson, Erik H. *Gandhi's Truth on the Origins of Militant Nonviolence.* New York: W. W. Norton, 1969.

Fermor-Hesketh, Robert. *Architecture of the British Empire.* London: Weidenfeld and Nicolson, 1986.

Fishman, Robert. *Urban Utopias in the Twentieth Century: Ebenezer Howard, Frank Lloyd Wright, Le Corbusier.* Cambridge: MIT Press, 1999.

Forrest, G. W. *Cities of India: Past and Present*. 1903. Reprint, Mumbai English Edition, 1999.

Frampton, Kenneth. *Modern Architecture: A Critical History*. New York: Oxford University Press, 1980.

———. "Towards a Critical Regionalism: Six Points for an Architecture of Resistance." In *The Anti-Aesthetic: Essays on Postmodern Culture*, edited by Hal Foster. Port Townsend, Wash.: Bay Press, 1983.

Gaekwad, Fatesinghrao Rao P. *Sayajirao of Baroda: The Prince and the Man*. Bombay: Popular Prakashan, 1989.

Gandhi, M. K. *The Story of My Experiments with Truth*. Boston: Beacon Press, 1957.

———. *Collected Works of Mahatma Gandhi*. New Delhi: Govt. of India, Ministry of Information and Broadcasting, 1959–84.

"Gandhinagar." *Journal of the Indian Institute of Architects* 37, no. 3. (July/Aug./Sept. 1971): 16.

Gazetteer of the Bombay Presidency: History of Gujarat. Vol. 1, part 1. Bombay: Government Central Press, 1896.

Ghirardo, Diane. *Architecture after Modernism*. London: Thames and Hudson, 1996.

Gillion, Kenneth L. *Ahmedabad: A Study in Indian Urban History*. Berkeley: University of California Press, 1968.

Government of India. *Report of the States Reorganisation Commission*. New Delhi: Govt. of India Press, 1955.

Guha-Thakurta, Tapati. *The Making of a New "Indian" Art: Artists, Aesthetics, and Nationalism in Bengal*. Cambridge: Cambridge University Press, 1992.

Hall, Peter. *Cities of Tomorrow*. Reprint, Oxford: Blackwell, 1994.

Hamesse, Jean-Elie. *Sectoral and Spatial Interrelations in Urban Development: A Case Study of Ahmedabad, India*. Göttingen, Germany: Edition Herdot, 1983.

Hardgrave, Robert L., and Stanley A. Kochanek. *India: Government and Politics in a Developing Nation*. 6th ed. Fort Worth, Tex.: Harcourt College Publishers, 2000.

Harle, J. C. *The Art and Architecture of the Indian Subcontinent*. New York: Viking Penguin; Harmondsworth, U.K.: Penguin Books, 1986.

Hunt, James D. *Gandhi in London*. New Delhi: Oxford University Press, 1993.

Irving, Robert Grant. *Indian Summer: Lutyens, Baker, and Imperial Delhi*. New Haven: Yale University Press, 1981.

James, Kathleen. "Louis Kahn's Indian Institute of Management's Courtyard: Form versus Function." *Journal of Architectural Education* 49, no. 1 (Sept. 1995): 38–49.

———. *Erich Mendelsohn and the Architecture of German Realism*. Cambridge: Cambridge University Press, 1997.

Jencks, Charles. *Le Corbusier and the Tragic View of Architecture*. London: Allen Lane, Penguin Books, 1973.

Joglekar, M. N., and S. K. Das. *Contemporary Indian Architecture: Housing and Urban Development*. New Delhi: Galgotia, 1995.

Joshi, Kiran. *Documenting Chandigarh: The Indian Architecture of Pierre Jeanneret, Edwin Maxwell Fry, Jabe Drew*. Vol. 1. Ahmedabad: Mapin Publishing, 1999.

Kahn, Louis. "Louis Kahn and the Living City." *Architectural Forum* 108 (March 1958): 114–19.

Kalia, Ravi. *Chandigarh: The Making of an Indian City*. Updated; New Delhi: Oxford University Press, 1999. Originally published as *Chandigarh: In Search of an Identity* (Carbondale: Southern Illinois University Press, 1987).

———. *Bhubaneswar: From a Temple Town to a Capital City*. Carbondale: Southern Illinois University Press; New Delhi: Oxford University Press, 1994.

Kamath, M. V., and V. B. Kher. *The Story of Militant but Non-Violent Trade Unionism*. Ahmedabad: Navajivan Mudranalaya, 1993.

Khan, Hasan-Uddin. *Charles Correa*. New York: Concept Media, 1987.

———. *Contemporary Asian Architecture*. Cologne, Germany: Benedikt Taschen Verlag, 1995.

Kirloskar, S. L. *Cactus and Roses: An Autobiography*. Pune: Kirloskar Press, 1982.

Konvitz, Josef W. *The Urban Millennium: The City-Building Process from the Early Middle Ages to the Present*. Carbondale: Southern Illinois University Press, 1985.

Kopf, David. *British Orientalism and the Bengal Renaissance: The Dynamics of Indian Modernization, 1773–1834*. Berkeley: University of California Press, 1969.

Ksiazek, Sarah. "Architectural Culture in the Fifties: Louis Kahn and the National Assembly Complex in Dhaka." *Journal of South Asian History* 5 (Dec. 1993): 416–35.

Land, Jon, Madhavi Desai, and Miki Desai. *Architecture and Independence: The Search for Identity—India, 1880 to 1980*. New Delhi: Oxford University Press, 1997.

Lim, William S. W., and Tan Hock Beng. *The New Asian Architecture: Vernacular Traditions and Contemporary Style*. Hong Kong: Periplus Editions, 1998. Original edition entitled *Contemporary Vernacular: Evoking Traditions in Asian Architecture* (Singapore: Select Books, 1998).

"Louis Kahn in India: An Old Order at a New Scale." *Architectural Forum* 125 (July–Aug. 1966): 38–49.

Majumdar, M. R. *Cultural History of Gujarat*. New York: New York Humanities Press, 1966.

Malabári, Behrámji M. *Gujarát and the Gujarátis: Pictures of Men and Manners Taken from Life*. London: W. H. Allen, 1882; New Delhi: Asian Educational Services, 1997.

Mason, Philip. *The Men Who Ruled India*. New York: W. W. Norton, 1985.

Mehrotra, Rahul J. "Making Legible City Form." *Architecture + Design* 7, no. 6 (Sept.–Oct. 1990): 18–25.

Mehta, J. L. *India and the West: The Problem of Understanding—Selected Essays*. With an introduction by Wilfred C. Smith. Chico, Calif.: Scholars Press, 1985.

Mehta, M. J. "Runchhodlal Chottalal and the Ahmedabad Cotton Textile Industry—a Study in Entrepreneurial History." Unpublished doctoral thesis, Gujarat University, 1979.

Mehta, Makrand. *Indian Merchants and Entrepreneurs in Historical Perspective*. New Delhi: Academic Foundation, 1991.

———, ed. *Regional Roots of Indian Nationalism*. New Delhi: Criterion Publications, 1990.

Mehta, Yashodhar. *Ranchhodalal and Bija Natko*. Ahmedabad, 1948.

Menon, V. P. *The Story of the Integration of Indian States*. New Delhi: Sangam Books, 1979.

Metcalf, Thomas. *An Imperial Vision: Indian Architecture and Britain's Raj*. Berkeley: University of California Press, 1989.

Misra, Satish C. *Muslim Communities in Gujarat: Preliminary Studies in Their History and Social Organization.* New York: Asia Publishing House, 1964.

Mittar, Partha. *Art and Nationalism in Colonial India, 1850–1922.* Cambridge: Cambridge University Press, 1994.

Nagar, Murari Lal. *Shri Sayajirao Gaikwad, Maharaja of Baroda: The Prime Promoter of Public Libraries.* Columbia, Mo.: International Library Center, 1992.

Nandy, Asish. *The Intimate Enemy: Loss and Recovery of Self under Colonialism.* New Delhi: Oxford University Press, 1983.

Pandey, Gyanendra. *The Construction of Communalism in Colonial North India.* New Delhi: Oxford University Press, 1992.

———, ed. *Hindus and Others: The Question of Identity in India Today.* New Delhi: Viking, 1993.

Pantham, Thomas. *Political Parties and Democratic Consensus: A Study of Party Organisations in an Indian City.* New Delhi: Macmillan of India, 1976.

Patel, Sujata. *The Making of Industrial Relations: The Ahmedabad Textile Industry, 1918–1939.* New Delhi: Oxford University Press, 1987.

Pearson, M. N. *Merchants and Rulers in Gujarat: The Response of the Portuguese in the Sixteenth Century.* Berkeley: University of California Press, 1976.

Perera, Nihal. *Decolonizing Ceylon: Colonialism, Nationalism, and the Politics of Space in Sri Lanka.* New Delhi: Oxford University Press, 1999.

Pouchepadass, Jaques. *Champaran and Gandhi: Planters, Peasants, and Gandhian Politics.* New Delhi: Oxford University Press, 1999.

Prakash, Vikramaditya. *Chandigarh's Le Corbusier: The Struggle for Modernity in Postcolonial India.* Seattle: University of Washington Press, 2002.

Rajyagor, S. B. *History of Gujarat.* Edited by P. N. Chopra. New Delhi: S. Chand, 1982.

Raval, R. L. *Socio-Religious Reform Movements in Gujarat during the Nineteenth Century.* New Delhi: Ess Ess Publications, 1987.

———. "Cultural Perspectives of the Emerging Nationalism in the Nineteenth Century Gujarat." In *Regional Roots of Indian Nationalism,* edited by Markand Mehta. New Delhi: Criterion Publications, 1990.

Rewal, Raj. "The Relevance of Tradition in Indian Architecture." In *Architecture in India.* Paris: Electa Moniteur, 1985.

Rice, Stanley. *Life of Sayajirao III, Maharaja of Baroda.* 2 vols. London: Oxford University Press, 1913.

Sanghvi, Nagindas. *Gujarat: A Political Analysis.* Surat: Centre for Social Studies, 1996.

Sardesai, G. S. *New History of the Marathas.* 3 vols. 2nd imp.; Bombay: Phoenix Publications, 1957.

Scully, Vincent J. *Modern Architecture and Other Essays.* Selected and with introductions by Neil Levine. Princeton, N.J.: Princeton University Press, 2002.

Segeant, Philip Walsingham. *The Ruler of Baroda: An Account of the Life and Work of the Maharaja Gaekwad.* London: J. Murray, 1928.

Sen, Amartya. *Development as Freedom.* New York: Vintage Anchor, 2000.

Sheik, Gulam Mohammed, ed. *Contemporary Art in Baroda.* New Delhi: Tulika, 1997.

Spodek, Howard. "On the Origins of Gandhi's Political Methodology in the Heritage of Kathiawad and Gujarat." *Journal of Asian Studies* 30 (1971): 365–67.

Steele, James. *Rethinking Modernism for the Developing World: The Complete Architecture of Balkrishna Doshi.* New York: Whitney Library of Design, 1998.

———. *Architecture Today.* London: Phaidon Press, 2001.

Stein, Joseph Allen. "The Responsibility for Environment." *Journal of the Indian Institute of Architects* 29, no. 1. (Jan.–Mar. 1963): 10–19.

Tadgell, Christopher. *The History of Architecture in India: From the Dawn of Civilization to the End of the Raj.* London: Architecture Design and Technology Press, 1990.

Thapar, Romila. *A History of India.* Vol. 1. Reprint; London: Penguin, 1990.

Tillotson, Giles H. R. *The Tradition of Indian Architecture: Continuity, Controversy, and Change since 1850.* New Haven: Yale University Press, 1989.

———. *Paradigms of Indian Architecture: Space and Time in Representation and Design.* Richmond, Surrey, U.K.: Curzon Press, 1998.

Treasures of Indian Textiles: Calico Museum, Ahmedabad. Bombay: Marg Publications, 1980.

Tripathi, Dwijendra. *The Dynamics of Tradition: Kasturbhai Lalbhai and His Entrepreneurship.* New Delhi: Manohar, 1981.

———. *Business and Politics in India: A Historical Perspective.* New Delhi: Manohar, 1991.

———. *Historical Roots of Industrial Entrepreneurship in India and Japan: A Comparative Interpretation.* New Delhi: Manohar, 1997.

———, ed. *Business Communities of India: A Historical Perspective.* New Delhi: Manohar: 1984.

Tripathi, Dwijendra, and Markand Mehta, eds. *Business Houses in Western India: A Study in Entrepreneurial Response, 1850–1956.* New Delhi: Manohar, 1990.

Twombly, Robert C. *Frank Lloyd Wright: An Interpretive Biography* (New York: Harper and Row, 1973.

———. *Louis Sullivan: His Life and Work.* New York: Viking Press, 1980.

Tyng, Alexandra. *Beginnings: Louis I. Kahn's Philosophy of Architecture.* New York: John Wiley and Sons, 1984.

Vale, Lawrence J. *Architecture, Power, and National Identity.* New Haven: Yale University Press, 1992.

———. "Designing National Identity: Post Colonial Capitals as Intercultural Dilemmas." In *Forms of Dominance: On the Architecture and Urbanism of the Colonial Enterprise,* edited by Nezar AlSayyad. Aldershot, U.K.: Avebury, 1992.

van der Veer, Peter. *Religious Nationalism.* Berkeley: University of California Press, 1994.

Ward, Philip. *Gujarat, Damn, Diu: A Travel Guide.* Cambridge, U.K.: Oleander Press, 1994.

Weeden, Rev. Edward St. Clair. *A Year with the Gaekwar of Baroda.* Boston: Dana Estes, 1911.

Wink, André. *Land and Sovereignty in India: Agrarian Society and Politics under the Eighteenth-Century Maratha Svarajya.* New York: Cambridge University Press, 1986.

Wolpert, Stanley. *A New History of India.* 4th ed. New York: Oxford University Press, 1993.

———. *Gandhi's Passion: The Life and Legacy of Mahatma Gandhi.* New York: Oxford University Press, 2001.

INDEX

Aalto, Alvar, 82

administration. *See* management

Afghanistan, 11, 13

Agha Khan Centre (Lisbon), 120

Agnew, Spiro T., 23

agroindustrial complexes, 55

ahimsa (nonviolence), 8, 12, 45–46, 54

Ahmed Shah, 38

Ahmedabad: architecture and buildings in, 38, 39, 57–59, 64–72; British rule of, 39–40; business and industry in, 3, 4–5, 7, 38–54, 59, 137n. 60; Calico Museum in, 58, 64; as capital in fifteenth century, 7; charitable trusts in, 53; communications links between Gandhinagar and, 105; compared with Baroda, 40; and Congress Party, 28–29; description of, 38–39; Doshi's buildings in, 67, 68; education in, 43, 45, 47, 49, 52–55; founding of, 38; Gandhi in, 40–45, 60; high court of Gujarat in, 107, 110; history of, 10, 13, 38–59; Indian Institute of Management in, 5, *following p.* 40, 50, 53, 54, 60, 69, 71, 72, 79–81, 84, 85, 87, 88, 95, 103, 128; "Indianness" of, 41; Jivraj Mehta in, 55–57; Kahn's buildings in, *following p.* 40, 57, 60, 69–72, 79–81, 84; Lalbhai family in, 45–54, 59, 60, 64; Le Corbusier's buildings in, *following p.* 40, 57–59, 60, 66, 69; Muslims in, 41, 109; newspapers in, 21, 96; and opium trade, 40; plague in, 40; population of, 40, 41, 42, 59, 115; as possible capital of Gujarat, 4–5, 30, 45, 59, 114–15; and recruitment of Kahn for Gandhinagar project, 3, 5, 60, 77, 84–95; Sabarmati Ashram in, 40, 42, 43, 58, 60, 65, 101; Sarabhai family in, 43–45, 50, 53–55, 60, 64; as temporary capital of Gujarat, 59, 60; violence in 2002 in, 109; working class and labor strikes in, 41–46, 49, 50

Ahmedabad Education Society, 53, 84

Ahmedabad International Airport, 105, 107

Ahmedabad Management Association, 54

Ahmedabad Millowners Association (AMA), *following p.* 40, 50, 57, 69

Ahmedabad Museum, 57, 69

Ahmedabad Spinning and Weaving Mill, 40

Ahmedabad Textile Industries Research Association (ATIRA), 53, 54, 65, 68

airports, 71, 105, 107

Alamgir I, 12

Ala-ud Din Muhammad Khilji, 11, 13

alcohol, 107

Alexander, Christopher, 71

Ali, Muhammad, 43

Ali, Shaukat, 43

Allahabad, 51, 124, 126

All-India Radio, 136n. 35

Alptigin, 11

AMA. *See* Ahmedabad Millowners Association (AMA)

Amarji, 12

Ambedkar, Bhimrao Ramji (B. R.), 26, 36, 46

America. *See* United States

American Civil War, 19–20, 40, 46
American Cyanamid, 47–48
Amin, Indubhai, 37–38
Anderson, Lawrence B., 66
Andhra, 23, 24, 27
Andrews, C. F., 44
Anhilwada Patan, 7, 9–10, 38
Apte, P. M., 102, 111
Arabs. *See* Islam and Muslims
archaeological sites, 9
Architectural Research Group, 74
architecture. *See* specific cities, buildings,
  architects, and architectural movements
Architecture, School of, 53, 71, 80
Aristophanes, 92
Aronovici, Carol, 99
arts and crafts movement, 67
Arya Samaj, 22
Asaval (Karnavati), 38
ashrams, 40, 42, 43, 58, 60, 65, 103
Asiatic Society of Bengal, 20
asmita (Gujarati identity), 21–22
Asoka edict, 9
Assam, 22, 100
ATIRA (Ahmedabad Textile Industry
  Research Association), 53, 54, 65, 68
Atomic Energy, Department of, 54
Atomic Energy Commission, 54
Atul Products Ltd., 48, 49, 52, 53, 59, 64
Audicyas, 10
automobiles, 62–63, 64, 102, 105

B. E. College, 71
Babuline Gripe Water, 56
Bagchi, B. P., 102
Baji Rao II, 17
Balrama, 9
Bangalore, 6, 54, 135n. 11
Bangladesh, 5, 81, 83–84, 89–90, 114,
  139n. 49
Banias, 38, 40, 41, 53, 55, 67, 70
banking and bankers, 41, 46
Baroda (city), 31–38, 40, 54, 55, 97, 117,
  135n. 5
Baroda College and Kalabhavan (art
  school), 31, 34
Baroda Museum, 35
Baroda State, 14, 25, 26, 37–39, 56–57

Bartholomew, Harland, 99
Bassein, Treaty of, 17
Batley, Claude, 67–68
Bauhaus school, 34, 65–66, 97
Beaux Arts, 66, 73, 74, 75, 98, 121,
  123–24
Bengal and Bengalis, 18, 22, 24, 26, 28, 51,
  83, 88, 123
Benninger, Christopher, 71
Berar, 32
bhadralok (intellectuals), 22
Bhagvati, Jagdish, 42
Bhalla, Jai Rattan, 71
Bhargava, Gopichand, 122
Bhatia, Gautam, 123
Bhavnagar, 57
Bhima, 10
Bhonsle, Shahji, 14
Bhonsle, Shivaji, 14, 21, 24
Bhopal, 109, 110
Bhubaneswar, Orissa: as administrative capi-
  tal, 3–4, 62; administrative control of
  construction of, 96; author's approach to
  study of, 1; Buch's criticism of, 109–10;
  Gandhi Memorial Pillar proposed for,
  103; government's vision for, 3–4; hous-
  ing in, 106; and Koenigsberger, 30, 62,
  64, 103, 106, 109–10, 113, 120; larger
  meaning of urban planning in, 1–4, 118;
  Nehru on, 122; Rajkumari Amrit Kaur
  on, 121–22; temples and religious monuments in, 3–4, 109–10; and Vaz, 6, 68,
  122
Bhutto, Sir Shah Nawaz, 25
Bhutto, Zulfiqar Ali, 25
bicycle paths, 105
Bihar, 48
Birdwood, Sir George, 121
Biruni, Al, 12
Blair, Joseph C., 99
Bobrowski, Tadeusz, 32
Bombay (city): architect in, 58; architecture
  and buildings in, 56, 78, 120; as capital
  of Bombay state, 37; and chemical industry, 48; education in, 40, 58, 67; industry
  in, 54; legal family from, 42; medical college and hospital in, 56; working class
  in, 56

Bombay (province): bifurcation of, 4, 59, 70; British rule of, 7, 15–17; education in, 20–21, 40, 52, 58; and Gujarat, 7, 16–17, 27–29, 52; Jivraj Mehta in government of, 38; merger of Baroda State with, 26, 37, 57; newspapers in, 21–22; and Saurastra, 25–28; and Swaraj Party, 51

Bombay Darpan (Bombay mirror), 22

Bombay Education Society, 20

Bombay Native Education Society, 20

Bombay Provincial Municipal Corporation Act (1949), 37

Bombay Reorganization Act (1960), 29

Bombay Samachar (Bombay news), 21

Bombay University, 21, 34

Booth, George, 71

Borden, William Alanson, 34

Brahmans, 10, 11, 18

Breuer, Marcel, 66

Britain: architecture and architects in, 31, 67, 82, 120, 121; and colonialism in India, 4, 7, 8, 14, 16–22, 39, 119, 120, 121; defeat of, by Dutch in Indies, 15; early contact with Gujarat by, 14–16; education in, 44–45, 51, 54, 124; Gandhi's struggle against, in India, 8, 14, 35, 50; hospital in London, 56; Indian elected to Parliament in, 32; Sarabhai family in, 44–45; textile industry in, 47

Broadacare City, 125

Brooklyn Institute of Technology, 49

Buch, M. N., 109–11

Buddhism, 9, 12, 46

Budhivardhak Sabha (Intellectual society), 22

Burnham, Daniel, 124

business. *See* industry and business

business management. *See* management

Calcutta, 24, 51, 54, 69, 71

Calico Mills, 69

Calico Museum, 58, 64

Calico Shop, 65

California, 71, 74, 75, 78–79

Cambay, 39

Cambridge University, 45, 51, 54, 64

Cantlie, James, 55

Capital Project Circle, 30–31, 61, 62, 81, 96. *See also* Gandhinagar

capitol complex: in Chandigarh, 107, 109; in Gandhinagar, *following p.* 40, 62, 102, 107, 112–18

Carl Wilhelm, Margrave, 102

caste system, 3, 35–36, 41, 44, 46, 121. *See also* untouchables

Catherine of Braganza, 16

Cavadas (Capa of Bhinnmal), 9–10

cement and concrete, 89, 108, 131

Centre for Environmental Planning and Technology (CEPT), 58, 71

CEPT. *See* Centre for Environmental Planning and Technology (CEPT)

Chakubhai, Chimanlal, 26

Chalukyan dynasty, 7, 12

Champaran, 42

Chandigarh, Punjab; administrative control of construction of, 96; author's approach to study of, 1; Bhargava on, 122; bifurcation of, between Punjab and Haryana, 3; business and industry in, 106; capitol complex in, 107, 109; compared with Gandhinagar, 107–8, 111; concrete used in construction of, 109; Correa's criticism of, 109; functions of, 111; housing in, 106, 109; Koenigsberger's critique of plan for, 64; larger meaning of urban planning in, 1–2; Le Corbusier as architect-planner of, 2, 3, 5, 6, 30, 48, 49, 62, 64, 66, 67, 69, 72, 79–82, 85, 86, 87, 89, 96, 99–100, 103, 107–8, 110, 113, 118, 120, 125; Mayer as first architect-planner of, 62, 66, 85, 86, 98, 120, 125, 126–27; and Mewada, 5, 96, 99–100, 102, 109; as model for Gandhinagar and other new cities in India, 102, 106, 109; and Nehru, 48, 79, 89, 108, 120, 121, 125, 127; neighborhood blocks (sectors) in, 105; opposition to statues of Gandhi in, 103; road system of, 63; urban sprawl in, 3

Chandragupta II, 9

charities, 53

Charles II, 16, 73

Chaudhry, Nirad C., 52

chauth tax, 13, 14

Chavan, Y. B., 28

chemical industry, 48
Chicago, 124, 126
Chimanbhai, Chinubhai, 43, 57–58, 66
China, 3, 9, 11, 15, 40, 51, 87, 108, 114
Chisolm, R. F., 34
Chotala, Runchhodlal, 40
Chowdhury, Jugal Kishore, 97
Christians, 40
Churchill, Sir Winston, 8
CIAM (Congrès Internationaux d'Architec-
    ture Moderne), 64, 75, 79
Cities of India (Forrest), 38
City Beautiful movement, 120, 123–24, 126
Clouds (Aristophanes), 92
colonialism: British colonialism in India,
    4, 7, 8, 14, 16–22, 39, 119, 120, 121;
    D'Souza on, 119; Le Corbusier on, 82,
    119; and New Delhi architecture, 31, 34,
    71, 100, 112, 119–21, 123–26
Columbia University, 74, 95
Communism, 120
concrete (in construction), 89, 109, 131
Congrès Internationaux d'Architecture
    Moderne (CIAM), 64, 75, 79
Congress Party, 24, 26–29, 32, 38, 51, 55, 114
Congress Working Committee, 24–25
Conrad, Joseph, 32
Constituent Assembly, 27
Coomaraswamy, Ananda, 58
Cornell University, 96, 97–99, 104
Correa, Charles: architectural practice of,
    58, 120; on architecture, 131–32; on
    Chandigarh, 109; in discussion group in
    Ahmedabad on urban design, 70, 84;
    education of and influences on, 58, 66;
    Gandhi Smarak Sanghralaya designed
    by, 58, 65, 66; and Gandhinagar project,
    84, 88, 92, 93, 99; and modernism, 5, 66,
    109, 131, 132; U.S. architectural projects
    of, 120
cottage industry. See swadeshi (indigenous
    goods)
cotton/textile industry, 19–20, 27, 39–43,
    46–47, 50–53, 58
Cranbrook College, 71
Creative Choice, 107
Critical Regionalism, 132
Curtis, William, 128, 129

Dalpatbhai, Sardar Seth Lalbhai, 45, 46
Dangs, 52
Darpana, 55
Das, C. R., 50, 51
Dave, Narmadshankar Lalshankar. See
    Narmad, Kavi
deconstructionism, 119
Delhi, 12, 19, 112. See also New Delhi
Delhi University, 108
democracy, 81–82, 85, 120–21, 127
Desai, Ichharam Suryaram, 22
Desai, Morarjibhai, 23, 27–29, 38, 57,
    59
Desmukh, C. D., 108
DeTurk, Charles, 99
Devi, Phoolan, 109
Dhaka, 60, 81–85, 88–89
Dhandhuka, Gujarat, 9
Dhar Commission, 27
Dhara Sabha, 37
dharma (duty), 47
Dheber, Shri Uchhrangrai, 26
Dhruva, Keshav Harshad, 47
Dickens, Charles, 67
doctors. See medicine and doctors
dome idea, 65
Doshi, Balkrishna Vithaldas: Ahmedabad's
    buildings by, 67, 68; architectural firm of,
    58, 67, 68, 120; and Batley, 67, 68, 77;
    and Centre for Environmental Planning
    and Technology (CEPT), 58, 71; in dis-
    cussion group in Ahmedabad on urban
    design, 70, 84; education of, 58, 66–67,
    88; and Gandhinagar project, 5, 61,
    84–86, 89–94, 99; and Indian Institute
    of Management (IIM), 69, 75, 79–81,
    85, 95; and Kahn, 5, 67, 68, 69, 70, 72,
    75, 77–81, 84–95; and Le Corbusier, 5,
    58, 67, 68, 70, 77–80; as lecturer at Uni-
    versity of Pennsylvania, 79; and mod-
    ernism, 66, 70, 79, 122, 130–31, 132;
    and Stein, 67, 71; trips to Philadelphia
    by, 77, 78–79, 85; on Western-inspired
    building designs, 5
Drew, Jane, 82
D'Souza, Dinesh, 119
Du Bois, W. E. B., 33
Dufferin, Lord, 37

Dulles, John Foster, 83
Dundas, Henry, 17
Durga, 10
Dutt, R. C., 38
Dwivedi, Manilal Nabhubhai, 22

Eames, Charles, 127
Eames, Ray, 71, 127
East India Company, 14–16, 39–40
East Pakistan, 5, 83
education: in Ahmedabad, 43, 45, 47,
    49, 52–55; in architecture, 53, 58, 60,
    65–67, 71, 73, 75, 80, 86, 88, 97–98; in
    Baroda, 32–35, 55, 97; of blacks in U.S.,
    33; in Bombay, 20–21, 52, 58; in Britain,
    44–45, 51, 54, 124; in business manage-
    ment, 49, 50, 54; in engineering, 65–66,
    95; English-language education in India,
    20–21, 32, 47; and Gandhi, 52; in
    Gujarat, 20–21; and Kasturbhai Lalbhai,
    49, 52–53; medical education, 55–56;
    Montessori school system, 45, 54; rural
    education, 55; Satellite Instructional
    Television Experiment for, 55; and Saya-
    jirao Gaekwad, 32, 33–36, 38, 97; sci-
    ence education for children, 55; in
    United States, 33–35, 49, 50, 66–68,
    70–73, 75, 84, 88, 96, 97–99; university
    education, 21, 23, 33, 34, 40, 43, 45,
    52, 54, 66–67, 68, 70, 88, 96, 97; and
    Vikram Sarabhai, 55; Western education
    for Indians, 34, 35, 49, 51, 52, 54, 55,
    65–66, 72, 88, 96, 97–99, 122–23, 124;
    of women, 21, 34, 45, 47
Edward VII, 33, 56
Eiffel Tower, 103
Einstein, Albert, 76, 77
Elliot, F. A. H., 32
Elphinstone, Mountstuart, 17, 18, 20
Elphinstone College, 21
England. See Britain
English language, 20–21, 24, 32, 47
Epic Mahabaratha and Puranas, 9

family planning, 55
famines, 3, 87
Fanon, Frantz, 119
fasting, 50

Federation of Indian Chambers of Com-
    merce and Industry, 50
Fergusson College, 66
Finance Act (1948), 53
Fleischer School of Art, 73
Forbes, Alexander Kinloch, 21
Forms and Functions of Twentieth Century
    Architecture (Hamlin), 74
Forrest, G. W., 38
Frampton, Kenneth, 132
France, 16, 100, 101, 103, 120, 124, 126
Fry, Maxwell, 82
Fuller, Richard Buckminster, 65

gaddi system of management, 51
Gaekwad, Fatesinghrao P. (Maharaja of
    Baroda), 32, 38, 135n. 5
Gaekwad, Jaisinghrao, 35
Gaekwad, Khanderao, 32
Gaekwad, Malharrao, 32
Gaekwad, Padmavati, 35
Gaekwad, Pilaji, 31
Gaekwad, Pratapsinghrao (Maharaja),
    25–26, 35, 37
Gaekwad, Sayajirao, III (Maharaja), 31–36,
    38, 56–57, 97, 135n. 5
Gaekwad, Shivajirao, 35
Gaekwads, 14, 31–38, 39, 57
Gandhi, Indira, 29, 83, 87, 114
Gandhi, Maganlal, 58
Gandhi, Mohandas Karamchand: in
    Ahmedabad, 40–45, 60; assassination of,
    43; deference to, 52; and education, 52;
    in elite class, 20; and fasting, 50; Gan-
    dhinagar planned as memorial to, 3, 4,
    5, 30, 88, 103, 122; goals of, 6; health
    problems of, 56; and Hindi as national
    language, 23; influences on, 14, 22; and
    Jivraj Mehta, 55, 56; and Kasturbhai Lal-
    bhai, 49, 50; and linguistic states, 22–23;
    in London, 55; monument to, on banks
    of Sabarmati, 5, 103, 116; and nonvio-
    lence, 8, 12, 35, 41–44, 50, 52, 60, 101,
    102, 117; political struggle against
    British by, 8, 14, 35, 50; and Sarabhai
    family, 43–45, 54; and sarvodaya (Gand-
    hian socialism), 52, 62, 106; in South
    Africa, 58; statue of, following p. 40;

Gandhi, Mohandas Karamchand (*continued*)
successor to, 25; and swadeshi movement, 4, 38, 41, 42, 44, 46–47, 50, 51,
52, 56, 104, 107; village emphasis of,
128, 131; and working class and labor
strikes, 42, 43, 49, 50; youth of, 8–9
Gandhi monuments, 5, 103, 116
Gandhi Samadhi, 103
Gandhi Samarak Sanghralaya, 58, 65, 66
Gandhidham, 63–64
Gandhinagar: administrative control of
construction of, 96; author's approach to
study of, 1; beginning of construction in,
17; Buch on, 109, 110, 111; business and
industry in, 106–7, 110, 111, 114; Capital Project Circle for, 30–31, 61, 62, 81,
96; capitol complex in, *following p.* 40,
62, 102, 107, 112–18; Chandigarh as
model of, 102, 106, 109; climate of,
61–62; communications links between
Ahmedabad and, 105; compared with
Chandigarh, 107–8, 111; construction
delays at, 96; corruption charges during
building of, 111, 115; cost of, 108, 113,
114–15; criticisms of, 111, 114–15; and
Doshi, 5, 61, 84–86, 89–94, 99; educational and research institutions in, 106;
financial arrangements with Kahn on,
85, 86, 87, 89–90, 92–94; functions of,
as administrative center of Gujarat, 104,
111; Gandhi monument in, 5, 103, 116;
geology of, 61; Hindu-Muslim conflict in
2002 in, 109; housing in, 62, 105–6, 112;
Indian effort in planning and development of, 4; InfoCity in, 107; infrastructure in, 111, 113, 115; Kahn not selected
for construction of, 94, 99; Kahn's choice
of architects and engineers for, 88, 92;
Kahn's proposed responsibilities for,
86–87; Kahn's recruitment as architect
for, 3, 5, 60, 77, 84–95, 120; Kahn's terms
for work on, 85–86, 92–94; and Kasturbhai Lalbhai, 60, 61, 84, 85, 86, 88–91,
94; larger meaning of urban planning in,
1–2; location of, *following p.* 40, 61; as
memorial to Gandhi, 3, 4, 5, 30, 88, 103,
122; Mewada as architect-planner for, 5,
6, 94, 96–97, 99, 102–6, 110, 112, 117;

Mewada's master plan for, 102–6, 112,
117; neighborhood blocks (sectors) in,
following p. 40, 105; and Newcombe,
112–13, 130; Patel's master plan for,
100–102; plan of, *following p.* 40, 62–63,
96; population of, 104, 114; public spaces
and civil areas in, 103–4; religious violence in 2002 in, 6; road system of, *following p.* 40, 61, 63, 104–5, 107, 113,
116; selection of, as site of capital, 4–5,
7, 30–31, 59, 81, 112, 134–35n. 1; and
Sindi refugees, 26; size of, 61, 104; tech-
nology park in, 102, 107; temple in, *fol-
lowing p.* 40
Gandhinagar Urban Development Area
(GUDA), 104
Ganesh, 101
Garden City movement, 31, 62, 64, 119,
120, 123, 125–27
Gaudas, 10
Gazetteer of the Bombay Presidency, 9, 13, 14,
18
George III, 15
Germany, 64, 101–2, 111
Ghazni, 11
Ghelebhai, Manchharam, 22
Girdharadas, Runchhodlal, 20–21
Giurgola, Ronaldo, 94
glass, 34, 70, 127, 131
Goetz, Herman, 34–35
Gokhale, Gopal Krishna, 56
Government of India Act (1858), 19
Government of India Act (1921), 51
Great Britain. *See* Britain
Greenbelt towns, 126
Griffin, Walter Burley, 69
Gropius, Walter, 66, 74, 97–98, 127
GUDA (Gandhinagar Urban Development
Area), 104
Gujarat: Ahmedabad as temporary capital
of, 59, 60; alienated lands in, 19; archae-
ological sites in, 9; British contact with
and rule of, 4, 7, 8, 14–24, 39; charitable
trusts in, 53; and compromise of 1955,
28; cotton production in, 19–20, 27; cre-
ation of new state of, in 1960, 7, 17, 30,
45; derivation of name for, 4, 7; division
of, based on Indian constitution of 1950,

26; education in, 20–21; elections of 1951 in, 26–27; elections of 1957 in, 26, 28–29; geographic area of, 4, 7–8; history of, 8–29; invasions of, by different cultures, 8, 10, 11–12; Maha (Greater) Gujarat, 20, 24; map of, *following p.* 40; Maratha rulership of, 13–14, 16, 17, 18, 21, 24, 31, 39; Muslim invasions and rule in, 8, 10–13; and Mutiny of 1857, 18; national anthem for, 20, 22; newspapers in, 21, 96; nineteenth-century regional movement in, 21–22, 23; political situation of, after independence, 65; religions in, 6, 10, 12, 13; riots of 1956 in, 28; sites proposed for capital of, 4–5, 30–31, 36, 37, 38, 45, 59. *See also* Ahmedabad; Baroda (city); Gandhinagar
Gujarat College, 43, 47, 51, 52, 54
Gujarat Pradesh Congress, 28
Gujarat University, 53
Gujarat Vernacular Society, 21, 46
Gujarat Vidyapith, 52
Gulf of Kutch, 57, 64
Guptas, 9

Hall, Cuthbert, 33
Hamlin, Talbot, 74
Harijans (untouchables), 36, 42
Harrison, Wallace K., 67
Harvard University and Harvard Business School, 33, 34, 35, 49, 50, 65–66, 70, 84, 88, 95, 120
Haryana, 3, 30. *See also* Chandigarh, Punjab
Hawkins, William, 14–15
Hewlett-Packard, 107
Hindi language, 3, 23, 24
Hinduism and Hindus: and Anhilwada Patan, 9; and Bengal Renaissance, 123; and caste system, 46; compared with Islam, 12–13; conversion of Hindus to Christianity or Islam, 21; in Gujarat, 12, 13; in Junagadh, 25; and Kashmir dispute, 55; and Marathas, 13–14, 16, 17, 18, 21, 24, 31, 37, 39; and nationalism, 6; nineteenth-century revivalism of, 22; and *sati*, 121; and Shaivism, 9, 10; Sindis, 24; temples of, 6, 10, 11, 12, 25, 49;

tensions between Muslims and, in Gujarat, 6; in Uttar Pradesh, 100
historicism, 101, 119
Hiuen Tsang, 9
Holkar, Yeshwant Rao, 17
hospitals, 36–37, 56, 62, 114
housing, 62, 64, 68, 105–6, 108, 109, 112
Howard, Ebenezer, 31, 64, 125–26
Howe, George, 74
Hubbard, Henry V., 99
Hudnut, Joseph, 66
Hulagu Khan, 8
Hussain, Diwan A. K. M., 25
Hutheesingh, Gautam, 48
Hutheesingh, Mohinibehn, 47
Hutheesingh, Surottam, 38, 43, 57
Hyderabad, 25

IAS. *See* Indian Administrative Service (IAS)
Ibn Asir, 11
ICS. *See* Indian Civil Service (ICS)
Idrisi, Al, 13
IIM. *See* Indian Institute of Management (IIM)
illiteracy, 3, 6, 42, 108, 109
Income Tax Law, 53
India: British rule of, 14, 17–22, 39, 119, 120, 121; constitution of 1950 for, 26; contradictions in postcolonial India generally, 48–49, 82; and dual identity of Western and Indian thought systems, 113, 120–23, 131; English education and language in, 20–21, 32, 47; Hindi as national language of, 3, 23, 24; independence for, 2, 6, 9, 37, 51; international travel by Indians, 113, 130; Islam's expansion across, 8, 10–13; linguistic nationalism in, 10, 22–24, 27–28; Mutiny of 1857 in, 18, 19; number of registered architects in, 120; partition of, in 1947, 24; regionalism in, 21–24; social political problems of, 3; subsidiary alliance system in, 16; villages in, 6, 128, 131. *See also* Gujarat; and specific cities, leaders, and architects
India International Centre, 71
Indian Administrative Service (IAS), 31, 110

Indian capitals. *See* Bhubaneswar, Orissa; Chandigarh, Punjab; Gandhinagar
Indian Civil Service (ICS), 31
Indian diaspora, 113
Indian Institute of Management (IIM), 5, *following p.* 40, 50, 53, 54, 60, 69, 71, 72, 79–81, 84, 85, 87, 88, 95, 103, 120, 128
Indian Institute of Science, Bangalore, 54
Indian Institute of Technology, 95, 120
Indian National Committee for Space Research, 54
Indian National Congress, 23, 24, 32, 35, 46, 57
Indian Union, 20, 26, 37
indigo, 42
Indo-China War (1962), 87
Indus Valley, 9
industry and business: agroindustrial complexes, 55; in Ahmedabad, 3, 4–5, 7, 38–54, 59, 137n. 60; and Ambalal Sarabhai, 43–45, 50; and Babuline Gripe Water, 56; in Baroda, 38, 54; in Bombay, 54; in Chandigarh, 106; chemical industry, 48; cotton/textile industry, 19–20, 27, 39–43, 46–47, 50–52, 58; in Gandhinagar, 106–7, 110, 111, 114; and Gujarati capitalism, 65; and Jains, 45–46; in Jamshedpur, 48; and Kasturbhai Lalbhai, 45–54; and nuclear power, 55; in Valsad, 48; and Vikam Sarabhai, 53–55
inflation, 3
InfoCity in Gandhinagar, 107
information technology, 107
international style, 2, 4, 58–59, 68, 73–74. *See also* modernism
Islam and Muslims: in Ahmedabad, 41; architecture of, 129; arrival of Muslims in Gujarat, 8; beginning of, 10–11; compared with Hinduism, 12–13; conversion of Hindus to Islam, 21; doctrines of, 12; expansion of, across India, 8, 10–12; and Gandhi, 43; invasions and Muslim rule of Gujarat, 8, 10–13; and Kashmir dispute, 55; mosques of, 6, 49; in Pakistan, 83
Ismail, Diwan Mirza, 135n. 11
Italy, 33, 126
I-tsing, 9

J. J. School of Art, 58, 67, 81, 88
Jagabhai, 46
"Jai Jai Garvi Gujarat" (Narmad), 20, 22
Jain, Kulbhushan, 84, 86, 120
Jain, Minakshi, 86
Jain, Uttam, 120
Jainism, 9, 12, 25, 38, 40–43, 45–47, 53, 70
Jaji Bai, 14
jajmani (patronage), 85
Jalal-ud Din, 13
James, King, 15
Jamnabai Saheb, Matushri, 32
Jamnagar, 57
Jamshedpur, 48
Japan, 107
Jarasandha, 9
Jeanneret, Pierre, 79
Jesuits, 15
Jews, 40, 68, 72, 75–76, 77, 78, 82
Jhangir, Emperor, 15
jihad (holy war), 12
Jinnah, Mohammad Ali, 83
John Company, 16, 39–40
Jones, Sir William, 20
journals. *See* newspapers and periodicals
Junagadh, 9, 25
Jung, Carl Gustav, 74, 76, 77
JVP Committee, 27

Kahn, Bertha, 73
Kahn, Esther, 76
Kahn, Leopold, 73
Kahn, Louis: Ahmedabad buildings by, *following p.* 40, 57, 60, 69–72, 79–81, 84; architectural philosophy of, 68, 72, 74–77, 79–82, 105, 122; and Architectural Research Group, 74; and Bangladesh buildings, 1, 139n 49; death of, 71, 81; and Dhaka project, 81, 82, 84, 85, 88–89; disappointments of, 81; and Doshi, 5, 67, 68, 69, 70, 72, 75, 77–81, 84–85, 88–95; education of, 73; financial negotiations by, for Gandhinagar project, 85, 86, 87, 89–90, 92–94; and Gandhinagar project, 3, 5, 60, 77, 84–95, 99, 120; Indian Institute of Management design by, *following p.* 40, 60, 69, 71, 72, 79–81, 84, 85, 87, 88, 95, 103, 128;

large-scale projects of, in Indian subcontinent, 60; and Le Corbusier, 72, 74,
77–79, 80, 82, 85, 128–29; and modernism, 74, 75, 82, 128; and National
Institute of Design (NID), 60, 81, 95;
not chosen for Gandhinagar project, 94,
99; patrons of, in Ahmedabad, 3, 5, 60,
128–29; personal beliefs and personality
of, 68–69, 72, 78, 80, 129; photograph
of, *following p.* 40; terms of, for Gandhi-
nagar project, 85–86, 92–94; U.S. archi-
tectural projects of, 75, 78–79; youth and
family of, 68, 72, 73, 75–76, 77
Kala Bhavan Technical Institute, 97
Kali, 10
Kandala, 26, 64
Kandala Port, 57
Kantawala, K. M., 86–92, 99
Kanvinde, Achyut P., 5, 65–66, 70, 88, 120
Kar, Surendranath, 58
Karachi, 25, 26, 57, 64
Karlsruhe, Germany, 101–2
Karnavati, 10, 38
Kashmir, 25, 55
Kathiawar, 25, 42
Kaur, Rajkumari Amrit, 121–22
Kennedy, Axel S., 48
Kennedy Airport, N.Y., 71
Kesari kings, 10
khadi (homespun cloth), 44
Khan, Liaquat Ali, 83
Khan, Momin, 13
Khan, General Muhammad Ayub, 82–83,
87
Khapardo, Ganesh Shridhar, 22
Kheda, 28–29
Khiljis, 11, 13
Khyber Pass, 9, 11
Kincaid, Evert, 99
Kishangarh, 100
Koenigsberger, Otto: beautification of
Mysore and Bangalore by, 135n. 11; and
Bhubaneswar project, 30, 62, 64, 103,
106, 109–10, 113, 120; Buch's criticism
of Bhubaneswar plan of, 109–10; critique
of Chandigarh plan by, 64; and educa-
tional and research institutions in city
plans, 106; and Gandhi Memorial Pillar

for Bhubaneswar, 103; and housing pro-
grams in Germany, 64; and Jamshedpur
project, 48; and neighborhood units, 64;
youth of, 64
Kohn, Bernard, 71, 99
Korzeniowski, Count Apollo, 32
Krishna, Lord, 9
kshatriya, 31
Kshatriyas, 45
Ksiazek, Sarah, 82–83
Kumar, Mandeep, 111
Kunst, Jaap, 74–75, 77
Kutch, 10, 26–29, 55

La Valliere, Louise de, 101
labor strikes. *See* working class and labor
strikes
Lalbhai, Chimanbhai, 47
Lalbhai, Kasturbhai: and Ahmedabad
architecture, 68, 70; and Ahmedabad as
possible capital city for Gujarat, 59; and
education, 47, 49, 51, 52–53; family and
ancestors of, 45–47; and Gandhi, 49, 50;
and Gandhinagar project, 60, 61, 84, 85,
86, 88–91, 94; and Indian Institute of
Management (IIM), 50, 85, 95; and
industry, 45–54, 64; and Kandala Port,
57; opinions of, on local and national
issues, 52; and Swaraj Party, 50–51, 52;
and Valsad, 49
Lalbhai, Seth, 46–47
Lalbhai, Shardabehn, 47
Lalbhai Dalpatbhai Arts College, 53
Lalbhai Dalpatbhai Institute of Indology, 53
Landscape Architecture in the Modern World
(Lohmann), 99
Laxmi Villas Palace, 31, 34, 35
Le Corbusier: Ahmedabad buildings
designed by, *following p.* 40, 57–59, 60,
66, 69; on centralized metropolis, 125;
and Chandigarh project, 2, 3, 5, 6, 30,
48, 49, 62, 64, 67, 69, 72, 79–82, 85, 86,
87, 89, 96, 99–100, 103, 107–8, 110,
113, 118, 120, 125; death of, 66, 78, 82,
97; disappointments of, 81; and Doshi, 5,
58, 67, 68, 70, 77–80, 97; in France, 58,
67, 74; influence of, 129–30; and Kahn,
72, 74, 77–80, 82, 85, 128–29; and

Le Corbusier, (*continued*)
Maisons Jaoul, 132; and Mewada, 5, 97, 99–100; Millowners Association Building designed by, *following p.* 40, 69; and modernism, 60, 66, 74, 108, 118, 125, 127–28; Nehru on, 127–28; personal beliefs and personality of, 78, 81, 82, 128; photograph of, *following p.* 40; and Sarabhai House, 57, 132; on temple architecture, 49; and United Nations Building, 67; Wright on, 69
Lescaze, William, 74
libraries, 21, 34, 49, 58, 62, 114
Lincoln, Abraham, 47
linguistic nationalism, 10, 22–24, 27–28
Litvag, Irving, 81
Lohmann, Karl B., 99, 100
Lok Sabha, 28, 37–38, 59, 114
London University, 97
Lorenz, Herbert Edward, 48
Lothal, Gandhinagar, Gujarat, 9
Louis XIV, 101
Lucknow, Uttar Pradesh, 100
Lutyens, Edward, 34, 123
Lynch, Kevin, 82

M. R. College, 52
Macaulay, Thomas Babington, 52
Mackesey, Thomas W., 98–99, 100
Madhya Pradesh, 109–10
Madras, 27
Magadha, 9
Maha Gujarat Adolan, 20, 24
Maha Gujarat Janata Parishad (Greater Gujarat people party), 27, 28–29
Maha Gujarat Parishad, 28
Maharaja Sayajirao University, 55
Maharastra, 28
Mahavira, Prince Vardhamana, 45
Mahida, Narendra Singh, 114–15
Mahmud, 11
Maisons Jaoul, 132
Majaraja Fatesinghrao Museum, 35
Malraux, André, 76–77
mamluks (slaves), 11
management, 49, 50, 51, 54. *See also* Indian Institute of Management (IIM)
Manekshaw, Sam, 83

Manibhai, 46
manooteedars (middlemen), 17
Mansart, Jules Hardouin, 101
Mant, R. N., 34
Maratha Chitpavan Brahman community, 35
Marathas, 13–14, 16, 17, 18, 21, 24, 31, 37, 39
Marathi language, 52
MARG (Bombay), 127
marriage, 34, 44, 47
Massachusetts Institute of Technology (MIT), 58, 65–66, 70, 88, 95, 120, 124
Master, Sathe, and Bhuta, 84
Matthai, John, 57
Mauraya, Asoka, 103
Mauryas, 9, 12
Mayer, Albert, 62, 66, 85, 86, 98, 120, 125, 126–27
Mecca, 15
medicine and doctors, 55–56
Mehsana, 28–29
Mehta, Ashok, 28
Mehta, Balwantrai, 57
Mehta, Hansabhehn, 55
Mehta, Jivraj Narayan, 29, 30, 37, 38, 55–57, 59, 90, 134–35n. 1
Mehta, Narayanbhai, 55
Mehta, Sir Pherozshah, 56
Mehta, Yashodhar, 136n. 35
Mehta, Zamakbehn, 55
Menon, V. P., 25
Mewada, H. K.: architect-planner career of, in 1950s and 1960s, 100, 110; and Chandigarh project, 5, 96, 99–100, 102, 109; education of, 97–99, 104; and Gandhi monument in Gandhinagar, 5, 103; Gandhinagar master plan by, 102–6, 112, 117; and Gandhinagar project, 5, 6, 94, 96–97, 99, 102–6, 110, 112, 117; and Le Corbusier, 5, 97, 99–100; on master plans, 110–11; and modernism, 6; on Patel's master plan for Gandhinagar, 100–102; personality of, 99, 100, 112; photograph of, *following p.* 40; youth and family of, 97
middle class, 23
Mies van der Rohe, Ludwig, 66, 74, 97–98, 127

Millowners Association Building, *following p.* 40, 57, 69

MIT. *See* Massachusetts Institute of Technology (MIT)

modernism: and "Architect and the Community" seminar in New Delhi (1965), 108–9; Bhatia on, 123; and Correa, 5, 66, 109, 131, 132; and Critical Regionalism, 132; critics and criticisms of, 74–75, 82; and Doshi, 66, 70, 79, 122, 130–31, 132; and India generally, 2–3, 5–6, 70, 129, 132; and international style, 2, 4, 58–59, 68, 73–74; and Kahn, 74, 75, 82, 128; and Le Corbusier, 60, 66, 74, 108, 118, 125, 127–28; meaning of, 109; and Mewada, 6; and Nehru, 121, 123, 124–25, 127–28, 131; and new construction materials, 2, 34, 66, 70, 89, 108–9, 127, 131; in U.S. architecture, 73–75, 97–98

moksha (salvation), 47

Montague, Edwin Samuel, 8

Montessori school system, 45, 54

Morocco, 96

mosques, 6, 49, 82, 89

Mughals, 13, 14, 15, 19, 31, 39, 44, 129

Muhammad, 12

Mukerjee, Sharda, 118

Mularaja, 10

Mumtaj, 44

Municipalities of Illinois (Lohmann), 99

Munshi, K. M., 24

Museum of Modern Art, New York, 74

museums, 35, 36, 56, 57, 58, 64, 69, 74

Muslims. *See* Islam and Muslims

Mussolini, Benito, 33

Mutiny of 1857, 18

Muzaffar Khan, 7

Muzumdar, B. K., 53

Mysore, 33, 135n. 11

Nadaji, 31

Nagar, Murali Lal, 135n. 5

Nagindas, Chimanlal, 43

Naidu, Sarojini, 43

Naoroji, Dadabhai, 32

Narayan, Shriman, 61

Narmad, Kavi, 20, 21–22

Nathwani, Narendra, 26

National Institute of Design (NID), 60, 71, 81, 95

nationalism, 10, 22–24, 27–28, 42–43, 46

Native Schoolbook and School Society, 20

Nazarbagh Palace, 36

Nehru, Jawaharlal: on Bhubansewar, 122; and Chandigarh project, 48, 79, 89, 108, 120, 121, 125, 127–28; on city planning and architecture, 123, 124–26, 131; and creation of Andhara, 24; death of, 87; economic policies of, 48, 122; and elections of 1957, 29; goals of, for India, 6; and Indian Institute of Management (IIM), 69; on Le Corbusier, 127–28; and linguistic provinces, 23, 24, 27; as mayor of Allahabad, 51; ministerial appointments by, 59; and modernism, 121, 123, 124–25, 127–28, 131; and national defense, 87; on need for trained personnel, 49; on New Delhi, 120, 121; and Patel, 25; photograph of, *following p.* 40; on plan for Chandigarh, 2; and "socialization of the vacuum," 52; and swadeshi movement, 38; and Temple of Somnath, 12; on urbanism, 6; on villages, 6

Nehru, Krishna, 48

Nehru, Motilal, 44, 50

Nehru, Pandit, 23

Nehru Foundation for Development, 55

neighborhood unit, 64, 98, 102, 127

Nelson, George, 127

Nepal, 42

Neutra, Richard, 71, 74, 127

New Delhi: architectural firm in, 84; architecture and plan of, 31, 34, 71, 100, 112, 119–21, 123–26; architecture conference in, 108–9; and Dhar Commission, 27; Gandhi Samadhi at Rajghat, 103; India International Centre in, 71; Mewada on, 100

New York, 34, 67, 74, 75, 97

Newcombe, Vernon Z., 112–13, 130

newspapers and periodicals, 21–22, 51, 96

NID (National Institute of Design), 60, 71, 81, 95

Niemeyer, Oscar, 67

Nixon, Richard, 114

Nolen, John, 99
nonviolence (*satyagraha*), 8, 12, 35, 41–44, 50, 52, 60, 101, 102, 117
nuclear power, 54, 55

Operations Research Group, 54
opium trade, 40
Orissa, 3, 10, 22, 24, 25. *See also* Bhubaneswar, Orissa
Oswals, 45
Outlook (New York), 34
Oxford University, 32, 34, 35
Oza, Bhavanishankar Atmaram, 56

Pakistan, 24, 25, 26, 51, 55, 57, 60, 64, 81–85, 87, 108, 114–15
Pancasar, 10
panchayats (council of five in Hindu village), 37, 57
Parbhundas, Kikabhai, 22
Parsis, 40, 48, 56
Patel, Hasmukh, 72, 99, 120
Patel, M. D., 96, 102
Patel, Raghav L., 100
Patel, Ratilal K., 111
Patel, Sardar Vallabhbhai, 9, 12, 20, 24–27, 37, 56, 57, 115
Patel, Vithalbhai, 115
patidar (Kanbi agriculturalists), 37–38
Patil, G. K., 61
peasants, 17, 30, 41–42
pedhi (banking) firm, 46
Pei, Ieoh Ming, 70
penicillin manufacturing, 54
Penn, William, 73
periodicals. *See* newspapers and periodicals
Perkins, Holmes, 78, 94
Perry, Clarence Arthur, 64, 98
peshwa, 14, 17, 19, 31, 39
Peshwa, Balajirao, 14
Phadnis, Nana, 17
Philadelphia, 72–75, 78, 79, 81, 85–86
Philadelphia Savings Fund Society Building, 74
Physical Research Laboratory (PRL), 53, 54, 68
Pite, W. A., 56
plague, 14, 37, 40, 56

plastics, 66
Polk, Benjamin, 71
Poona (Pune), 14, 17, 19, 31, 39, 66–67
Poona, Treaty of, 17, 39
Porbandar, 9
Portugal, 15
postmodernism, 79, 119
poverty, 6
Prabhawalker, A. R., 88
praja mandals (People's councils, or forums), 37, 56–57
Prasad, Rajendra, 12
Pray, James S., 99
Premchand, Karamchand, 43
Principles of City Planning (Lohmann), 99
PRL. *See* Physical Research Laboratory (PRL)
Pune, 14. *See also* Poona (Pune)
Punjab and Punjabis, 7, 24, 26, 29, 30, 39, 80, 83, 84, 121–22. *See also* Chandigarh, Punjab
Puranic tales, 11

R. C. Technical Institute, 52
Radburn plan, 126
railroads, 31, 46, 48, 61
Raipur Mills, 47
Rajasthan, 7, 28, 100
Raje, Anant, 70, 81, 84, 86
Rajghat, New Delhi, 103
Rajkot, Saurastra, 26, 42
Rajput clans, 45
Raman, Sir C. V., 54
Ranchhodalal and Bija Natko (Mehta), 136n. 35
Ranjitram, 24
Rao, Diwan Sir T. Madhav, 32
Rashtriya Janata Party, 107
Ray, Satyajit, 123
Raymond, Antonin, 69, 97
refugees, 26, 57, 63, 65, 114, 135n. 11
regionalism, 21–24
residential areas. *See* housing
Rewal, Raj, 120, 132
Rice, Norman, 74
Rice, Stanley, 32
Rig-Veda, 11
Ripon, Viceroy, 37, 56–57

road systems, *following p.* 40, 61, 63, 102, 104–5, 107, 113, 116

Robertson, Howard, 67

Roe, Sir Thomas, 15, 16

Roy, Arundhati, 123

Roy, Rammohan, 123, 127

Rozdi, Saurastra, 9

Rudradaman rock, 9

ryots (peasants), 17, 30, 41

Saarinen, Eero, 71

Sabarmati Ashram, 40, 42, 43, 58, 60, 65, 101

Sabarmati River, 5, 103

Sabikhi, Ranjit, 120

Sahib, Jam, 57

Said, Edward, 119

Sakandagupta, 9

Salk Institute, 75, 78–79

Samantasimha, 10

Samyukta Maharastra Samiti (United Maharastra party), 26–27, 28

Sangath office complex (Doshi), 67

Sarabhai, Ambalal, 43–45, 50, 51, 53

Sarabhai, Anasuya, 43, 45, 54

Sarabhai, Gautam, *following p.* 40, 58, 64, 65, 69, 70, 95

Sarabhai, Gira, 58, 64, 69, 70

Sarabhai, Kartikeya, 54

Sarabhai, Mallika, 54, 55

Sarabhai, Mirdula, 54–55

Sarabhai, Sarladevi, 44

Sarabhai, Vikram, 45, 51, 53–55, 69, 70, 84, 85

Sarabhai family, 60, 64

Sarabhai house, 57, 132

Sarabhai industries, 54

Sarabhai Research Centre, 54

sarafs (bankers), 41

Saraswati, Swami Dayanand, 22

Sardesai, G. S., 35

sardeshmukhi tax, 13, 14

sarvodaya (Gandhian socialism), 52, 62, 106

Sasaki, Hideo, 99

Satellite Instructional Television Experiment, 55

sati (immolation of Hindu widow), 121

Satraps, 9

satyagraha (nonviolent, noncooperation movement), 8, 35, 41–44, 50, 52, 60, 101, 102, 117

Satyagraha Ashram. *See* Sabarmati Ashram

Saurastra, 9, 25, 26–29, 37

savarajya, 14

Schiller, J. C. F., 92

Schindler, Rudolf, 74

science, 53, 54–55

Shah, Jhan, 44

Shah, M. G., 102

Shahibagh, 44

Shaivism, 9, 10

Sharma, M. N., 102

Shastri, Lal Bahadur, 87

shaukar (businessman), 17, 26

Shiva, 9, 10, 11

Shodhan, Shyamubhai, 57

Shodhan house, 57

Sika, 57

Sikhs, 29

Sind and Sindi, 10, 26, 39, 83

Sindhia, Daulat Rao, 17

Singh, Kuldip, 120

Sitarammaiya, Pattabhi, 27

Sitaramulu, Potti, 23, 27

Smithson, Peter and Alison, 82

socialism: democratic socialism, 120–21; Gandhian socialism, 52, 62, 106

Solanki, Mularaja, 7

Solankis (Chalukyans), 10

Soma (deified juice), 11

Somnath, 11, 12

Somnath, Lord. *See* Shiva

Sompura, Mr., 110

South Africa, 58

Soviet Union, 87, 114

Spain, 120

Spivak, Gayatri, 119

SRC. *See* State Reorganization Commission (SRC)

Staatliches Bauhaus, 34

Standard Pharmaceuticals Ltd., 54

State Reorganization Commission (SRC), 27, 28

steel, 34, 131

Steele, James, 68

Stein, Clarence, 98

Stein, Doshi, and Bhalla, 71
Stein, Joseph, 67, 69, 71
Stevens, Wallace, 77
Stonorov, Oskar, 74
subsidiary alliance system, 16
suburbanization, 64, 79, 81–82
Suez Canal, 20
Sulaiman, 12
Sullivan, Louis, 124
Sun Yat-sen, 55
Sunderdas, Seth Gordhandas, 56
Surat, 14–17, 21, 22, 39
Suthar, Kalidas K., 97
svadharma (native religion), 14
svaraj (self-rule), 14. See also *swaraj*
swadeshi (indigenous goods), 4, 38, 41, 42,
    44, 46–47, 50, 51, 52, 56, 95, 104, 107,
    121, 128
Swaminathan, Mrinalini, 54, 55
swaraj (self-rule), 46–47, 104, 121. See also
    svaraj
Swaraj Party, 50–51, 52
Swaroopananda, Swami Nitya, 69
swatantra, 22

T. T. Nagar, 109, 110
Tagore, Rabindranath, 44, 58, 123
Taj Mahal, 44
Taliesin, Wis., 64–65
Tamils, 27
Tata, Sri Jamsetjee Jeejeebhoy, 48
taxation, 13, 14, 40, 51, 52, 53
technology park in Gandhinagar, 102, 107
Telesis, 71
television, 55
Telugus, 27
Temple of Somnath, 10, 11, 12, 25
temples, 6, 10, 11, 12, 25, 31, 36, *following*
    p. 40, 49, 53
textile industry. *See* cotton/textile industry
Thakare, Bal, 23–24
Thapar, P. N., 80
Times of India, 51, 114
tinkathia system, 42
To-Morrow: A Peaceful Path to Real Reform
    (Howard), 31, 125–26
Treaty of Bassein, 17
Treaty of Poona, 17, 39

tree planting, 48
Tripathi, Mansukram Suryaram, 22,
    137n. 60
Trowbridge, Alexander, 98
Tughlaqs, 13
Tuskegee Institute, 33, 34, 97
Tyng, Alexandra, 72, 74, 76, 77
Tyng, Anne G., 75

Udayram, Ranchhodbhai, 22
Ulsidas, Nagindas, 22
umma (Islamic brotherhood), 12
Union of States of Saurastra, 25
United Nations, 48, 97, 112, 130
United Nations Building, 67
United States: American Cyanamid in,
    47–48; architecture in, 64–65, 67, 71,
    73–75, 78–79, 97–98, 103, 120, 124,
    126; blacks in, 33, 34; Civil War in,
    19–20, 40, 46; education and universities
    in, 33–35, 49, 50, 66–68, 70–73, 75, 84,
    88, 96, 120; information technology in,
    107; Kahn's youth in, 72–73; policy of,
    toward India, 114; United Nations
    Building in, 67; Wright as architect
    in, 64–65, 69, 125, 127
United States of Kathiawar, 25
university education. *See* education
University of Bombay, 21, 34
University of California, Los Angeles, 75
University of Chicago, 33, 68
University of Illinois, 97, 99
University of Michigan, 120
University of Pennsylvania, 73, 75, 78, 79,
    86, 94–95
University of Tennessee, 97
untouchables, 35–36, 41, 42, 46, 121
urban planning. *See* Bhubaneswar, Orissa;
    Chandigarh, Punjab; Gandhinagar; and
    specific architects
Urban Studies and Planning, School of, 53
Utkal Union Conference, 24
Uttar Pradesh, 100

Vadodara. *See* Baroda (city)
Vaghela, Shankersinh, 107
Valabhi kingdom, 9
Valabhipura, 9

Vale, Lawrence, 83
Valsad, 48, 49, 52, 59, 64
Van Pelt, John V., 98
Vanaraja, 9–10
Vartaman (newspaper), 21
Vastu-Shilpa Foundation for Environmental
  Design, 58, 67, 68
Vaz, Julius, 6, 68, 122
Véret, Jean-Louis, 67
Verma, P. L., 80
Vers une architecture (Le Corbusier), 125
Versailles Garden, France, 100, 101
Victor Emmanuel, King, 33
Victoria, Queen, 33
Viderbha, 28
Vivekananda, Swami, 47
Les Voix du Silence (Malraux), 76–77

Washington, Booker T., 33, 35
Washington, D.C., 103, 111, 124, 126
Washington Memorial, 103
Webber, Major, 35
Weeden, Rev. Edward St. Clair, 32
Weese, Harry, 71
Wellesley, Richard Colley, 16, 17
White, Andrew Dickson, 98

White, Stanley, 99
Wittet, George, 56
Wodeyar, Chamarajendra (Maharaja of
  Mysore), 33
Wodeyar, Krishnaraja (Maharaja) , 33
women: education of, 21, 34, 45, 47; mar-
  ginalization of, 3; and marriage, 34, 44,
  47; at social occasions with husbands, 44
Wonder House, 58
Wood, Charles, 23
working class and labor strikes, 41–46, 49,
  50, 65
World Trade Center attack, 65
World War I, 47, 55, 65
World War II, 47, 51, 54, 66
World's Columbian Exposition (Chicago),
  124
Wright, Frank Lloyd, 64–65, 69, 125, 127
Wright, Henry, 99
Wurster, William Wilson, 66

Yagnik, Indulal, 20, 28
Yale University, 75

Zaveri (Jawahari), Shantidas, 45